LESS IS
MORE

TEACHING LITERATURE WITH SHORT TEXTS — GRADES 6–12

KIMBERLY HILL CAMPBELL

STENHOUSE PUBLISHERS
PORTLAND, MAINE

CONTENTS

Foreword by Leila Christenbury.......................................vi

Acknowledgments...ix

CHAPTER 1 Teaching Literature with Short Texts.................................1

CHAPTER 2 Structures and Strategies That Support
the Teaching of Short Texts...9

CHAPTER 3 Short Stories 42

CHAPTER 4 Essays 77

CHAPTER 5 Memoir 116

CHAPTER 6 Poetry 144

CHAPTER 7 Children's Literature and Picture Books............................175

CHAPTER 8 Graphic Novels 199

Index...217

Foreword

Kimberly Campbell is a thoughtful, intentional teacher, and the case she makes for short texts in *Less Is More* is compelling. With insight and example she walks us through her classroom, introduces us to her students, and shows how short texts can transform the indifferent into engaged readers and writers.

I wish I had known Kimberly Campbell when I was first teaching high school. Back then, I was confronted with numerous students who were resolute nonreaders both in and outside of school. Some of this was due to skill issues, and some of it was due to indifference—if not resistance—to what was occurring in our classroom. So when I assigned extensive reading for the next day, it was almost guaranteed that virtually no one in the class would complete—or probably even attempt—the work. I quickly found that positive reinforcement was not a powerful inducement for these students, and the threat of failing grades was similarly ineffective; the novel's chapters and the long essays remained either partially or completely unread, and the subsequent classes limped along.

I was a conscientious if not particularly skillful beginning teacher, and I worried about my classroom. It was painfully obvious to me that for both my students and myself, teaching and learning were not occurring. I concluded that there was no way to transform the situation directly, so I moved around it. Rather than continue to fight with my students and lose the battle almost every day, I decided to regroup and began using short texts that we could all experience at the same time.

In class, together, students and I would read silently or, more frequently, read aloud, and short stories, poems, and brief essays, both fiction and nonfiction, became our staples. The benefits were huge and virtually immediate: completing the reading was inescapable, and, when we read aloud, students could not only see the text but hear it read with real interpretive intonation, greatly enhancing comprehension. The activity immediately following the reading activity—discussion or writing—was reinforcing and organic; there was no gap between the reading and the response. Interest improved, grades rose, and student and teacher satisfaction soared.

Kimberly Campbell knows all this and makes the point in *Less Is More* that using shorter texts addresses a number of instructional issues about which most of us conscientious teachers fret. For Campbell, short texts are a "great equalizer" that can serve to address the varying reading abilities of students in our classrooms. In addition, with short texts a teacher can more easily use a variety of genres: the short story, the essay, the memoir, the poem, children's books, and graphic novels. With short texts teachers can directly incorporate reading strategies, use literature circles, and, for challenged readers and English language learners, convert the text to an audio recording and even into a second language translation. Texts can indeed be read aloud or read silently in class, but with shorter pieces, teachers can also be confident that students likely will complete these more manageable reading assignments on their own.

Clearly, I believe in the genius of small things, but this is not to argue that only short texts are acceptable in our classrooms. There is a place for the 5,000-line epic, the five-act play, and the 500-page novel. Some students will want to read *Middlemarch* or *Bleak House* or even *Harry Potter and the Order of the Phoenix*, and they should. Some teachers will want to incorporate some longer texts into their curriculum, and they should be welcome to do so. Certainly sustained concentration on a long text is a skill that will stand students in good stead long after they leave our classrooms.

But I do not feel that such longer texts should be the absolute center, the sine qua non, of the curriculum. As Kimberly Campbell notes, many of our colleagues face mandated English curriculums that consist entirely of canonical works, novels, long (mostly Shakespearian) plays, and virtually no poetry or short fiction and nonfiction. When students are confronted solely and consistently with texts that are complex and lengthy, there is resistance, a tendency to disengage and to look for shortcuts that may help complete a required assignment but that circumscribe or even totally avoid actual reading. Surely we as teachers do not want to contribute to the epidemic of nonreading that plagues so many English classrooms. Indeed, many students are skillful at doing almost anything with a long, canonical text but actually read it, at least as we expect it to be read. And, thanks to innumerable resources readily available on the Internet, this kind of nonreading can be almost undetectable.

Given a text that is manageable, though, most students are far less tempted to skip the assignment or to cram, skim, or run to the mother of all reading challenges, SparkNotes. Real learning can occur through tackling a shorter piece and examining a text that is, for many students, ultimately more manageable. In addition, exposure to a variety of literary genres—many of which are short texts—can do nothing but enhance a student's interest in lifelong reading. Finally, a classroom literature community is easier to construct and maintain when students are actually reading and thus are legitimately engaged.

Shakespeare instructed us that brevity is the soul of wit; Wordsworth found freedom in the sonnet's scanty plot of ground. For many of our students, exploring the small can also be intensely satisfying. Kimberly Campbell knows this, and *Less Is More* is a practical and smart discussion of how students and their teachers can find pleasure and profit in short pieces of literature that are well written and satisfying to complete. We can ask for no more.

— **LEILA CHRISTENBURY**

Acknowledgments

T his book would not exist if my colleague, friend, and teacher Ruth Shagoury did not encourage and nudge me. Ruth's nudge led to Brenda Miller Power, friend and then editor at Stenhouse, who met with me over coffee and re-configured my ramblings into the vision for this book. Even after she moved on to new professional adventures, she continued to read my drafts and find my voice. She served not only as volunteer editor but also as cheerleader. Bill Varner, currently my editor at Stenhouse, entered the picture to move the book from draft to reality, asking good questions and providing constructive feedback but always taking time to let me know how much he believed in the book. The fact that he loves coffee and shares his favorite blends with me is an added bonus. I am grateful to each of these amazing people.

I also want to recognize all the other wonderful folks who supported my work and this book:

My son, John, and his friend Chubs, who taught me that I needed to be more expansive in my thinking about what can be read and studied in English classrooms. John is also my resident expert on graphic novels.

My daughter, Kinsey, who shared her wisdom regarding short stories, poetry, and graphic novels for girls. She also helped me navigate the library and order books online.

My writing group—Ruth Shagoury, Melanie Quinn, and Melina Dyer—who listened patiently to outlines that became drafts that became revised drafts. I am grateful for their feedback and their gracious fellowship.

The teachers and graduate students studying to be teachers who asked good questions and shared their ideas and insights regarding the use of short texts in middle school and high school classrooms. I am honored to share the teaching profession with all these wonderful folks. I am particularly grateful to the following teachers who invited me into their classrooms or were interviewed by me for this book: Sharon Klin, Jamie Williams, Kristi Latimer, Gayle Van Lehman, Lisa Souther, and Stephanie Cromer.

All the middle school and high school students who have shared the classroom with me and taught me what they needed as readers, writers, and members of a learning community.

My colleagues at Lewis & Clark College Graduate School of Education and Counseling who shared their favorite short texts with me and encouraged me to keep writing.

The teacher-researchers who inspired me with stories of their learning about teaching, particularly Nancie Atwell, Linda Rief, Leila Christenbury, Linda Christensen, Cris Tovani, Heather Lattimer, and my writing and teaching hero, Tom Romano.

Jim Whitney, the calm voice on the other end of the phone who talked me through computer crises and provided the photographs for this book.

My parents, Gil and Vonnie Hill, who taught me that you must finish what you start. I heard their voices urging me to keep at it on those days when finding the right word, any word, felt impossible.

And finally, to Michael, my husband, who tolerated my use of the dining room as my office; understood that when I was staring into space rather than listening, it was because my head was writing; and did not flinch when I added up the total cost of all the books I purchased as resources for this book. He always supports and believes in me.

CHAPTER 1

Teaching Literature with Short Texts

Yet a story's very shortness ensures its largeness of accomplishment, its selfhood, and purity.

–LORRIE MOORE

Picture the scene twenty years ago. I am reading aloud Roald Dahl's wonderfully twisted short story "Lamb to the Slaughter" to my junior high students. In the story made famous in an Alfred Hitchcock television program, a woman clubs her husband with a frozen leg of lamb, then covers the crime by roasting the meat as she chats innocently with the police detectives. I read it aloud as the students follow along with their copies, rain streaming down the lone window in the classroom. When I am finished, there is a hushed silence, which erupts thirty seconds later into questions, comments, theories, reactions. Students call out, "Do you think the wife will really get away with it?" "I think the husband deserved it." "Who wrote this story? I love how the cops at the end are eating the murder weapon." "Can we hear the story again so we can listen for clues?" "Cool story—got any more by this guy?" And I did have more. We went on to read "The Way Up to Heaven" by Roald Dahl, which students also admired for its surprising revenge ending. We then explored Shirley Jackson's "The Lottery," a story that haunted students for the remainder of the year. Its misleading lead, which paints a portrait of an idyllic summer day as a community gathers, sets up the shocking ending in a way that intrigued the seventh and eighth graders.

We read many short stories that first year of my teaching career, and every year after. As an English major, I didn't read very many short stories in college. Literature courses I took focused on novels and the occasional poem. As I entered my first classroom as a teacher, in a junior high located on Main Street in a small, rural Oregon town, I pictured myself sitting in a circle, engaged in a lively discussion with my eager young students about whatever novel we were reading. I was shocked to discover that the junior high had no classroom sets of novels for my students to read. Literature was not the focus of the junior high curriculum; the emphasis was on writing, spelling, and grammar. In fact, sentence diagramming was a mandate; students were required to pass sentence-diagramming tests.

While hunting for a teacher's edition of the grammar book so I could learn how to diagram sentences in an effort to support my students, I stumbled across a dusty copy of a short story collection. Hidden inside the tattered green cloth covers were stories—stories that became the glittering gems in an otherwise tedious march through formulaic writing prompts, weekly spelling pre- and post-tests, and the grammar focus of the month.

Short stories provided more than a distraction from the grammar and writing formulas. Students were identifying the elements of short stories: character, setting, plot, and theme. They were discovering literary elements: irony, foreshadowing, and point of view. They were noticing writing craft: a compelling lead, surprise endings, and the use of descriptive language. They were also making text-self connections, identifying with characters, and seeing how the character's decisions were related to their own lives. Short stories were a way into literature for these students. They are a way into literature for most students.

When I moved from teaching at the junior high to teaching at the high school, I brought my passion for short stories with me. Fortunately, the literature anthologies I was required to use, although unwieldy in size and weight, were rich with short stories. I supplemented the anthologies with short stories I had grown to love. Poetry was another form of short text that had served my junior high students well. Again I used the anthology but also used my limited copying budget to provide students with poetry not contained in the anthology. In addition to the anthology reading, novels were a literature focus. And the novels that were required were the same novels I had read in high school: *Great Expectations, To Kill a Mockingbird, Lord of the Flies, Of Mice and Men, The Great Gatsby, The Scarlet Letter.* Each year we also taught at least one play: *Romeo and Juliet, Julius Caesar, Raisin in the Sun, Death of a Salesman, Our Town, Macbeth, Hamlet.*

Although many of these longer works were favorites of mine, I was struck by the difference in how students read and responded to these longer texts. The participation level during discussions of longer texts was significantly less than when we were discussing short texts. When I queried students about the assigned reading in longer texts, they were candid in sharing that they had read the text but could not retain all the details, so they did not feel comfortable talking in class. And some students admitted that they had not done the reading. Students were frank about the sense of frustration they felt as they read; they were overwhelmed by the complexity of the multiple characters, settings, and plot twists. But the more common response to longer texts was an intense dislike for the text—a dislike that grew in intensity the longer we worked with the text.

I empathized with the students' complaints. As an English major I had read many books that I disliked. But I also recognized that despite my dislike for the text, I learned from these authors. And although I did not want my students to be frustrated, I did want them to be pushed as readers so they could develop reading skills that would support reading complex texts. So I clung to the inclusion of longer texts, but I worked to pick books I thought would have greater interest for more students than the traditional texts seemed to have; for example, I traded *Great Expectations* for *A Separate Peace* in my freshman English class. I also paid attention to reading strategies, although I realize now, after reading Cris Tovani's wonderful work *I Read It, but I Don't Get It* (2000), that there was much more I should have done.

But the distinction between who we were as a literature community when we read and discussed short stories and poetry and who we were when we were immersed in reading a novel continued to fascinate me. Students dug deep when they spoke about short stories and poetry. They referred to the text in support of their answers. They spoke about the craft of the writing, noting how figurative language, foreshadowing, irony, and point of view contributed to the literature's effect. Students were engaged in literature appreciation and analysis. And the

3

short texts we read were often complex and required close attention using the reading strategies we were exploring, in particular text-to-self, text-to-text, and text-to-world connections.

I found myself using more and more short texts because their length supports in-class reading—reading that can be supported with reading strategies. And short texts' length supports in-class discussion, often on the same day the short text is read, in development of an appreciation for literature. An emphasis on short texts allowed me to include classic authors as well as multicultural and contemporary works. Rather than reading less with short text, my students were reading more. I also appreciated the fact that reliance on reading supplements such as SparkNotes and online summaries and essays was reduced. I was saddened to discover that there are online essays about short texts, particularly short stories, but these can be avoided if I am creative in my framing of the response to literature (see section entitled "Writing in Response to Literature" in Chapter 2 for more on this).

Beyond Fake Reading

Short texts were also a response to fake reading. I found that in-class reading of short texts allowed me to observe my students as readers. And, if needed, I could intervene, with individuals and with the whole class. For one of my students—I'll call him Fred—reading in class resulted in my discovering that he could not read. It was early fall, and I had just assigned an in-class reading of Nathaniel Hawthorne's short story "The Minister's Black Veil." This is not an easy read, so I had talked with students about focusing their attention on the references to the veil; they were marking these references with sticky notes (see Chapter 3 for more on this story and reading strategy). I circulated as students read, noting how they were using the sticky notes. I noticed Fred shifting in his chair; his eyes moved from the page in the book to the desk of the student next to him. I watched as he picked up his sticky note, looked again at the student sitting next to him, and placed the sticky note in the same place as the other student. He then stared down at the book for several minutes. I asked Fred to stay after class and talk with me. As he sat down in the chair next to my desk, I noted his anxiety. "Fred, thanks so much for staying after class today. I haven't had the opportunity to work with you before, so I wanted to spend a few minutes finding out more about you as a reader. Over the course of the year I ask all of my students to sit down and read with me.

So today is your day. I would like you to read the first paragraph of the story we read in class today aloud to me. I know reading aloud is a different reading skill than silent reading, but this is helpful information for me and I really like hearing this story." Fred did not look up from the floor; his eyes had been focused on the green carpet in my classroom since he sat down. I handed him the literature anthology. Silence. I waited. More silence. "Fred, would you prefer to read the first paragraph silently and tell me what you read? We can start there?" Silence. "Fred, tell me how I can help you."

Fred responded, his eyes still focused on the floor, "Mrs. Campbell, the words in this story are really confusing. I . . . " His voice broke as he turned to look at me. "I don't think I know how to read." I thanked Fred for his honesty as my eyes welled up with tears, and I assured him that I would help him learn to read.

I acknowledge that Fred's situation is unique. But Fred, whose first language is English, had attended public school since the first grade. He was then a junior in high school. And Fred could not read. He was a charming, sociable boy who had developed coping skills to cover his lack of literacy skills. Fred's story is just one example of the range of abilities my students brought to literature reading. I worked with students who could read in their native language but not English, students who could not read in their native language or English, and students who were native English speakers but, like Fred, struggled with reading. Asking these students to read a novel that would challenge a reader with excellent reading skills is not why I became a teacher. Short texts were the way for me to address the varying reading abilities in my classroom. I read short texts aloud to the whole class and to small groups. I taught reading strategies that we then applied in class as we read short texts. I formed literature circles that read a variety of short texts with different reading challenges. I arranged to have short texts read on tape and even translated into my students' native languages. Short texts served as the great equalizer.

Meeting the Objectives for Teaching Literature

Please know that this move to the inclusion of—even dominance of—short texts in my literature classroom was slow and at times agonizing for me. I adore reading novels. My bookshelves are heavy with novels. I want my students to discover the joys of immersing themselves in a book, of embracing the complexities of a well-crafted novel. But the realities of my classroom made me question whether the

5

dominance of novels served my students well. Immersing my students for weeks at a time in a novel was unwieldy. Rather than digging deep, students' discussions often skimmed over the surface of hundreds of pages of reading, or they relied on me to tell them what matters in the book. And I certainly did not resist telling them. At times I found myself having a discussion about the novel with myself!

But was I serving my students well by making literature reading more accessible? Was I lowering my expectations? I worried that my emphasis on short texts was promoting the equivalent of literary fast food.

As I wrestled with the question of which literature to read, I realized I had neglected to ask myself the more important question: what do I want my students to know, understand, and be able to do as a result of their reading of literature? I began to compile a list of objectives for reading literature:

- Students will develop a variety of reading strategies in support of comprehension.
- Students will identify literary terms and examine how these terms contribute to the craft of writing.
- Students will develop skills in support of analyzing literature.
- Students will develop discussion skills that enable them to converse with peers about the literature they read.
- Students will discover connections with the literature they read: text to self, text to text, and text to world.
- Students will recognize the role literature plays in telling the story of cultures.
- Students will read literature as a model for the kinds of writing they are doing.

When I looked at this list of objectives, I realized that I needed to expand rather than narrow my list of literature choices. In addition to short stories, poetry, and the occasional novel or play, I needed to include literature that modeled the kinds of writing my students were doing: responses to literature, persuasive and expository essays, personal narratives, and memoirs. The National Council of Teachers of English (NCTE) and International Reading Association (IRA) standards also support this broad range of literature in calling for a "wide range of literature from many periods and genres" (Standard 2, 1996; see further discussion of standards in Chapter 2). This variety of writing is reflective of what is published

6

as literature. Bookstores and libraries recognize that literature is not limited to the novel. I also needed to include texts that reflected the changing landscape of literature—literature written for young adults and graphic novels, illustrated stories that bring together the best of comic books and great literature.

My classroom practice changed because my students demonstrated they needed a different approach to literature. They wanted to read well-crafted, accessible texts that supported the development of their reading skills and modeled writing craft they could emulate in their own writing. They wanted a greater variety of texts so that they could connect with the texts we read but also be introduced to ideas and cultures that went beyond their experience. They wanted short texts that they could read and reread—discovering all the possibilities of great writing. They wanted a classroom that reflected the rich range of literature that exists outside of the classroom. As one of my resistant readers, Jason, noted, "I got to admit, it's weird to be in this class. I am actually saying stuff about what we read because for the first time, I have actually read the stuff." And when we did read a novel as a class, *Their Eyes Were Watching God*, Jason announced to the class, "This is the first English-class book I have ever finished."

Short texts allowed all of my students to come to the literature table—where we dined not on fast food, but on a delicious buffet that represented the smorgasbord of literature genres available to us as readers.

It's my hope this book will support your interest in and efforts to bring short texts into your classroom, to build on what you are already doing. I've included an overview chapter, which discusses the structures and strategies I used in my literature workshop to support our short texts study. The subsequent chapters focus on short texts by genre. Each chapter includes an overview of the genre and a series of teaching strategies in support of the genre, including reading strategies and strategies to analyze literary elements and writing craft. Informal assessments are woven into the teaching strategies. Recommended texts are listed in sidebars as well as in resource lists at the end of each chapter. Many of the works in these lists, especially older works, have been published in many different editions and collections over the years. I've included the editions that I've used, so the publication dates are often not the original publication dates. When you look for these older works, you'll find they're available in many different collections and editions. Please note that I did attempt to reference collections that contain a number of the shorter text selections. As I compiled these lists I was aware that

I was just scratching the surface of the rich literature resources available to us. I hope these lists will build on the literature you are already using.

I am confident you'll adapt and tweak the teaching strategies and resources I describe to meet the needs of the diverse students with whom you work. My hope is that you'll find the time to send me a note or an email and let me know what you're doing with short texts. I wanted to include a pound of really good coffee with every book, but the publishers said this would not be practical. So I trust you are sipping a good cup of coffee or tea as you read (I drank Sumatran-blend coffee while writing this book). May you find confirmation for what you are already doing as well as inspiration to use more short texts in your classroom.

WORKS CITED

Dahl, Roald. 2006. "Lamb to the Slaughter." In *Collected Stories*, ed. Jeremy Treglown. New York: Everyman's Library.

——.1990. "The Way Up to Heaven." In *The Best of Roald Dahl*. New York: Vintage.

Dickens, Charles. 2002. *Great Expectations*. New York: Penguin Classics.

Fitzgerald, F. Scott. 1999. *The Great Gatsby*. New York: Scribner.

Golding, William. 1959. *Lord of the Flies*. New York: Perigee Trade.

Hansberry, Lorraine. 1994. *A Raisin in the Sun*. New York: Vintage.

Hawthorne, Nathaniel. 1952. "The Minister's Black Veil." In *Fifty Great Short Stories*, ed. Milton Crane. New York: Bantam Classics.

——.1981. *The Scarlet Letter*. New York: Bantam Classics.

Hurston, Zora Neale. 1998. *Their Eyes Were Watching God*. New York: HarperPerennial Classics.

Jackson, Shirley. 1991. "The Lottery." In *The Lottery and Other Stories*. New York: Noonday Press.

Knowles, John. 1984. *A Separate Peace*. New York: Bantam.

Lee, Harper. 2002. *To Kill a Mockingbird*. New York: HarperPerennial Classics.

Miller, Arthur. 1988. *Death of Salesman*. New York: Penguin.

Moore, Lorrie. 2004. "Introduction." In *The Best American Short Stories: 2004*, ed. Katrina Kennison. Boston: Houghton Mifflin.

Shakespeare, William. 1973. "Hamlet," "Julius Caesar," "Macbeth," "Romeo and Juliet." In *The Riverside Shakespeare*. Boston: Houghton Mifflin.

Standards for the English Language Arts. 1996. Urbana, IL: National Council of Teachers of English, and Newark, DE: International Reading Association.

Steinbeck, John. 1981. *Of Mice and Men*. New York: Bantam Books.

Tovani, Cris. 2000. *I Read It, but I Don't Get It: Comprehension Strategies for Adolescent Readers*. Portland, ME: Stenhouse.

Wilder, Thornton. 1998. *Our Town*. New York: HarperPerennial.

CHAPTER 2

Structures and Strategies That Support the Teaching of Short Texts

In an act of swift engagement with his or her subject matter, the skilled essayist can imbue even the briefest text with the immediacy, momentum, and intellectual agility one expects from a longer work. **—BERNARD COOPER**

I was fortunate to work in a school where my colleagues were supportive of using short texts. But I recognize this approach to teaching literature is the exception rather than the rule. As I look at curriculums, particularly high school curriculums, I see the dominance of novels. A beginning teacher with whom I work is faced with a curriculum for senior English that includes eight novels and two Shakespeare plays. According to the syllabus for the course, "a few short stories" will be read. Poetry is not listed. Nonfiction is nonexistent. She would like to find ways to weave some short texts, particularly nonfiction, into her classroom. Another colleague faces the challenge of using a mandated literature anthology. Although he supports many of the selections in the anthology—some of these

9

selections are included in this book—he is looking for additional short text resources. A third colleague, now chair of her department, is working with her fellow
English teachers to shift the focus of the literature curriculum from a novels-only
approach to a curriculum that includes novels but also incorporates a variety of
genres through the use of short texts. All three of these teachers want support
for their efforts to incorporate short texts. They want to know how to respond to
questions from colleagues, students, administrators, and parents. In the first section of this chapter I provide research on and a rationale for using short texts. The
remainder of the chapter focuses on selecting short texts and the structures and
strategies I have developed, with the gracious help of wonderful colleagues and
students, in support of using short texts to read, analyze, and enjoy literature.

Making the Case for Short Texts

Paulo Freire (1987) calls into question our curriculum expectations of reading
multiple novels in a semester:

> I believe much of teachers' insistence that students read innumerable books
> in one semester derives from a misunderstanding we sometimes have about
> reading. In my wanderings throughout the world there were not a few
> times when young students spoke to me about their struggles with extensive
> bibliographies, more to be devoured than truly read or studied.... Insistence
> on a quantity of reading without internalization of texts proposed for
> understanding rather than mechanical memorization reveals a magical view
> of the written word, a view that must be superseded. (24)

Freire's reminder that we need to focus on the "why" rather than the "how much"
of reading is consistent with research on supporting adolescents as readers. This
research, which builds on lessons learned from teaching adolescents to write,
recognizes the importance of choice, relevance, differentiation, and modeling
(Allen 1995; Allen and Gonzalez 1998; Atwell 1998; Bean 2002; Bomer 1995;
Langer 2001; Tovani 2000, 2004). Using short texts to teach literature supports
each of these key components.

MORE READING CHOICES

Creating room for student choice within the requirements of literature-heavy
curriculum expectations is challenging. Short texts allow us to present students

with a list of title choices from within a genre. I remember the excitement the seniors in one of my English classes felt when they selected a short story entitled "Demon Lover" from a list of title options. Their subsequent dismay when the story did not live up to their interpretations of the title led to a rich discussion of the importance of titles as well as the craft and content of the story. I was struck by the students' framing of this discussion. They began their critique of the story with statements about how they felt misled by the title. They went on to point out places in the story where the author could have, even should have, made a different choice, a choice they would have found more interesting. They homed in on the story's characters—what worked and what didn't work. They were critics of this particular story, but not all stories. Rather than a tirade about how all literature is boring, they focused on how this story both met and did not meet their expectations as readers. When it came time to make the next story selection from a list of titles, they asked if they could skim the stories before choosing.

The use of short texts also supports literature circles. I implemented literature circles in my classroom so that students could have a choice about what novel they read and could experience shared reading with a group. I was so excited as I watched students select novels and form their literature circles. I will admit that my excitement lessened when I realized I now had to read all of the books they had chosen so I could support their discussions. Over the course of the literature circle unit I read frantically and convinced myself that students were engaged in rich discussions about the various books they were reading—discussions I heard snippets of as I circled the room, eavesdropping. But the group presentations on the literature circle novels painted a very different picture. I was dismayed when I began to ask questions of a literature circle group that had just presented a video about the book they had read. No one in the group could answer any of my questions; one of the students finally admitted that they had "skimmed the last three-quarters of the book." In a follow-up discussion with this group, students commented, "We figured you would not have read all the books so you would not notice." I have talked to a number of English teacher colleagues who have admitted their own struggles with reading all of the novels selected by students for literature circle reading, and have worried about students' depth of understanding if they were not able to check students' comprehension. As one colleague lamented, "I recently found myself online looking for shortcuts to get up to speed on the novels my students were reading in literature circles."

11

Focusing the literature circle on short texts gives teachers the opportunity to have read everything the students are reading in order to support literature circle conversations and check students' comprehension. It's also been my experience that reading short texts, which can be done in class, often results in more in-depth student discussions because the reading is immediate and manageable.

The use of short texts also means classes can examine a wider variety of authors and texts. Students' range of choices can include canon literature but also expand to include literature beyond the canon.

MORE RELEVANCE TO ADOLESCENTS' LIVES

Reading short texts allows for a greater variety of literature in the classroom and creates room for including texts that speak to the diverse students with whom we work. A balance of classics and more contemporary texts, including those from popular culture, is consistent with research on making reading relevant for adolescents—not just relevant recreational or self-selected reading but reading as a whole class (Bean 2002, Gallo 2001, Langer 2001). It is disheartening to note that in a recent newspaper article regarding book choices at area high schools in Portland, Oregon, students reported that they believed the primary criteria for selecting whole-class texts was that the choice be "long and boring."

As noted previously, I am not suggesting there is no place for long books, and I am not ready to concede that they are all boring! But I do recognize the power of selecting literature that has relevance for students. Short texts allow for the inclusion of literature based on contemporary issues that impact students' lives. Seeing connections between what they read and their own lives encourages students to see literature as part of their world, not just something one studies in school. "If educators are serious about developing students' lifelong love of reading, they need to incorporate in the curriculum literature that is captivating and issue-based" (Bean 2002).

MORE POSSIBILITIES FOR DIFFERENTIATED INSTRUCTION

Short texts in classrooms also provide a response to the ever-growing and ever-changing need for differentiated instruction. As noted in Chapter 1, within our classrooms today we have students with a wide range of reading abilities and cultural experiences. Selecting a long text that will address the variety of students we encounter is daunting at best. It is unrealistic to assume that in a class of thirty to thirty-five ninth graders all students have the same reading ability. Asking a group of differentiated readers to read *To Kill a Mockingbird* sets up some of our students for failure. As Cris Tovani notes, "If we are constantly giving students text that is too hard for them to read, they may get through it, but probably not without cheating. Many of my students who are struggling readers feel defeated before they even begin" (2004, 40). Ideally we would have the time and resources to select novels that are accessible for all the readers in our classrooms. But the reality is we don't have the time or resources. Short texts make differentiation possible: a selection of short stories with varying lengths and complexity is one option. Or, if all students are reading the same story, providing strategies that support reading the text during class is more doable for a short text.

I am not suggesting we lower our standards. But requiring students to read a text that is not accessible is not being rigorous. Our job as teachers is to teach the students in our classrooms—all of them. It is not to teach a particular text. Laurie Halse Anderson, author of young-adult literature, including the novel *Speak*, which has the longest waiting list of any book at Portland-area middle school and high school libraries, reminds us that our goal is not to produce students who can deconstruct text:

> *The goal is to produce, at graduation, every single child in America who can read and read well, and who will read broadly, who will read for fun, who will read for enlightenment, for work, who will read for safety, who will read to get information in emergency situations, who will read for information, who will read to make intelligent political decisions, and who will read for cultural understanding. (2005, 56)*

Anderson goes on to suggest that we need to do away with the term "reluctant reader." They are not reluctant readers. They are readers faced with "high barriers (presented by the canon) and high standards," and they are too smart "to willingly endure boring books" (57). Our job is to create a classroom where students want to read and can read. A classroom where the teacher is focused first on the students and how to connect students with curriculum rather than our current model where curriculum, which in many cases has not changed in the last twenty years in terms of the literature assigned, is the driving force.

Short texts make it possible to draw on a wider variety of literature so that we can factor in our students' reading interests and abilities. The variety of short

13

texts also makes it possible for us to select literature that will challenge our students rather than overwhelm them. Psychology and brain research indicates that students learn best when they are faced with a moderate challenge (Bess 1997; Csikszentmihalyi, Rathunde, and Whalen 1993; Howard 1994; Jensen 1998; Vygotsky 1978, 1996). My task as a language arts teacher is to provide texts that are not so difficult that my students shut down in frustration and not so easy that my students don't push their thinking. I want the students in my class to use their minds well as they interact with literature. Short texts provide me with more possibilities for supporting a moderate challenge. For specifics on how to differentiate instruction, I recommend Carol Ann Tomlinson's book *The Differentiated Classroom* (1999), which is listed in the resource section at the end of this chapter.

MORE EFFECTIVE WRITING MODELS

Short texts also allow us to connect what students read with what students write. Research shows that immersing students in good models of the writing we want them to do is important (Atwell 1998, Bomer 1995, Zinsser 1988). Although students can certainly learn about writing craft from novels, they can imitate both structure and writing craft if they are reading what they are being asked to write: short stories, memoirs, essays, poetry, even children's books and graphic novels.

I found that I needed to be explicit with students about how the literature we were reading could be used to "mentor" their writing. I then watched with wonder as students drew on the literature we read to inform their own writing. Darcy noted her own use of "stream of consciousness," based on a Faulkner story; Jess shared how Eudora Welty's use of descriptive detail in "A Worn Path" helped him bring the characters in his own short story to life. Sarah's richly detailed poem was inspired by the close reading we did of Elizabeth Bishop's "The Fish." Josh announced to the class that he was so angered by an editorial we read about why sixteen-year-olds should not drive, he was going to stay up all night writing a response. His essay not only provided a compelling alternate view, but also drew on the structure of the essay that inspired his response.

Connecting the short texts we read to the writing students did changed the way the students in my classroom viewed literature. Students responded to the literature as writers. They talked about the literature using the language of writing craft. They connected their own struggles and celebrations as writers with the authors they read. I witnessed students beginning to see themselves as fellow writers with the authors we were reading.

NCTE/IRA STANDARDS

The use of short texts to support literature study is also consistent with the *Standards for the English Language Arts* (1996). The standards call for a broad approach to text reading:

1. Students read a wide range of print and nonprint texts to build an understanding of texts, of themselves, and of the cultures of the United States and the world; to acquire new information, to respond to the needs and demands of society and the workplace; and for personal fulfillment. Among these texts are fiction and nonfiction, classic, and contemporary works.

2. Students read a wide range of literature from many periods and in many genres to build an understanding of the many dimensions (e.g. philosophical, ethical, aesthetic) of human experience. (3)

Using short texts to support the study of a wide range of texts is consistent with the standards' stance regarding the need for extensive literary experiences. "Students should learn that virtually any type of text—essay, diary, or film, as well as sonnet, short story, or play—can contain powerful literary expression" (1996, 17). Although I don't profess to be an expert on all of the state standards, I have found that most are consistent with the standards developed by the National Council of Teachers of English and the International Reading Association.

Classroom Structure and Student Supports

Drawing on the research supporting a workshop approach to writing and reading (Atwell 1998, Rief 1992, Romano 1987), I created a literature workshop. This workshop provided time in class to read, write, and discuss literature. In the process of developing this workshop approach, I discovered that I needed to provide instruction in and modeling of strategies that would support students in reading literature, writing in response to literature, and discussing the literature we read. In addition to literature workshop, I also provided time for students to write in a writing workshop and to read self-selected books in a reading workshop. Each of these workshops supported the work we did in the other workshops.

Short texts are extremely effective tools for teaching literature, but I learned that students need supports of brief prereading activities, previewing by the teacher, or useful postreading prompts (writing or discussion) to grow as readers through short texts. I could not simply assign the text and then expect my students to answer my questions after they completed the reading. I needed to structure a process that identified for students what I wanted them to examine and the strategies I wanted them to use. I needed to provide the means of accessing the literature in support of analysis. Too often in my enthusiasm to dig in and really explore a text, I found myself asking a question, pausing, and, when no answer was forthcoming, answering it myself. As one of my juniors responded one day when I queried the class about why they had not done the assigned reading, "Why should we read? If we wait long enough, most English teachers get frustrated and rather than trying to discuss the reading, they just tell us what it means." Ouch!

FRAMING OBJECTIVES
To counter the "let me tell you what the text means" tendency, it is imperative to know why I am teaching a particular text. Am I teaching the text to apply reading strategies in support of comprehension? To introduce or analyze literary elements or terms? To connect personal experiences with the text? Connect the text to other texts? To introduce an author? To serve as a model for writing? I need to frame a primary objective for each text: what I want students to know, understand, and be able to do (Wiggins and McTighe 2005). Once the primary objective is identified, I focus on assessment: How will I know what students know, understand, and can do? In developing assessments, I focus on creating and sustaining readers and writers. Although I recognize that I have diverse learners in my classroom who will need diverse approaches, I also recognize the importance of engaging students in what real readers and writers do beyond the world of school.

16

ASSESSMENTS
I think of assessment in two ways:

- Formal: the assessments I use to evaluate students' mastery of objectives and standards

- Informal: the assessments I do every day as students are engaged in the work of reading and writing

Formal assessment is the road map for my planning. My goal is to design a formal assessment that allows students to demonstrate their mastery of the objectives I have determined. How will I know what students know, understand, and can do? Designing the formal assessment at the beginning of the unit plan guides me in developing activities and informal assessments that will support students in developing the skills needed to demonstrate mastery. As noted previously, I want the assessments I use to engage students in reading and writing. I ask three questions of any formal assessment I plan to use. The first two are based on Grant Wiggins's book *Educative Assessment* (1998), and the third is a question I designed:

1. Could a student do well on this assessment for reasons that have little to do with mastery of the unit objectives?

2. Could a student who had participated in the learning activities of the unit do poorly on the assessment for reasons that have little to do with mastery of the objectives? (32)

3. Would a reader or writer outside of the world of school be engaged in this type of activity/assessment?

These questions help me avoid assessments that do not accurately assess students' mastery of my predetermined objectives. These questions also help me in designing activities for students that support the skills needed for the assessment. For example, it is tempting to evaluate students' understanding of short stories by asking students to write a short story as their formal assessment. But when I examine this assessment using the three questions, I see the flaws in this expectation:

1. It is possible that a student could write a short story without focusing on all the elements and writing craft we have studied during the short story unit.

2. A student could know and understand the elements of a short story and the ways authors use writing craft yet struggle to apply this understanding in the crafting of his or her own story. I would need to build in support for short

17

story writing as part of the unit. Also, I would need a process for students to show me how their story reflected their understanding of short story elements and literary craft.

3. To answer this question I always do the assessment I am asking of students. This decision to assess the assessment by doing it myself changed my teaching! In the case of writing a short story, I discovered it was incredibly challenging and would require significant in-class writing workshop time for support. I also discovered that understanding short stories didn't mean I could write a short story. Finally, I acknowledged that my response to reading short stories outside of school has never been to write a short story.

So what assessment did I design to formally assess students' understanding of short stories? I used several, but a favorite was the following in-class writing prompt:

We have been examining short stories for the past several weeks, identifying the elements of short stories and the ways authors draw on writing craft to bring these elements into focus. It is now time for you to put your understanding of short stories to use. For purposes of this task today, you are a textbook editor and your job is to determine which stories are to be included in your new and improved textbook for (middle school or high school) students. Select one of the short stories we have read and write a letter to its author about why you are including or rejecting his or her story for your new textbook. I ask that you be specific in your letter, referencing the elements and writing craft terminology we used in our study with examples from the story that illustrate these elements and writing craft. I will not be assessing you on the letter format you use, so put your time and energy into your analysis and critique of the story.

In response to the assessment questions noted above, I determined that this in-class writing task requires students to draw on the stories we read in class and our discussions of story elements and writing craft. I would allow students to use their literature learning logs (described in a later section) in support of this task. The design of the task is consistent with the low-stakes writing we did in class, so it doesn't require additional knowledge of writing, such as proper letter format, to complete the task. I do note that if letter writing had been a focus of the class, proper use of this format could be part of the evaluation criteria. Finally, although it is true that as a reader and writer outside of school I don't write letters as a textbook editor, I do read and critique stories. And since part of our focus as students of literature is to analyze and articulate what makes a story work well or less well, this task has real-world application.

I recognize that in answering the three assessment questions, I have to take into account that assessment requires me to evaluate students' understanding in ways that serve school standards. There will always be tension between the community of readers and writers I envision and the realities of the middle school and high school classrooms with curriculums, state and district standards, and testing expectations. But I maintain that asking questions of the assessments we design, doing the assessments ourselves, and designing activities that support students as they move toward formal assessment will help keep us focused on the goal: a classroom community that supports students in developing the skills and desire to be lifelong readers and writers. (For more on linking assessment with planning and teaching, I recommend Wiggins and McTighe's *Understanding by Design* [2005].)

Once I have the big picture of the unit—objectives and formal assessment—I design activities and the teaching strategies needed to support these activities as well as informal, ongoing assessment of the activities that provide me with data regarding students' understanding.

In-Class Reading

I made assumptions about my students as readers. I assumed they had strategies they could use when faced with difficult text. I assumed that if they read an assignment they understood it. I assumed that if they did not complete a reading assignment it was a reflection on their work ethic, or lack of work ethic. I was wrong every time!

The first time I assigned an excerpt from Thoreau's *Walden* to a class of juniors, I had the opportunity to challenge my assumptions. I had assigned an excerpt from "Where I Lived and What I Lived For" as homework. This assignment was a mere four and a half pages in the literature anthology. The next day in class I chose to check for comprehension with some questions that would also facilitate our classroom discussion. I asked students to respond to the following:

1. What details do you remember regarding Thoreau's house at the pond?

2. Thoreau writes about morning as his favorite time of day. What is his reasoning? Do you agree or disagree?

3. What do you know about the reasons for Thoreau being at Walden Pond? What do you want to know more about?

As I briefly explained each question, I let the students know they could use their books in support of their answers. I heard a student mutter, "Like that will help us." As I scanned the room I could see students glancing at each other as if to say, "Did you understand the reading?" I took a deep breath and asked the question I didn't want to ask: "How many of you did the reading assignment?" A majority of the students raised their hands or at least started to raise their hands. One brave student, I think it was Cheryl, offered the following explanation: "Okay, so I read this, at least my eyes moved across the words on the page, but I didn't understand it—not any of it." Other students chimed in, "I had the same experience." And, "What's with this guy? He makes nature sound like a college textbook." Before I had a revolt on my hands, I asked students to think about strategies they could have used in response to this challenging reading. I was met with silence. So I provided some prompts:

Did you reread when you realized you had not understood the first reading?

Did you go to the end of the excerpt and use the textbook questions as a guide?

Did you jot down questions about places in the reading that were confusing?

Did you try to summarize a paragraph or section before going on to the next section to check your understanding?

Did you try talking to a classmate about the reading before class?

Not one of my students answered yes to any of my questions. Susan shared, "I did keep reading, all of the assignment, but I never understood any of it." I observed other students nodding in agreement. These students demonstrated what Cris Tovani writes about in her book *I Read It, but I Don't Get It* (2000). Many of our students equate reading with the act of eyes scanning words; they go through the motions of reading but not the thinking of reading (see Chapter 2 in Tovani 2000 for more on this).

And my classroom also contained "resistant readers." Jason admitted, "When I don't understand the first page, I just stop reading. What's the point of continuing? It's just a waste of time." Again I saw students nodding. Bill added, "I figured you wouldn't give us a quiz; you usually don't. So we would discuss it and I would figure it out from the discussion." I also recalled the earlier comment from a student, "If we wait long enough, English teachers will just tell us what the reading means."

Arrggh! I wanted to talk about literature, not teach reading. But my students needed to learn reading strategies that would support text analysis and the discussion of literature. They needed me to teach them. In support of my students' reading, I drew on the strategy I used to teach them writing: modeling my own process. I asked students to open their books and follow along as I read aloud the first paragraph of the *Walden* excerpt I had assigned. As I read I stopped and talked about my thinking process.

I observed that Thoreau is detail oriented. He points out that he is "spending days and nights" in his "abode in the woods." He goes on to share that his first full day and night was "Independence Day." This reminds me of the way my mother tells stories—full of details that I often think are not important, but I discover later that all the details really do matter. So, I made note of "Independence Day" and planned to look for other details that would show me why this detail is important.

After modeling my thinking process with the first paragraph, I asked students to read the second paragraph in class. Before they read I asked them to jot down a question they had from the first paragraph or an aha, such as, "Will Thoreau say more about the area near his house?" I also asked them to mark with sticky notes places in the text where they felt confused. My final request was that they write down a quote they found that illustrates Thoreau's attention to detail. This built on our discussion from the first paragraph.

Students then shared their sticky note sections and quotes with a partner. As I circulated, I heard lively discussions of Thoreau's writing. I pointed out to students that they had moved from "not understanding" to discussing. And we agreed that slowing down our reading and paying attention to our process—and to developing strategies—served us well.

I continued to work with students to develop reading strategies. As discussed previously, the focus or objective of the lesson was a starting point for determin-

21

ing what reading strategies I would teach. As I made these decisions I was mindful not only of my objectives with respect to literary analysis but also how I could best support the diverse range of students in my class. I wanted the literature we read to be accessible to all the students in my class. So, in addition to the reading strategies noted in subsequent chapters, I drew on the following in support of students' understanding of short texts:

- Reading the text aloud to the class. I discovered that middle school and high school students like to be read to. Sometimes I read the text aloud without providing a copy of it. More typically, I read as students followed along with a copy of the text—or reread the text, or identified sections of the text after I had read it aloud.

- Short texts read aloud on tape or CD. My husband is a former radio DJ, so he helps with this, but I also found it helpful to ask students who read aloud well to help with recording. This work can be framed as an extra-credit option if needed, but it's been my experience that students will volunteer to help with this. Podcasts provide another version of read-alouds. PodcastDirectory.com provides a directory of what texts are available on podcast.

- Until I know my students' reading skills and strategies, we do all our short text reading in class.

- As illustrated in later chapters of this book, I let students know what I want them to focus on as they read. They will learn to mark texts, take notes, and write before and after they read. I want them to know that reading is more than just their eyes scanning the page; it's an interactive process between reader and text.

- For students who need more time to read, I provide them with a copy of the text before we will be reading it in class or allow them to take it home for rereading.

- If we are reading a longer or more complex text, I provide students who may be challenged by the text with a copy in which I have marked the key sections on which I want them to focus. Obviously this needs to be done with discretion so I don't draw attention to these students.

- Although the focus of this book is on whole-class story reading, literature circles work well with short texts. Many of the activities in this chapter could be done in literature circles by using the sidebar list of texts, which reflect a variety of lengths and reading challenges. I also want to note literature circles' power to support the reading of the same short text by the entire class. I found students benefited from a close examination of a whole-class text in a small group that met more than once (see discussion in Chapter 3 for more on literature circles).

- I model the teaching and reading strategies described in this book. These strategies incorporate a variety of techniques that illuminate the text for students. I utilize these strategies and the informal assessments noted above rather than multiple-choice quizzes that focus on comprehension. It's my hope students will continue to use the strategies they develop with short text in support of reading longer texts in language arts and other disciplines.

(See the resource list at the end of this chapter for recommendations of texts that address reading strategies.)

Sticky Notes

I have been amazed at the variety of ways sticky notes can be used to support literature study. They can note certain places in texts; they can be color-coded and used to identify literary terms or elements. For example, students might use blue sticky notes to mark places in a story that address character and green sticky notes for setting references. Sticky notes can also be used to jot down questions or quotes while reading.

I have also been amazed by students' reactions to sticky notes; they like using them. I watched my own daughter using sticky notes as she read and commented on her use of them. She responded with, "Don't you just love sticky notes; they are so multipurpose." I concur. Just a few days later a beginning teacher shared with me her surprise at students' enthusiasm for sticky notes. She provided the notes, and students thanked her profusely for being willing to use her own money for sticky notes. They then proceeded to use the sticky notes with enthusiasm, and the lesson was well supported by the sticky note element. I note the irony of my using a sticky note to write a note to myself about including a discussion of sticky notes in this chapter. So, if you haven't yet discovered the wonder of sticky notes, I urge you to get yourself to an office supply store and stock up: the more colors, sizes, and shapes the better. Throughout the genre chapters of this book, I describe uses for sticky notes. In the words of Martha Stewart, sticky notes are "a good thing."

Writing in Response to Literature

I write to know what I am thinking. I want students to discover this for themselves. So the writing we do in response to literature is primarily low-stakes writing (Elbow 1997). I want students to explore, experiment, and take risks without worrying whether or not they are doing it right. I use a variety of structures and prompts to encourage students to write about literature. The writing may focus on comprehension, examining writing craft, or connecting texts to one's self, other texts, or the world. We may be exploring literary analysis strategies. Writing in response to literature supports students' understanding and provides me with data I can use to monitor and adjust my teaching. Listed below are brief descriptions of the writing structures/strategies I use. You'll see further descriptions of these strategies in the chapters on short text genres.

READING CHECK-IN

I will admit to using the multiple-choice quizzes provided in the teacher resource guide that accompanied the literature anthology I was required to use. I wanted to check students' comprehension, and this was a quick way to do so. But when I looked at students' performance on these quizzes I was concerned. More than 50 percent of my students earned failing grades on the ten-question quizzes. So I decided I would try taking one of the quizzes myself. I am embarrassed to tell you that I was able to get only seven of the ten questions right when I took the quiz on the story "The Pit and the Pendulum." A closer examination of the quiz helped me see that the quiz required meticulous attention to plot details. Although I had read and comprehended the story, the quiz did not reflect my level of comprehension. So I developed alternative reading quizzes that would provide me with information about students' comprehension. On occasion, these were in multiple-choice formats—a format that doesn't serve me well in showing what I know. But I recognize that this format is part of the standardized testing students face, so I want students to have some experience with it. I used multiple-choice quizzes as a lesson in test taking more than as a measurement for comprehension.

The more typical reading check-in was a single question that students responded to in a five-to-ten-minute quick write. This single question was designed in support of the objectives for the short text. I note here some questions that worked well for a variety of objectives and short text genres:

What surprised you in the reading for today?

What do you think we should explore about this text in our discussion today?

If you were asked to create a title for this text, what would you call it and why?

What advice would you give the main character (or author)?

What does this author do well as a writer? Less well?

Summarize the theme or message of this text in five sentences and in one sentence.

If you were making a film of this text, what actor would you cast to play the main character? Why?

How does this short text compare with the text we read yesterday? What are the similarities? The differences?

If you could interview the author of this text, what would you ask?

Draft a question that you would ask to check students' comprehension of this text and then answer your own question. (An alternative to this is to have students draft questions and then collect them and use one of their questions as the reading check-in.)

LITERATURE LEARNING LOGS

I want students to have a place where their writing about literature is housed so they can revisit and reflect on their thinking—and so they can use their literature logs in support of formal assessments. After experimenting with a variety of formats, I found that using a spiral notebook exclusively as a literature log worked best for students. I will be honest in admitting that collecting and responding to these literature logs was a daunting task; the logistics of carrying as many as 150 spiral notebooks and developing a system for students to mark the pages was overwhelming. But the enormity of this task forced me to think carefully about why I was collecting and writing responses to these literature logs. Over time, I gave myself permission not to collect learning logs. I did do some in-class scanning of logs, and I periodically asked students to write reflections based on their learning logs—but they turned in the reflection rather than the log. And, as noted above, I modeled for students and encouraged them to use their learning logs in

25

support of class discussions and assessments (I kept my own literature log). The literature log supported the work we did in studying literature, so I did not need to read and write responses in students' logs. Literature log writing included the kinds of topics I use for reading check-in as well as quote and question in support of discussions (see section titled "Discussion"). I also asked students to write on the following topics in their logs:

- Based on the title of the short text, what predictions can you make?
- Find an example of the literary terms we've been discussing this week.
- Consider point of view: Who is telling this story? How might the story be different if told from a different point of view?
- What do you want to know more about with regard to this text?
- Think metaphor: if this text were a piece of clothing, what would it be and why?
- Other metaphor options: weather, color, animal, food (with grateful acknowledgment to Elbow and Belanoff 2000, 9, for this metaphor approach)
- What music do you think would be good to listen to while reading this text?
- Based on the short texts we have read, what are the characteristics that you think make for a good short story, essay, memoir, poem, children's book, graphic novel?
- Write a three-to-five-sentence summary of what you have read.
- I also used literature learning logs in support of reading process, so I asked students to stop after every two to four paragraphs and jot down what they notice in the text, what they wonder, or any discoveries they have made about their own reading process.
- Literature logs were the place to note new vocabulary words. Although it is not the focus of this book, I do see an important role for literature in vocabulary development. I asked students to list words that were new to them. We then created a class list of vocabulary based on student-selected words. I found students "owned" these words and were committed to learning them in a way I never saw with lists I generated. (For resources and strategies in support of vocabulary development, see Janet Allen's book *Words, Words, Words: Teaching Vocabulary in Grades 4–12* [1999].)

EXIT NOTES/ENTRANCE NOTES

These notes provided a manageable way for me to check students' thinking. Like the reading check-in described above, students were asked to write for five to ten minutes in response to a prompt. But the focus of these notes was not limited to reading comprehension. I used exit and entrance notes to assess students' process, to check understanding after a class discussion, or to provide students with the opportunity to practice metacognition. Some prompts I have used include the following:

- What worked well in your small group's discussion today? What do you think would make your small-group work more even more effective?
- Based on your group discussion today, what do you know about the author's use of writing craft?
- What questions do you still have about this text?
- Based on our class discussion, how would you define *theme*?
- In the memoir we read, the author shares the lesson she learned about family. How does her lesson inform your thinking about family?
- What was your favorite short text selection in this unit and why?
- What was your least favorite and why?

DIALOGUE JOURNALS

Talking, writing notes, commenting under their breath while I am talking— these are adolescent behaviors I have not always embraced. But I fully embrace talking and writing about the literature we are studying. Dialogue journals were a way for me to structure students' conversations with each other. I utilized a variety of formats but found a four-column approach worked best. I provided students with unlined sheets of paper. Students folded the paper in half, short side to short side or hamburger bun style. They then folded the half in half again. When the paper is opened back up, there are four columns. In Column 1, students list one or two quotes from the text. Specifics regarding this quote selection come from the lesson objectives. For example, I might ask students to list quotes that illustrate the author's use of descriptive writing. In Column 2, students explain why they chose the quotes. Students then exchange their dialogue journals with a peer. I often control this exchange process by collecting the journals and redistributing them. This may seem heavy-handed, but in a

27

classroom with diverse learners, I want to ensure that the peer-to-peer response serves all students well. So I might choose to have an ELL student respond to another ELL student. After students have exchanged dialogue journals, their task is to write a response in Column 3. What do they learn from reading their peer's thinking? We then return the dialogue journals to the original authors, and in Column 4 students write what they learn from reading their peer's response. I will then collect the dialogue journals and skim through them to glean information to inform my teaching.

ESSAYS

I appreciate James Moffet's reminder that the word *essay* comes from the French term *essai*, which means "to attempt" (Moffett 1983, 171). I want students to see essay writing as a place where they try out their thinking. My emphasis is on supporting students' idea development. What do they want to say? Students write about writing craft; they write about personal connections with texts; they develop essays that compare and contrast texts; they link the texts we read to world issues. Essays are an opportunity for students to show their exploration of ideas and text, to wrestle with their thinking. I discovered that reading essays and examining how authors structured their writing to convey their thinking was an effective way to learn about structure in essay writing. Chapter 4 discusses the study of essays as literature. I also recommend Tom Romano's books *Clearing the Way* (1987) and *Crafting Authentic Voice* (2004) in support of essay writing (see the resource list at the end of this chapter for more on Romano's books).

Discussion

My dream is a classroom where each student is so engaged in our conversation about the literature that when the bell rings no one reacts; the conversation just continues. Although I certainly have experienced class discussions that leave me giddy about the level of engagement, I have also facilitated class discussions that leave me wondering if good classroom discussions are even possible. I do know that preparation is a necessary first step for good discussions. Students need to have read the text and done some thinking about what they want to discuss. A simple strategy that has served me well is quote and question.

QUOTE AND QUESTION

I ask students to prepare for our upcoming class discussion by writing down a quote from the text that they find striking. I also ask them to develop a question they think is worthy of discussion. I cannot stress enough the importance of modeling this practice with students. A mistake I made in the past is assuming that students knew how to home in on a pithy passage or craft a question that fosters conversation. I certainly struggle to do this well, which has led to some of my less-than-stellar class discussions. I can confirm that even as students are developing their skills at selecting quotes and framing questions, the fact they have something written down ahead of time provides a starting point for each student to join in the conversation.

Whether the conversation will be with a small group or the entire group is always an intriguing teaching decision. As someone who is shy about sharing my ideas with a large group, I appreciate opportunities to talk in small groups. I also recognize the benefit of creating a classroom conversation that allows all voices to be heard. I have yet to develop a formula that tells me when to use which kind of group arrangement. I tend to use small groups in support of early explorations, such as the first discussion of a particular text or genre. Large groups come later as students develop more confidence about what they know. However, I have also used small groups to support conversations where we dig deep into a text we have been studying, and large-group discussions can serve as an introduction to a text or genre. I am learning that the setup and expectations of the small- or large-group discussion require my attention. What structures will support students' engagement?

SMALL-GROUP STRUCTURES THAT SUPPORT DISCUSSION

As mentioned earlier, requiring each group member to bring to the discussion something he or she has prepared is essential. This ensures there is a starting point for the conversation. I have also learned that the number of students in a group can impact the group's effectiveness. My experience is that groups of three or four students work best. How the students are assigned to groups varies. I have found that the least effective strategy for group assignments is allowing students to choose their own groups. I recently had a freshman girl tell me that she hated her English class because she was in a class where she did not know a lot of people and it was hard to find a group. She found it awkward to ask her peers, "Hey, can I

29

be in your group?" And I certainly have observed groups made up of friends who were engaged in conversation, but not about the literature.

There are a number of resources available on small-group setup, including literature circle discussion strategies. You'll find a list of these resources at the end of this chapter.

LARGE-GROUP STRUCTURES IN SUPPORT OF DISCUSSION

Again, preparation is key. But the struggle I have with large-group discussions is ensuring that all students have the opportunity to speak. I have discovered three strategies that address this challenge.

Silent Graffiti

This strategy invites students to converse as a whole group through writing. The goal is to have students respond to prompts, quotes, or questions that are posted on butcher paper around the room. Each student is given a felt pen and asked to write responses to the prompt on the butcher paper as well as respond to their peer's responses. I will admit that I enjoy the silence of this process. For those of you wondering how you could implement this strategy with large classes or with classes of students you don't think are ready to wander with felt pens in their hands, an alternative setup is to have students do this activity in small groups.

Carousel Graffiti

This variation of silent graffiti utilizes a small-group format to facilitate a whole-group discussion. Students are divided into small groups, three or four students in each group. Each group is provided with a large piece of butcher paper and a felt pen. For assessment purposes I find it helpful to have each group use a different color of felt pen so I can trace responses to each group based on color. Depending on the lesson objective and students' skill at developing questions, the questions are either provided by me or developed by each group. After each group has its question written on the top of the butcher paper, a scribe and a "carrier of the question" are selected for each group. These roles rotate with each rotation of the carousel so that responsibilities are shared. The carousel commences with the carrier of the question delivering his or her butcher paper to an adjacent group. Each small group then reads, discusses, and jots down its response to the question. After the designated time for response, I announce it is time to "carousel" and a new scribe and carrier of the question are selected. The questions move to the next group, and the process continues. Students in each group respond not only to the original question but also to the other groups' responses. Each group responds to each question. I find it works best to allow eight to ten minutes for the first question response and then to gradually reduce the amount of time for each group to respond to subsequent questions (five to seven minutes). Eventually the question makes its way back to its original group. The original group is then asked to synthesize the responses and report their synthesis to the whole group. This allows students to see the development of each question and how their responses contributed to this development. In a large class, I have used two carousels so that students are divided into two groups, and then each of these groups is divided again so that I have two separate carousels going on in the same classroom.

Fishbowl

A third strategy I have used is a discussion technique that focuses attention on a small group discussing in an inner circle while the rest of the class listens and takes notes from their position in the outer circle. This technique is sometimes called "fishbowl" (see Baloche et al. 1993). The idea is for a small group of students to converse while their peers listen in. Again, students are instructed in how to prepare for the conversation. I set up the room so a small group of five to seven students is in the center and places for the remaining students surround this inner group. I select the first "inside" group and ask them to take seats in the inner circle. The "outside" students are instructed to take notes on the conversation they hear. I let students know they will be using the notes they take when they switch roles with the inside group, so it is important that they be good listeners. Depending on the size of the class, we will have multiple rotations of the inside and outside groups. Each student in the class is a member of the inside group once. I tell inside group students that once they have spoken in the inside group, they need to wait until their fellow group members speak before they can speak again.

31

Although I sometimes need to intervene with the inside group, for the most part I have the privilege of being an observer of this discussion. I appreciate how this structure allows all voices to be heard and supports students in developing active listening skills. I also find that the notes students take during the discussion, which I typically collect, provide data I can use to inform my teaching. I don't use these large-group discussions all the time but I find their use supports my goal of creating a community of learners who engage in conversation about literature. See the list at the end of this chapter for resources to use in supporting discussion.

Literary Theory

I know there is debate among English teachers about the approach we should use to teach literature. In my own classroom and in crafting this book, I chose to focus on an approach that is not linked to any one literary theory; my focus is on the structure and craft of each text. This is not to suggest that history, feminism, new criticism, and reader response are irrelevant. In fact, I would humbly suggest that I touch on all of these during my yearlong exploration of literature with students. But my starting place is examining genre, structure, and writing craft. I want students to be immersed in the text. I want them to explore the text as it stands as well as make connections between the text, other texts, their own lives and writing, and the world.

My goal is to create a classroom community that encourages students to articulate responses to literature as readers and writers. I want students to describe the structures and craft they see in a specific text and to connect these observations with other texts they have read. I want students to ask questions about the author and how his or her life reflects history and culture. I want students to explore the links they see between the author's text and their own lives and culture. I want students to develop their keen eyes as writers, drawing on the craft lessons they find in the texts we read. Most important, I want students to develop response habits that enable them to both enjoy literature and feel confident about their ability to interact with it. I want students to see how reading literature helps them discover the stories of their own lives. As Robert Probst notes:

In the process of reading, responding, articulating questions, and contemplating possible answers, the reader may gradually define herself. The knowledge she gains is not something that the literary work has given her—it is something of her own that the work has enabled her to create. As she reads and thinks, she inscribes herself upon the world, declaring what she believes and what she denies, what she values and what she rejects. (2004, 18)

Selecting Short Texts

In the past few years I have seen an increased focus on reading levels. It's been my experience that the methods of rating the text reading levels are at best highly suspect. Rather than worry if a text is sixth-grade or tenth-grade level, I choose texts that illustrate what I want students to know and understand: a reading strategy, an element of the genre, an example of writing craft, or a text I want them to connect to their own lives, another text, or the world. The teaching strategies I describe for each genre of short text support the diverse groups of students with whom I have worked.

In selecting the texts I reference in this book, I was cognizant of the challenge of bringing texts into the classroom. I scoured a number of literature anthologies, so I am hopeful some of the text selections are in the textbooks already sitting on your classroom shelf. I also wanted to explore texts that have not yet been discovered by textbook publishers. For these texts, I consulted colleagues and students, and I searched the stacks of my local library and bookstore. I also checked online resources. Having taught both middle school and high school, I am aware of the need to consider district and community standards with regard to content. I trust each of you to make your own decisions about what is appropriate for your classroom.

I also recognize the reality of seeking out resources and finding the funds to support the use of the resources you find. I found the majority of the short texts I reference in my local public library or on websites. I will admit to making a few purchases of short text collections; my husband would tell you that I purchased more than a few.

At the end of each chapter I list my favorite resources and text collections. The collections listed are ones in which I found multiple short text selections to use.

Literature Anthologies and Short Text

A reality for many of us who work in middle and high schools is the literature anthology. Its use can be daunting for teachers and students. It weighs more than is reasonable to carry in a backpack. It looks like school—the pages are glossy, there are illustrations, and there are the inevitable questions and skills sections at the end of each story. Teachers often use the quizzes prepared and provided by the publisher to check for reading comprehension. This setup doesn't lend itself to creating a classroom of authentic reading.

To test my theory, I experimented with two classes of freshmen: one class read the short story as it was presented in the textbook, complete with pictures and end-of-text questions, which I did not assign. The other class read the same short story, but I made a classroom set of copies from a short story collection—no pictures or questions. The students who read the copied version reported they "liked the story," and their animated discussion was evidence of this. The students who read the same story in the textbook described the story as "okay, but kind of boring." If you have the choice to use copied stories rather than textbook versions, I encourage you to do so.

For those of you using textbooks, I empathize. I discovered some strategies that helped my students see past the textbook and discover the literature that might be of use to them. First, I demonstrated for my students why we had the textbook. I piled up books of short stories, poems, novels, plays, and nonfiction works to show them how many books it would take to even begin to capture the rich variety offered by the literature anthology. I asked them to skim the literature anthology's table of contents and jot down selections or authors that they recognized or that piqued their interest.

This skimming of the table of contents led me to think about the importance of incorporating choice in literature selections. I began to experiment with giving students choices with respect to which selections we read in the literature anthology (see discussion in upcoming chapters on the role of titles and leads in selecting what we read).

Embracing Genre with Short Texts

I support the inclusion of well-crafted genres that by their very design are short: short stories, essays, poetry, and children's books. I also support the use of excerpts from longer texts; you'll see this in the chapter on memoir. In selecting excerpts, I worked to honor the author's original work by selecting entire sections or chapters so that students could experience the author's style and perhaps even seek out the entire work for further reading. I also used excerpts from graphic novels. I am advocating the inclusion of graphic novels, a genre that has the potential to draw students into the world of storytelling while supporting complex reading skills development. The following sections provide a brief rationale for each genre chapter.

SHORT STORIES (CHAPTER 3)

A short story, rather than requiring long periods of time to read, invites readers to look closely, to dig deep. Unlike longer works, which can be challenging for adolescents to analyze, the brevity of short stories supports a level of scrutiny that enables students to develop their skills as literary analysts. Short stories provide us with the opportunity to explore literary terms and the elements of fiction in support of writing craft.

As Carole Hamilton and Peter Kratzke (1999) note in their edited collection of essays supporting short story use in the classroom:

Teachers challenge students to care, widening the tiny cracks in their students' intellectual and emotional armor and opening the way to deeper insight. The short story provides the perfect occasion to do that, for it resists facile assumptions, presenting an enigma, not an explanation. The short story demands contemplation and rewards interrogation, offering up its sweetest secrets to those who probe it in earnest. (1)

The more I teach short stories, the more I appreciate this genre. As a reader and teacher of short stories, I have experienced what Raymond Carver, one of my favorite short story authors, describes; short stories "send a chill along the reader's spine" (1994, 273).

ESSAYS (CHAPTER 4)

It is striking to me that we expect our students to write essays—literary, expository, and persuasive—but we typically do not require students to read essays. Why is this genre so limited, or even missing, in our middle school and high school curriculums? Introducing students to well-written essays serves a variety of purposes:

1. It demonstrates to students that this genre exists beyond the world of school.

2. It provides models for students' own essay writing.

3. It allows for the exploration of writing craft and theme in an accessible, nonfiction format.

MEMOIR (CHAPTER 5)

When students read memoir they see how stories of life, from the small moment to the life lesson, inform and even inspire. Childhood, family, hobby, career come into focus as students compare and contrast their own life stories with the memoirs they read. In the process, students examine writing craft in the memoirs—craft they can use in their own writing. My hope is that they also discover that although we each have our own story to tell, we also are linked with others in shared story.

POETRY (CHAPTER 6)

Poetry is the ultimate short text. Poems, by their very length and nature, illustrate that short doesn't mean easy. I want students to wrestle with the complexities of poetry. I appreciate how poems serve as the great equalizer for students of widely varying reading abilities. Comprehending a poem requires multiple readings; this is true for all readers. Literal comprehension is not the goal when reading poetry. I enjoy watching students who have struggled with literal comprehension discover that poetry encourages them to take risks in interpreting the text.

CHILDREN'S BOOKS (CHAPTER 7)

Children's books hold promise for the middle school and high school classroom. They support the continued development of students' visual literacy. But they also do more than that. Children's literature encourages students to tap into their early memories of reading. Students who are new to the English language or who struggle with reading often find children's literature more accessible, and a whole-class focus on children's literature takes away any stigma that these are "easy books." Children's literature also provides opportunities for literature study—examining structure, writing craft, and the connection between children's literature and the tradition of storytelling. Studying children's literature also supports cultural explorations.

36

GRAPHIC NOVELS (CHAPTER 8)

Supporting students' development of multiple literacies is important, as is providing students with reading that represents popular culture. Graphic novels allow for the examination of plot, character, theme, and writing craft. They also invite students to become knowledgeable consumers of popular culture.

WORKS CITED

Allen, Janet. 1995. *It's Never Too Late: Leading Adolescents to Lifelong Literacy.* Portsmouth, NH: Heinemann.

———. 1999. *Words, Words, Words: Teaching Vocabulary in Grades 4–12.* York, ME: Stenhouse.

Allen, Janet, and Kyle Gonzalez. 1998. *There's Room for Me Here: Literacy Workshop in the Middle School.* Portland, ME: Stenhouse.

Anderson, Laurie Halse. 2005. "Loving the Young Adult Reader Even When You Want to Strangle Him (or Her)!" *The ALAN Review,* Winter: 53–58.

Atwell, Nancie. 1998. *In the Middle: New Understandings About Writing, Reading, and Learning.* 2nd ed. Portsmouth, NH: Heinemann.

Baloche, Lynda, Marilyn Lee Mauger, Therese M. Willis, Joseph R. Filinuk, and Barbara V. Michalsky. 1993. "Fishbowls, Creative Controversy, Talking Chips: Exploring Literature Cooperatively." *English Journal* 83 (2): 43–50.

Bean, Thomas W. 2002. "Making Reading Relevant for Adolescents." *Educational Leadership* 60 (3): 34–37.

Bess, J. Ed. 1997. *Teaching Well and Liking It: Motivating Faculty to Teach Effectively.* Baltimore, MD: Johns Hopkins University Press.

Bomer, Randy. 1995. *Time for Meaning: Crafting Literate Lives in Middle and High School.* Portsmouth, NH: Heinemann.

Bishop, Elizabeth. 1983. "The Fish." In *The Complete Poems: 1927–1979.* New York: Farrar, Straus and Giroux.

Carver, Raymond. 1994. "On Writing." In *The New Short Story Theories,* ed. Charles E. May. Athens: Ohio University Press.

Cooper, Bernard. 1996. "Preface: The Disproportionate Power of the Small." In *In Short: A Collection of Brief Creative Nonfiction,* ed. Judith Kitchen and Mary Paumier Jones. New York: W.W. Norton.

Csikszentmihalyi, Mihaly, Kevin Rathunde, and Samuel Whalen. 1993. *Talented Teenagers: The Roots of Success and Failure.* New York: Cambridge University Press.

Elbow, Peter. 1997. "High Stakes and Low Stakes in Assigning and Responding to Writing in the Disciplines." In *Assigning and Responding to Writing in the Disciplines,* ed. Mary Deane Sorcinelli and Peter Elbow. San Francisco: Jossey-Bass.

Elbow, Peter, and Pat Belanoff. 2000. *Sharing and Responding,* 3rd ed. New York: McGraw-Hill.

Freire, Paulo, and Donaldo Macedo. 1987. "The Importance of the Act of Reading." In *Literacy: Reading the Word and the World.* Westport, CT: Bergin and Garvey.

Gallo, Don. 2001. "How Classics Create an Aliterate Society." *English Journal* 90 (3): 33–39.

Hamilton, Carole L., and Peter Kratzke, eds. 1999. *Short Stories in the Classroom.* Urbana, IL: NCTE.

Howard, Pierce. 1994. *The Owner's Manual for the Brain.* Austin, TX: Leornian.

Jensen, Eric. 1998. *Teaching with the Brain in Mind.* Alexandria, VA: ASCD.

Langer, Judith. 2001. "Beating the Odds: Teaching Middle and High School Students to Read and Write Well." *American Educational Research Journal* 38 (4): 837–80.

Lee, Harper. 2002. *To Kill a Mockingbird.* New York: HarperPerennial Classics.

Moffett, James. 1983. "On Essaying." In *Fforum: Essays on Theory and Practice in the Teaching of Writing*, ed. Patricia L. Stock. Upper Montclair, NJ: Boynton/ Cook.

Probst, Robert. 2004. *Response and Analysis: Teaching Literature in Secondary School.* Portsmouth, NH: Heinemann.

Rief, Linda. 1992. *Seeking Diversity: Language Arts with Adolescent*s. Portsmouth, NH: Heinemann.

Romano, Tom. 1987. *Clearing the Way: Working with Teenage Writers.* Portsmouth, NH: Heinemann.

Poe, Edgar Allan. 1984. "The Pit and the Pendulum." In *The Complete Stories and Poems of Edgar Allan Poe.* New York: Doubleday.

Standards for the English Language Arts. 1996. Urbana, IL: National Council of Teachers of English, and Newark, DE: International Reading Association.

Thoreau, Henry David. 1995. *Walden.* New York: Houghton Mifflin.

Tovani, Cris. 2000. *I Read It, but I Don't Get It: Comprehension Strategies for Adolescent Readers.* Portland, ME: Stenhouse.

———. 2004. *Do I Really Have to Teach Reading? Content Comprehension, Grades 6–12.* Portland, ME: Stenhouse.

Vygotsky, Lev. 1978. *Mind in Society: The Development of Higher Psychological Processes*, ed. Michael Cole, Vera John-Steiner, Sylvia Scribner, and Ellen Souberman. Cambridge, MA: Harvard University Press.

———. 1996. *Thought and Language.* Rev. ed., ed. and trans. Alex Kouzlin. Cambridge, MA: MIT Press.

Welty, Eudora. 1982. "A Worn Path." In *The Collected Stories of Eudora Welty.* New York: Harvest Books.

Wiggins, Grant. 1998. *Educative Assessment: Designing Assessments to Inform and Improve Student Performance.* San Francisco: Jossey-Bass.

Wiggins, Grant, and Jay McTighe. 2005. *Understanding by Design.* 2nd ed. New York: Prentice Hall.

Zinsser, William. 1988. *Writing to Learn.* New York: Harper and Row.

RECOMMENDED RESOURCES IN SUPPORT OF TEACHING SHORT TEXTS

Teaching Literature

Allen, Janet. 1995. *It's Never Too Late: Leading Adolescents to Lifelong Literacy.* Portsmouth, NH: Heinemann.
A research chronicle that offers inspiration and proven methods. Readers will find case studies, photographs, quotes from educators, surveys, activities, and step-by-step strategies for teaching reading (and writing) to the most reluctant middle and high school students.

Barchers, Suzanne. 2005. *In Short: How to Teach the Young Adult Short Story.* Portsmouth, NH: Heinemann.
Strategies for teaching fifteen young-adult short stories—includes each story.

Boomer, Randy. 1995. *Time for Meaning: Crafting Literate Lives in Middle and High School.* Portsmouth, NH: Heinemann.
Thoughtful and practical advice about how to confront the realities of today's classrooms: overcrowded curriculums, unfriendly colleagues, choppy schedules, and resistant learners. Chapter 5 focuses on classroom arrangements for becoming better readers.

Gillespie, Tim. 1987. "Irony and Teaching: Three Students, Three Stories." In *Oops: What We Learn When Our Teaching Fails*, ed. Brenda Miller Power and Ruth Shagoury Hubbard. York, ME: Stenhouse.
Reflection on what we can learn from students and their stories of our classrooms.

Hamilton, Carole L., and Peter Kratzke, eds. 1999. *Short Stories in the Classroom*. Urbana, IL: NCTE.
A collection of essays in which authors explore teaching a variety of short stories, by authors such as Toni Cade Bambara, Tim O'Brien, Sherman Alexie, and Alice Walker.

Lattimer, Heather. 2003. *Thinking Through Genre: Units of Study in Reading and Writing Workshops 4–12*. York, ME: Stenhouse.
This book profiles six different units of study: memoir, feature article, editorial, short story, fairy tale, and response to literature. It provides an example of each genre, unit planning guides, sample lesson plans, examples of student work, and assessment measures. Very practical.

Purves, Alan C., Theresa Rogers, and Anna C. Soter. 1995. *How Porcupines Make Love III: Readers, Texts, Cultures in the Response-Based Literature Classroom*. 3rd ed. White Plains, NY: Longman.
A classic, albeit irreverent text for understanding the reader-response-based approach to literature teaching in the middle and secondary grades.

Teaching/Supporting Discussion

Copeland, Matt. 2005. *Socratic Circles: Fostering Critical and Creative Thinking in Middle and High School*. Portland, ME: Stenhouse.
A practical guide that includes strategies for and examples of Socratic circles.

Chistenbury, Leila. 2006. "The Craft of Questioning." In *Making the Journey: Being and Becoming a Teacher of English Language Arts*. 3rd ed. Portsmouth, NH: Heinemann.
In this chapter, Christenbury shares strategies for supporting students in developing and responding to discussion questions.

Daniels, Harvey. 2002. *Literature Circles: Voice and Choice in Book Clubs and Reading Groups*. 2nd ed. York, ME: Stenhouse.
Strategies, structure, tools, and stories to launch and guide literature circles effectively.

Daniels, Harvey, and Nancy Steineke. 2004. *Mini-lessons for Literature Circles*. Portsmouth, NH: Heinemann.
Forty-five mini-lessons designed to support literature circles.

Gilmore, Randy. 2006. *Speaking Volumes: How to Get Students Discussing Books and Much More*. Portsmouth, NH: Heinemann.
Although focused on longer texts, this book provides detailed directions for implementing a variety of discussion techniques.

Teaching Reading

Allen, Janet. 1999. *Words, Words, Words: Teaching Vocabulary in Grades 4–12*. York, ME: Stenhouse.
Offers practical, research-based solutions for helping students fall into new language, learn new words, and begin to use those words in their speaking and writing lives. It also provides research that questions

the practice of teacher-selected words and memorization.

Burke, Jim. 2000. *Reading Reminders: Tools, Tips, and Techniques.* Portsmouth, NH: Heinemann.
Practical strategies designed to improve students' reading skills. Designed to be read on the run, this book provides Jim Burke's one hundred best techniques for teaching reading.

Gallagher, Kelly. 2003. *Reading Reasons: Motivational Mini-Lessons for Middle and High School.* Portland, ME: Stenhouse.
Practical mini-lessons that focus on both the why and how of reading.

Tovani, Cris. 2000. *I Read It, but I Don't Get It: Comprehension Strategies for Adolescent Readers.* York, ME: Stenhouse.
This book contains great strategies to support adolescent readers.

———. 2004. *Do I Really Have to Teach Reading? Content Comprehension, Grades 6–12.* Portland, ME: Stenhouse.
Great strategies to support adolescent readers across content areas.

Wilhelm, Jeffrey D. 1997. *"You Gotta BE the Book": Teaching Engaged and Reflective Reading with Adolescents.* New York: Teachers College Press.
A lively mix of theoretical argument and classroom storytelling in which Wilhelm explores how dramatic and artistic responses to literature support students' learning.

Teaching Writing in Response to Literature

Lattimer, Heather. 2003. "Response to Literature." In *Thinking Through Genre: Units of Study in Reading and Writing Workshops 4–12.* York, ME: Stenhouse.
This book profiles six different units of study: memoir, feature article, editorial, short story, fairy tale, and response to literature. It provides an example of each genre, unit planning guides, sample lesson plans, examples of student work, and assessment measures. Very practical.

Romano, Tom. 1987. "Writing Amid Literature, Part One: Other Than Essays" and "Writing Amid Literature, Part Two: Restoring a Reputation." In *Clearing the Way: Working with Teenage Writers.* Portsmouth, NH: Heinemann.
Examples of ways students may interact and write about literature in nonessay and essay format.

———. 2004. *Crafting Authentic Voice.* Portsmouth, NH: Heinemann.
Rich in voice, this book provides inspiration as well as practical suggestions for nurturing students' voices as writers.

———. 2000. *Blending Genre, Altering Style: Writing Multigenre Papers.* Portsmouth, NH: Heinemann.
Practical advi ce regarding genres, subgenres, writing strategies and stylistic maneuvers students can use in crafting multigenre papers—an alternative to literary essays and research papers.

Planning and Assessment

Campbell, Kimberly. 1996. "You Can't Always Judge a Book by Its Cover." In *Oops: What We Learn When Our Teaching Fails*, ed. Brenda Miller Power and Ruth Shagoury Hubbard. York, ME: Stenhouse.
Lessons about structuring and assessing literature circles in support of choice-reading.

Tomlinson, Carol Ann. 1999. *The Differentiated Classroom: Responding to the Needs of All Learners.* Alexandria, VA: ASCD.
This book provides a variety of strategies in support of differentiated instruction and assessment.

Wiggins, Grant. 1998. *Educative Assessment: Designing Assessments to Inform and Improve Student Performance.* San Francisco: Jossey-Bass.
A thoughtful discussion of planning and assessment with an emphasis on backward design.

Wiggins, Grant, and Jay McTighe. 2005. *Understanding by Design.* 2nd ed. New York: Prentice Hall.
Further exploration of backward design with an emphasis on supporting students' understanding.

CHAPTER 3

Short Stories

Novels and stories are renderings of life; they can not
only keep us company, but admonish us, point us in new
directions, or give us the courage to stay a given course.
They can offer us kinsmen, kinswomen, comrades,
advisers—offer us other eyes through which we might see,
other ears with which we might make soundings.

–ROBERT COLES

W hat?" Milo's loud query pierced the quiet of my freshman English class. I smiled as we shifted from silent reading to class discussion. "So, let's check in with Milo and see what inspired his passionate question." Milo is the kind of student you hope for and dread. He was funny, articulate, and had no inhibitions. All of us in sixth-period English 9 always knew what Milo was thinking. On this particular day, Milo was thinking about a kindergarten student.

"Are you telling me that there really is no kid named Charles? So all that stuff the kid describes to his parents . . . all that stuff . . ."

Susan chimed in, "I knew it; I just knew it. The kid, Laurie, who tells all those stories, he was doing all the stuff."

Jennifer added, "I thought something was weird. Why would the whole class have to stay after school? Can you even keep kindergarten students after school?"

42

Ben jumped in. " I noticed that the kid wasn't good at home either. Remember that part . . . [he flips pages of the literature anthology as he talks] Yeah, here it is. The kid, Laurie, says to his dad:

"Look up."
"What?" his father said, looking up.
"Look down," Laurie said. "Look at my thumb. Gee you're dumb." He began
to laugh insanely.

Our conversation continued as freshman students talked about, reread, and talked some more about "Charles," a delightful story by Shirley Jackson that details the antics of a mischievous kindergarten student as told by Laurie to Laurie's parents. The parents are shocked to find out at parent conferences that there is no child named Charles in the class. This surprise ending elicited Milo's outcry and led to the kind of engaged conversation about story and writing that reminds me of why we teach literature. Students saw themselves in the story and shared their own classroom memories. They asked to reread the story so they could look for clues that supported the surprise ending—and they found clues. They looked at the dialogue between Laurie and his parents. They wondered what the parents would do when they got home and confronted Laurie. I wondered if Milo had not been a Laurie himself when he was in kindergarten. And I recognized once again the power of a well-crafted short story.

The short story is an "eminently teachable genre" (Hamilton and Kratzke 1999, xii). Because it is short, it can be read in class where teachers can provide support for struggling readers if needed. Short stories can be read in one sitting. Rather than facing a classroom of students in which less than half have read the assigned chapters of the novel chosen from the required reading list, short stories allow me to join with my students in reading and then closely examining a short story. Virtually all the literature elements used in novels can be analyzed more easily and efficiently with short stories, in a way that includes the varied readers in today's classrooms.

Short Story Selection

I worked to find stories that reflect my commitment to teaching a variety of stories: classic, contemporary, multicultural, and young-adolescent literature. I also worked to find stories that are easily accessible. I know the challenge of pulling

43

together a variety of short texts to use in the classroom. I began with literature textbooks borrowed from colleagues and my own children (I think I used my son's literature textbook more than he did). I looked at websites containing copies of short stories that can be downloaded and made good use of the local library. I scoured local bookstores as well as online bookstores. My best source of story titles was interviews with students and colleagues. It's my hope you'll find that the list of short story collections at the end of this chapter provides you with a starting place for using short stories in your classroom.

As for the reading levels of these stories, as noted in Chapter 2, it's been my experience that the methods of rating the reading levels of stories are at best highly suspect. Rather than worry about the reading level rating, I chose stories that I have used in classrooms with a range of readers—stories that illustrate an element or example of writing craft I want students to explore. The teaching strategies I describe for each of these stories served to support the diverse groups of students with whom I worked. At the end of the chapter I have included a list of short story collections and resources, knowing that I have only scratched the surface of the rich and varied stories out there just waiting to be read.

Teaching the Elements of Short Stories

CHARACTER

I want students to discover the people in the stories they read, to understand how the character serves as the entry point to the story. I want them to see how writers bring characters to life through physical description, gestures, actions and inactions, dialogue, and responses to situations and other characters. Analyzing character supports plot and theme analysis as well as writing craft. I want students to see that in both novels and short stories, complex characters are the heart of good fiction.

Teaching Strategy: Column Notes

In support of understanding character, I select a short story with two well-defined characters. I want students to pay attention to each character's physical characteristics and details and to compare and contrast characters. I also want them to pay attention to the interactions between characters. Jotting down what they observe as they read provides students with a starting place for character analysis based on textual evidence.

I ask students to make two columns on their paper. They write the first character's name at the top of the first column and the second character's name at the top of the second column. For each character, they are to note descriptions, actions, and dialogue.

These column notes help facilitate our discussion of the characters and their interactions.

The story "Winter Dreams" by F. Scott Fitzgerald works well for character analysis. The story is written in six sections, each one representing a different phase of Dexter Green's relationship with the beautiful and difficult Judy Jones. The contrast between Dexter and Judy is compelling.

The students in my junior English class were particularly struck (pun intended) by a scene in Section 2 of the story where Judy Jones hits another golfer in the abdomen with her wayward golf ball. This leads to the following confrontation:

> "You hit me in the stomach!" declared Mr. Hedrick wildly.
> "Did I?" The girl [Judy Jones] approached the group of men. "I'm sorry. I yelled, 'Fore!'"
> "Her glance fell casually on each of the men—then scanned the fairway for her ball.
> "Did I bounce into the rough?"

Students highlighted this scene because it is so telling regarding Judy Jones, who after this confrontation announces to her playing partner, "Here I am! I'd have gone on the green except that I hit something."

During our discussion of the characters Dexter and Judy, I appreciated how students drew on Judy's golf incident as evidence of her insensitivity to others. The details of the incident led students to share details from their own stories: of golf, of insensitivities they have endured, and of their own insensitivities. My sister would want you to know that I have my own insensitive golf story to share, and I always shared it with students when we read this story. When I was about six years old I was practicing my golf swing in our front yard. I swung the club back and hit my sister, who was just a toddler, in the mouth with the golf club. There was lots of screaming and blood, and my mother was furious. I kept trying to explain that I did not mean to do it; I did not know my sister was behind me. Finally, in exasperation, I threw down my club and announced, "Well, I said, 'Fore.'"

In the process of sharing our own stories, we saw how the characters in a story can serve as inspiration for reconnecting with our stories. We also identified and appreciated how authors use physical details, actions, dialogue, and interaction between characters to bring characters to life in a story. Listed in the sidebar are stories with two distinct characters that work well for character analysis.

USING TWO-COLUMN NOTES IN SUPPORT OF CHARACTER EXPLORATION

STORY/AUTHOR	PROMPT	CHARACTERS	
"The Catbird Seat" James Thurber	Note the interactions between these two characters	Mr. Martin	Mrs. Ulgine Barrows
"The Little House" Shirley Jackson	What do we learn about the dead aunt? How is she different from Elizabeth?	Elizabeth	Her dead aunt
"The Life You Save May Be Your Own" Flannery O'Connor	What do you learn about the characters from their squabbles with each other?	Mr. Shiftlet	Lucynell
"Man and Daughter in the Cold" John Updike	What do we learn about Becky from her speech and actions? What does Ethan, Becky's father, show us about Becky through his reflections about her?	Ethan, the father	Becky, the daughter
"Everyday Use" Alice Walker	How do these sisters differ? As individuals and with respect to their relationship with their mother and their African American heritage?	Dee	Maggie
"The Other Pin" Chris Crutcher	What do we learn about each of these characters through their friendships, physical characteristics, and interactions with each other?	Petey	Chris Beyers

SETTING

A story's time and place, as well as its cultural, social, and moral environment, may be clearly defined and essential to the story. In American literature, Willa Cather's story "A Wagner Matinee" is known for its contrasting setting: the stark Nebraska homestead and the music of the concert hall set the scene for this story of discovery as a nephew learns to appreciate his aunt's choices in life. Willa Cather's use of figurative language highlights the story's setting.

Teaching Strategy: Music as Setting

In an effort to bring students into this story's setting, I brought in an audiotape of Wagner's music. I wish I also had thought to bring in photographs of Nebraska's landscape. As we listened to the music, I asked students to jot down times when music has been important in their lives. We then shared our stories of music. Before we read the story, I asked students to think of an older relative or friend and tell the story of what this person really cares about; for example, music, a hobby, or a sport. I wanted students to be in the setting of this story in terms of the emotional environment.

We then listened to the music again, and I slowly turned it down and began to read the story aloud.

The connection between music and setting is intriguing. I was delighted to discover a recent collection of short stories that highlight this connection, *What a Song Can Do: 12 Riffs on the Power of Music*, edited by Jennifer Armstrong. I highly recommend this collection.

Teaching Strategy: Focus on Setting

In addition to music, authors draw on place and time to establish setting. I find students often overlook setting, looking instead at the who and what of the story. I want them to know the importance of setting, to see how it frames the story and provides insight into the characters, plot, and theme. To support this effort I select stories with well-developed settings and ask students to focus on how the author creates the setting, looking in particular at place, time period, and time of year.

I provide students with blank eight-by-fourteen-inch sheets of paper and crayons or markers and invite them to sketch, draw, or note the images and words that the author uses to create setting. I want them to see setting as a picture in their head. To build on the music connection, I encourage students to think about how they might use music or sound effects if they were making an audio recording of this story. I once had a group of students create and perform guitar music to support their report to the class on the novel *Ricochet River*. I can see that stories would also lend themselves to musical accompaniment.

47

FOCUS ON SETTING

STORY/AUTHOR	CREATING THE SETTING
"The Fall of the House of Usher" *Edgar Allan Poe*	*Time of year* *The storm* *The house*
"The Outcasts of Poker Flats" *Bret Harte*	*Time period* *Local color of the region*
"Sophistication" *Sherwood Anderson*	*Time period* *Time of year* *Town of Winesburg, Ohio*
"Sonny's Blues" *James Baldwin*	*Harlem* *Light/dark* *Greenwich nightclub*
"A Sound of Thunder" *Ray Bradbury*	*World of the dinosaurs* *The year 2055*
"Faces: A Story from Syria" *Elsa Marston*	*Turkish bath* *Streets of Damascus* *Raeef's flat* *Family dinner*

PLOT

What happened? As students delve into short stories I want them to notice how the story unfolds. What are the tensions? The conflicts? What happens to change or resolve the conflicts or tensions? Is the conclusion surprising? Satisfying? Unresolved? I want students to feel the uninterrupted, focused intensity of short stories—what Poe called the "single effect" (see discussion on "The Pit and the Pendulum" in the section titled "Imagery" for more on the "single effect"). Every word is chosen to support the story's central design. It's as if the short story author grabs hold of the reader and says, "Pay close attention; everything in this story matters."

I know that plot diagrams can be used in support of close attention to a story's events, but I am troubled by the prevalent use of this device. I support the use of a visual form to illuminate a story's events, and I support the exploration of how these events build to the resolution or climax of the story. But I want to be sure that students see the plot diagram as a device that supports their story analysis, so there is not one "correct" plot diagram. To be honest, I avoid plot diagrams. I think my resistance is related to my math phobia of charts and graphs. I do note that Jim Burke's "Plot the Action" form (2000) is an interesting approach to the plot diagram. Rather than utilizing a rising plot line leading to the story's climax, it is a straight line on which students label each event in the story. They are then asked to evaluate each event on a five-point scale as to "negative (mood, action, condition, life) or positive (change for the better, important event, realization)" (A-19). This approach would support further discussion regarding how different readers interpreted each event's significance.

One of my favorite stories for illustrating plot is Gina Berriault's "The Stone Boy." Students are riveted by this story of how an everyday event leads to tragedy and exposes the flaws of family. In the story two brothers are going hunting. The younger brother, Arnold, accidentally shoots his older brother. Rather than running home to tell his parents, he chooses instead to pick peas. The sheriff arrives and questions the brother. During his questioning the sheriff learns the shooting happened when Arnold's gun caught on the wire fence under which he was crawling. He also learns that Arnold was more focused on completing his chores than reporting the accident. As readers, we see Arnold's inner struggle and how his family's focus on daily responsibilities keeps him from grieving. In teaching the story I provide very little introduction, other than to ask what the title suggests to them (see the "Titles" section of this chapter for more on short story titles). I let students know that our focus is on plot: the story's events. (Note: This story was turned into a film, with a screenplay written by the author.)

Teaching Strategy: Marking Plot

In support of plot, I want students to "see" the action of the story. So I use colored adhesive dots—the kind I might buy to use as price tags for a garage sale, which is how I first came up with this idea. I explain to students that each of them will be given a sheet of colored dots, and I want them to mark key events with the dots as they read the story. I then ask them to go back and revisit each dot. As they review each event marked, they need to consider the following questions:

What happened?

Who was involved?

Did this event have a significant effect on a character or characters? (e.g., require him or her to act, make a decision, change a decision, see a situation with a new eyes)

49

Did this event change the direction of the story?

After this analysis, which can be done in writing or as a small-group discussion, each student selects the top five events (I increase this number if it is a longer or more complex story) and discusses in a small group why he or she made these selections. I then pose the following question to each group: Based on your discussion of the key events in this story, what do you think was the turning or tipping point of the story? Be prepared to explain your group's answer with support from the text.

Using this strategy supported students' search for the turning point event in "The Stone Boy." Was it Arnold's accidental shooting of his brother, Eugie, which happens early in the story? Or was it Arnold's decision to go pick peas rather than tell his family about Eugie's death? Or was it when the sheriff questioned Arnold and learned that the gun went off when it caught on the wire fence as Arnold attempted to crawl under? Or was it the chilling scene when Arnold knocks on his mother's door, seeking comfort, and she tells him to go back to bed? During our whole-group discussion students returned to the text, and their dots, looking for answers in the story's plot, answers that would help them understand why Arnold would shoot his brother and choose to pick peas rather than tell his parents. I would then write the title, "The Stone Boy," on the board and ask students to do a five-to-seven-minute quick write on how the plot is an exploration of the title.

CONFLICT

The next day we would take our plot exploration and the quick write about the "The Stone Boy" to explore conflict—how the story's events are used to illustrate a struggle or conflict. With regard to "The Stone Boy" most students concluded that the primary conflict was an internal struggle between the side of Arnold that was devastated by the fact he accidentally shot his brother and the side of Arnold that walled off any feelings and focused on practical matters. As Arnold explained to the sheriff, he didn't report the shooting because the sun was coming up and he needed to pick peas: "It's better to pick peas while they're cool."

Regardless of the strategy used to visualize plot, it's important to provide students with opportunities to focus their reading on the story's events—and then explore how the story's plot is driven by conflict. Most texts on literature analysis identify five kinds of conflict or struggle:

Character vs. Nature

Character vs. Character

Character vs. the Forces of Society

Character vs. Supernatural Forces

Character vs. Self (an internal struggle of opposing tendencies within the
character), as illustrated by "The Stone Boy"

In the sidebar chart I have noted stories that work well for exploring plot and conflict. I have also listed what I consider to be the type(s) of conflict in the story, recognizing that many plots involve multiple types of conflict.

SHORT STORIES AND CONFLICT

STORY	TYPE OF CONFLICT
"Flight" *John Steinbeck*	*Character vs. Nature* *Character vs. Forces of Society*
"True Love" *Isaac Asimov*	*Character vs. Computer*
"Harrison Bergeron" *Kurt Vonnegut*	*Character vs. Forces of Society*
"A Summer's Reading" *Bernard Malamud*	*Character (George) vs. Character (Mr. Cattanzara)* *Character vs. Self (George)*
"The Summer of the Beautiful White Horse" *William Saroyan*	*Character (Aram, the narrator) vs. Character (Cousin Mourad) vs. Character (Horse owner, John Byro) vs. Character (Uncle Khosrove)*
"Checkouts" *Cynthia Rylant*	*Character (Girl) vs. Character (Bag Boy)*
"Raymond's Run" *Toni Cade Bambara*	*Character (Squeaky) vs. Character (Gretchen)* *Character vs. Self (Squeaky)*
"Colony" *Rick Wernli*	*Characters (Schoolteacher and boy) vs. Characters (Colonists)* *Character (Boy) vs. Character (Girl)* *Character (Boy) vs. Colony*
"How Did I Get Away with Killing One of the Biggest Lawyers in the State? It Was Easy." *Alice Walker*	*Character (Narrator) vs. Character (Bubba)*

51

THEME

Theme is the "so what?" of the story, the message. But I would argue theme is more than just the message. It's the "why" we read. Although I hope my students will be engaged, even entertained, as they read, I want them to see how stories help them understand their own lives and the world. I want them to see the message of the individual story and how this message or theme reflects larger themes or messages. A lofty goal, I realize, but it gets to the heart of why we read and analyze literature; it's not just about structure and craft. I also like the way the exploration of theme pushes readers. In most stories, the theme is not stated directly. The reader must pay close attention and dig deep in an effort to reveal the theme(s).

In my work with middle school and high school students, theme was the dessert moment of the story. We enjoyed it after we had spent time examining the other elements such as character, setting, plot, and the author's use of writing craft (see the next section for further discussion of writing craft). A teaching strategy that worked well for students was when I presented them with selected quotes from the story and asked them to write in class about how these quotes were messages or lessons that extended beyond the story.

Tillie Olsen's "I Stand Here Ironing" is a favorite story of mine, and one that works well in helping students read deeply for theme. This story is framed as a mother's response to a phone call requesting information that will help the caller in his or her efforts to support the mother's daughter. As the mother irons and talks on the phone, she examines her efforts to be a mother to her daughter. Within this heartfelt scrutiny there are moments of frustration, even bitterness, but also tenacity—on the part of both mother and daughter. I want students to focus on the mother's language, to see how her story has meaning for her but also has meaning that extends beyond the story.

Robert Coles speaks to the power of this story in his wonderful book *The Call of Stories* (1989). He notes that the story appeals to a wide range of students. "The story prompts young readers to look at their own past—to take stock of the troubles they have had and the opportunities, too, and to reflect on how they have managed in the less than two decades of their lives" (50). I respectfully suggest that because students connect personally with the story, they are willing to delve into the close reading of the text the following quote assignment requires. I would also suggest that close reading supports the kind of intense personal connections students have shared. It's surprising to me how often students take on a defensive stance in support of the mother!

Teaching Strategy: Advice Quotes in Support of Theme

I ask students to read " I Stand Here Ironing" in class and as they read to write down quotes that offer insight into the mother and daughter but also seem to be advice to us as readers. With some groups of students I have found it helpful to add that I expect at least three quotes. Other groups needed me to limit the number of quotes to no more than five. As noted previously, explorations of theme come after we have worked with short stories so that students have experience with selecting quotes.

I then ask students to read through their quotes and star a quote they would like to explore in a discussion with peers. I find that this activity is bolstered by the use of stick-on stars. (It's true that I probably spend more than is reasonable at office and craft supply stores.)

Students then move into discussion groups of three or four (I prefer triads, but the numbers don't always work). The goal of this discussion is to share the quote they starred—read it aloud and talk about what it tells us about the mother and daughter and how it serves as advice. As students work in groups I circulate and look for quotes that I think will support a discussion of theme. In the case of "I Stand Here Ironing," I found that students repeatedly selected the following quotes:

"School was a worry to her. She was not glib or quick in a world where glibness and quickness were easily confused with ability to learn."

"She was a child seldom smiled at. "

"She is a child of her age, of depression, of war, of fear."

"Let her be. So all that is in her will not bloom—but in how many does it? There is still enough left to live by."

After circulating and reading over students' shoulders, I hand a piece of chalk or a whiteboard marker to two or three students who have selected quotes that will allow us to further explore theme. I invite these students to write their quotes on the board. (I don't know what it is about writing on the board, but I find students, even juniors and seniors, consider it an honor.) I then ask students to reflect on their reading and their small-group discussion and explore one of the quotes on the board in writing. Their task is to write about the broader message of the quote. What was Olsen saying about life beyond this story?

I use these quick writes in one of two ways. I ask students to underline a key sentence or two from their quick write, and we use these underlined sections as the starting point for a class discussion. Or I collect the quick writes and mark sentences or ideas I find compelling. The next day I return them and invite (call on) students to share the lines I marked during our discussion. I find that returning highlighted quick writes to students, and giving them time to read through their writing, along with my comments and highlighting, leads to more student participation during the whole-group discussion of the story's theme. In the process of reading through students' work I can also assess their individual understanding of the story.

In the sidebar I have listed stories and suggested quotes in support of theme exploration.

QUOTES IN SUPPORT OF THEME

STORY	QUOTE IN SUPPORT OF THEME EXPLORATION
"Sophistication" Sherwood Anderson	"Man or boy, woman or girl, they had for a moment taken hold of the thing that makes the mature life of men and women in the modern world possible."
"Man and Daughter in the Cold" John Updike	"Ethan tended to flinch from youth—its harsh noises, its cheerful rapacity, its cruel onward flow as one class replaced another, ate a year of his life, and was replaced by another."
"Marigolds" Eugenia Collier	"I said before that we children were not consciously aware of how thick were the bars of our cage. I wonder now, though, whether we were not more aware of it than I thought. Perhaps we had some dim notion of what we were, and how little chance we had of being anything else."
"The Pin" Chris Crutcher	"I wonder briefly how many other kids in the bleachers are rooting for me to make a statement for those of us whose time has come to measure ourselves against our fathers."
"A Crush" Cynthia Rylant	"Love is such a mystery, and when it strikes the heart of one as mysterious as Ernie himself, it can hardly be spoken of."
"Shortcut" Nancy Werlin	"Now she knew why the shortcut had been safe. And she knew something else too: they had let her use the shortcut. They had let her be safe."
"Satyagraha" Alden R. Carter	"But I believe you can resist in another way. Mahatma Gandhi called it satyagraha, to stand firmly with truth and love without ever resorting to force."

Short Stories that Model and Inspire Writing Craft

Reading good literature serves as a model for writing. I am explicit in drawing students' attention to the craft of writing.

LEADS

I want to be drawn in as a reader. I want a story's opening to grab me and compel me to keep reading. I admire great leads as a reader and a writer. I want students to recognize and to write their own great leads so I focus students' attention on how authors start stories. In Grace Paley's short story "Samuel" she begins with "Some boys are very tough. They're afraid of nothing." As the lead continues, it offers more examples of "tough boys" and foreshadows what is to come in the story. I find the writing compelling, as is the story's plot. The fact that the story is very short makes me admire it even more.

Teaching Strategy: Reading Leads Aloud and Quick Write Response

I emphasize leads by reading just the lead aloud. I read the lead once and ask students to jot down what struck them or hooked them. If I think the students may need some support for this initial writing, I will list questions such as the following on the board:

> What do you know based on the lead?
>
> Are there any characters who interest you? Annoy you? Remind you of someone you know?
>
> Do you have any clues as to where the story takes place?
>
> What do you think might happen in the story?
>
> Can you tell if the story is going to be funny, serious, suspenseful, tragic?

I then ask students to draw a line under their initial writing, and I hand out the story (or ask students to open their books to the story). If I have a class with students who are skilled at reading aloud, I will ask a student to read the lead. I give students two or three minutes to add any reactions to their initial writing about the lead and draw another line under what they have written. We then read the story silently.

Once students have completed their reading, I ask them to look back at the lead and their initial writing. What do they notice about the lead now that they have read the story? How did it set up the story? If needed, I will supply questions in support of this writing:

Did the lead introduce the narrator?

Did it set the scene or setting of the story?

Did the lead pull you in with a dramatic event?

Did you feel as if the lead began in the middle rather than at the beginning?

Did the lead begin by telling you the ending?

Did the lead start slowly?

Did the lead mislead you?

Examine the writing craft of the lead: Does it start with a descriptive detail? A question? An anecdote? Dialogue? A surprising fact?

As a follow-up to this examination of leads, I have tried asking students to re-write the lead to a short story, with mixed results. But I have found it works well to build on this lead study in writing workshop. I ask students to think about the work we did with leads in short stories and to apply what they know about leads to their own writing piece. (See the discussion on leads in Chapter 5, "Memoir," for more on this topic.)

STORIES WITH INTRIGUING LEADS

STORY	FOCUS OR TYPE OF LEAD
"The Lottery" Shirley Jackson	Misleading lead with focus on setting
"The Streak" Walter Dean Myers	Introduction of narrator
"The Harringtons' Daughter" Lois Lowry	Descriptive, intriguing details that foreshadow the ending
"Duel Identities" David Lubar	Dramatic event
"Imagined Scenes" Ann Beattie	Dialogue
"Yes, Young Daddy" Frank Chin	Letter
"Tell Me Who You Hang Out With and I'll Tell You What You Are" Eleanora Tate	Single-sentence lead that serves as foreshadowing

IMAGERY

Building on our previous explorations of detail in support of character and setting, I invite students to focus on how authors use imagery to paint a picture for the reader. Edgar Allan Poe's story "The Pit and the Pendulum," which details a prisoner's impending death from a slowly descending pendulum designed to "cross the region of the heart," pushes students to look closely at imagery.

Teaching Strategy: Reading with an Eye for Detail

As we read this story I want students to note the story's setting and pay attention to the way Poe uses details to create suspense and place us, the readers, in the pit with the narrator, allowing us to see and hear what he sees and hears—and fears. As students read I ask them to note what the narrator sees, hears, and feels by listing "See," "Hear," and "Feel" columns in their journal and then noting phrases or passages of detail in each column. I tell them to pay particular attention to the rats, which makes some students, and me, shudder. And I ask them to pay attention to Poe's description of the pendulum. I also ask them to note or mark with a sticky note any places they find confusing or unclear. This sticky note option gives students permission to be confused as readers. We use the spots they marked to talk about reading strategies they used to figure out the story. I have also found that marking confusing spots gives students permission to move forward as readers. Many of them discover that they figure out the sections they marked as they continue to read.

In an effort to model how to deal with confusion as we read and because it has been my experience that students struggle to understand the story's opening paragraphs, we read these aloud. I use this read-aloud, followed by a class discussion, as a way to remind students what strategies they have as readers and to introduce the guidelines described above for noting descriptions and marking confusing passages. We then transition into quiet reading time. My goal is to have students read the story in class in one sitting. Because the story is a challenging read, I want them to feel their fellow readers' support, and I want to be on hand if students become frustrated to the point they need to talk with me.

Please know I learned the importance of reading this story in class the hard way. I had assigned the story as homework and found myself struggling to hold all the details in my head as I read. The next day in class I had planned to give students the ten-question multiple-choice quiz supplied by the literature anthology publishers, but I wisely chose to take the quiz myself first. The fact that I missed three questions made me rethink my lesson plan. And students' anger as they entered class the next day, demanding to know what was wrong with this guy Poe and what I was thinking assigning a story that made no sense led me to develop the in-class reading plan. This one-sitting reading is consistent with Poe's belief regarding short stories. Poe wrote, "In the whole composition there should be no word written, of which the tendency, direct or indirect, is not to the one pre-established design" (2006, 725). Poe went on to state that the "pre-established design," which he also called the "single effect," would be best discovered if the story were read in one sitting. It's my hope that our structured reading plan during one class period will honor Poe's stance.

In our discussion of the story, which often took place the next day because this story takes quite a bit of class time to read, students used their journal notes to share what they noted about descriptive detail. They were struck by Poe's use of rich detail, commenting that they see, hear, smell, and touch what the narrator is experiencing. A favorite line of many students was "At the same time my forehead seemed bathed in a clammy vapor, and the peculiar smell of decayed fungus arose to my mouth."

We also discussed the pendulum and the way Poe shows its descent, "Down—steadily down it crept," followed by successive paragraphs beginning with the word *down*. Students were intrigued by this technique, and I saw them trying it in their own narratives and short stories. Using the technique is more important to me than the fact that they know the literary term *anaphora*.

FORESHADOWING

I love to read mystery novels and search for clues of "who done it" and why, so I cannot teach short stories without teaching foreshadowing. "Hints or clues of what is to come later in the story" is the definition of foreshadowing my students developed. As we read we delight in discovering foreshadowing. As one student said, "It's like a secret between the author and me."

Teaching Strategy: Reading Like a Detective

To support the discovery of this secret between reader and author, I rely on two readings of the story. As noted previously, I am a proponent of short stories because their length allows for repeated reading with an emphasis on a particular literary element or technique. In the case of foreshadowing, I ask students to read like detectives, noting places that contained important clues. In support of this "detective reading" I provide students with sticky arrow-shaped flags and note cards.

We then gather in investigative groups, and students review their flagged sections, looking for common patterns among group members. Typically I assign the investigative group members so that I can be sure I have a mix of reading abilities represented in each group. Then they reread the story in the group with an eye to the clues they had identified as key and write these key clues on note cards. I chose note cards because my favorite detective, Kinsey Milhone, created by Sue Grafton, always uses note cards to record key clues as she solves a case.

After investigative groups determine their clues, we regroup as a class and share our note card clues. From this discussion, we identify how the author used foreshadowing in support of character, plot, conflict, and even theme.

"The Life You Save May Be Your Own" by Flannery O'Connor, a tragic story of misfits, is rich with tragic irony and foreshadowing. The story tells of a drifter who marries a retarded girl in order to steal her mother's car. After the wedding he abandons the girl at a roadside diner. He then picks up a boy who has run away from home and tries to talk him into returning to his family by telling his own story: "My mother was a angel of Gawd. . . . He took her from heaven and giver to me and I left her." The boy retorts, "My old woman is a flea bag and yours is a stinking pole cat." And the boy jumps from the car. The story ends with the drifter driving through a thunderstorm and praying, "Break forth and wash the slime from this earth!"

Students have no trouble finding examples of foreshadowing in this story. As one junior noted, "I knew from the beginning description of Mr. Shiftlet that things were not going to turn out well." From our investigation of foreshadowing, a lively discussion usually ensues around which of the characters the title applies to most directly. We typically do not come to a consensus, but it is delightful to watch as students make their cases, citing details from the story that demonstrate their appreciation of the story's descriptive details. This story is a great lead-in to an exploration of irony. Listed in the sidebar are stories that illustrate foreshadowing.

STORIES WITH FORESHADOWING

STORY	FORESHADOWING CLUES
"Flight" John Steinbeck	Pepe's knife
"The Far and Near" Thomas Wolfe	Recounting of four fatal accidents Details of the children in the wagon
"Tell Me Who You Hang Out With and I'll Tell You What You Are" Eleanora Tate	"I knew something was snaky about that girl from the way that she flicked out her tongue."
"Duel Identities" David Lubar	"I committed my first act of self-destruction in less than five minutes into third period."
"Charles" Shirley Jackson	Laurie tells his parents the whole class had to stay after school because Charles was bad.
"In Line: A Story from Egypt" Elsa Marston	"Halfway home from school, on a lovely clear day in December, I did something really daring."
"The Hand of Fatima: A Story from Lebanon" Elsa Marston	"What did it mean, the Hand of Fatima? Luck . . . protection? A token of her father's love, surely. But also, she feared, a claim for obedience."
"Great Expectations" M. E. Kerr	"Ah, but then, as Onodaga John liked to say, Fate frolicked into the picture."

IRONY

I teach "The Story of an Hour" by Kate Chopin because I love it! I am pleased to report that students enjoy it as well. The details of a fragile wife who learns of her husband's death only to lock herself away in her room has a surprise ending that often leads to a gasp in the room. "The Story of an Hour" is a short, short story so I read it aloud or have students read it to each other in small groups. After they have read the story I ask them to write for five to seven minutes on the surprise ending: Were you surprised? What do you think caused Louise Mallard's death? After students write I ask them to go back and find details from the story that support their answer. Our discussion leads to the opportunity to revisit the literary term *irony*, a contrast between appearance and actuality. Depending on the group of students and my big-picture objectives, I might invite students to explore the three main types of irony: irony of situation, verbal irony, and dramatic irony. "The Story of an Hour" is a good example of irony of situation.

I would be remiss if I did not note that in exploring the irony of the wife's untimely death, students move into a discussion of marriage and the role of women, exploring text-society connections. I find students want to talk more about the message of this story and about its author, Kate Chopin.

Teaching Strategy: Rereading to Spot Irony

As discussed earlier, an advantage of short stories is that they can be reread with a focus on writing craft or literary technique. To support reading for irony, I often have students do some practice writing using short, silly prompts that require them to write a vignette illustrating irony. For example:

Prompt: Healthy Heather
Healthy Heather is committed to a lifestyle of organic eating and regular exercise. She gets up at 5:00 every morning and heads outside for a one-hour run.

Sample Student Vignette:
Healthy Heather is committed to a lifestyle of organic eating and regular exercise. She gets up at 5:00 every morning and heads outside for a one-hour run. On Thursday, at 5:35 a.m. Heather was tragically struck and killed. The driver of the truck that hit Heather was making a routine delivery of

61

Hostess Snacks to the local 7-Eleven. He indicated he took his eyes off the road for just a split second to reach for his Starbucks coffee cup.

From this writing, we go back to the story and reread, using focus questions like those detailed for "The Story of an Hour." Listed in the sidebar are examples of stories that work well for rereading—with an initial focus and then a rereading with a focus on irony. This two-focus reading supports students who are unsure about what to look for while reading by giving them specifics on which to focus. For more experienced readers, it focuses their attention on the author's craft. As an extension, I sometimes ask students to note what writing craft they see being used in support of irony.

REREADING TO SPOT IRONY

STORY/AUTHOR	FOCUS FOR FIRST READING	FOCUS FOR REREADING
"The Landlady" Roald Dahl	Time line of events	Landlady's strange behavior
"Charles" Shirley Jackson	Stories boy tells about Charles	Boy's behavior at home
"Lamb to the Slaughter" Roald Dahl	Interactions between husband and wife	Wife's actions to get dinner on the table Officers' comments during investigation
"Separation" Mary Gordon	Mother and teacher interactions	Mother and son interactions
"The Chaser" John Collier	Alan and the shop owner	Shop owner's descriptions of the potions he sells and Alan's reactions—or lack of reactions

POINT OF VIEW

Who is telling the story? Does our narrator have direct knowledge of the story because he or she is a participant? What are the limitations of the narrator's point of view? I often introduce point of view by reading the children's book *The True Story of the Three Little Pigs!* (see Chapter 6 for a discussion of this book and teaching strategy). As students explore point of view I want them to think about how it affects what we know as readers—to think about whether the narrator is limited in his or her point of view; to think about how the story might be different if told from a different point of view. My hope is that students will see that point of view controls what we know as readers.

"Today they got Sally. . . . I saw Doug Booker before she did." This first-person narrated story, "A Letter from the Fringe" by Joan Bauer, grabs the readers' attention and holds on as Dana shares the struggles of the not-it crowd being picked on by the "In-Crowd Individuals" (ICIs). With humor and sensitivity readers are taken into the thoughtful world of Dana and her friends, who serve as taunting targets for the "In-Crowd Individuals." As Dana recounts her experiences, she also shares her insights about what it means to be "on the fringe" as well as her wonderings about the "In Crowd." The use of first-person narration allows the readers to see, hear, and feel what Dana sees, hears, and feels.

Teaching Technique: How Might This Story Be Told Differently?
Before students read I ask them to pay close attention to the story's narrator, Dana. After they have read I ask them to write in response to the following questions:

> What do we learn about Dana from her story?
>
> How does she see her friends?
>
> How does she see the "In Crowd"?
>
> What does she learn from her conversation with Parker?

I then ask them to pick another character from the story and explore how the story would be different if told from that point of view. They share this writing in a pair-share. I then pose the following questions to each pair: How would the story change if it was told from a different narrator's point of view? Would it make a difference if this narrator was one of the characters in the story? Does the narrator's gender make a difference?

Focusing on point of view leads to a broader whole-class discussion of the role of cliques in schools. I have also found that it can lead to an interesting exploration of gender. On more than one occasion the girls in the class have explained with poignant anger the challenges of being girls in today's middle and high schools.

63

STORIES AND POINT OF VIEW

STORY	POINT OF VIEW
"Big Joe's Funeral" *Walter Dean Myers*	*First-person*
"How Did I Get Away with Killing One of the Biggest Lawyers in the State? It Was Easy." *Alice Walker*	*First-person*
"A Summer's Reading" *Bernard Malamud*	*Third-person limited*
"First Love" *Gary Soto*	*Third-person limited*
"He" *Katherine Anne Porter*	*Third-person omniscient*
"Sophistication" *Sherwood Anderson*	*Third-person omniscient*
"Squid Girl" *Todd Strasser*	*Second-person*

STREAM OF CONSCIOUSNESS

"Barn Burning" by William Faulkner illustrates the power of writing about the place where you live. As Faulkner noted, "My own little postage stamp of native soil was worth writing about and . . . I would never live long enough to exhaust it" (1968, 255). This story illustrates setting and the power of writing what you know. It also illustrates Faulkner's use of stream of consciousness and interior monologues. I ask students to pay particular attention to his use of italics. Why does he want to draw the reader's attention to these sections?

I point out a selected, italicized passage and ask students to pay particular attention to this passage as they read. It begins with *"Hits big as a courthouse* he thought quietly. . . ." After they have read, I ask them to write responses to the following questions with regard to this passage:

1. What do we learn about the character? What is the young boy, Sarty, thinking? Feeling?

2. What sensory experiences are described?

3. What is the effect of the long, long sentences Faulkner uses? (my all-time
favorite question)

I find it helpful to have students respond to these questions on their own
first and then to gather in small groups. I hand each group a piece of butcher
paper with a topic on the top: Sarty's Thinking, Sarty's Feelings, Sarty's Sensory
Experiences, Effect of Long Sentences. Students are instructed to show their
thinking on these topics and to find examples from the passage to support their
positions. Because all of the students have written on all of the topics and our focus is on one common passage, I find students are willing to question each group
as it presents its analysis. If you have a large class, it works well to have more than
one group working on each of the topics.

I must be candid and admit that I don't care much for Faulkner's writing style.
I hope this will not cause you to think less of me (particularly after the golf club
admission). But I recognize students should have some familiarity with who
Faulkner is in the literary world and should know about stream of consciousness
writing. I know this because Darcy, more than a month after we had read "Barn
Burning," pointed out to me during a writing conference, "Look, here is where I
used that technique where you show the character's inner thoughts; you know,
like in that story we read about the barn that burned." I don't know if Faulkner
would be pleased, but I certainly was.

SHORT STORIES WITH INTERESTING PUNCTUATION OR STYLE

STORY/AUTHOR	WRITING CRAFT TO EXPLORE	EXAMPLE IN TEXT
"The Jilting of Granny Weatherall" Katherine Anne Porter	Stream of consciousness Lack of transitions	"Well, I didn't do so badly, did I? But that would have to wait. That was for tomorrow. She used to think of him as a man, but now all the children were older than their father, and he would be a child beside her if she saw him now."
"Separation" Mary Gordon	Indented passages of interior monologue	The game was shut your mouth. The game was shut your mouth and keep it shut. The game was shut your mouth and give them what they wanted.
"Squid Girl" Todd Strasser	Fragments, single words, and lists	"Here's what nature offers: Bugs. Bats. Crabs. And the compost toilet. Here's what nature does not offer: Shopping. Mall. TV. Computer. Telephone.
"Yes, Young Daddy" Frank Chin	Story told in letters written in dialect	"Hi Dirigible, Guess hoo! Ya man, It's me, you know hoo-ooo! That fat lazy thing that lives somwere across the bay."
"Santa Claus in Baghdad: A Story from Iraq" Elsa Marston	Narrator's inner thoughts written in italics	He looks dopey, with his skinny shape and bony face, but he's a good teacher. I'd rather have a dopey-looking teacher than somebody who looks good but doesn't know how to teach.

TITLE

I struggle with titles in my own writing, so I appreciate authors who are skilled in selecting titles. To highlight the power and importance of title, I periodically ask students to select the next story we are going to read based solely on the title.

Teaching Strategy: Selecting a Story Based on Title

On the board I list story titles. I find four to six title choices work best. I read the titles aloud and ask students to list their top two picks. Next to each choice I ask students to jot down what it was about the title that inspired their choice. Typically I conduct this activity at the end of a class period so I can read through their selections and determine the class choice for the next class period.

The next day I share the results with the students by again listing all the titles and the number of votes each received as first and second choice. I then announce the story that won the most votes and share with students the comments made in support of the winning title.

Before they begin reading, I ask students to write down the title of the story on the top of their journal page. As they read I want them to stop and note any moments in the story that relate to the title.

As mentioned in Chapter 2, the first time I did this activity the seniors with whom I worked selected "Demon Lover." I was amused by their vehement reaction to what they considered a misleading title. This led to an animated discussion about the power and importance of titles. Throughout this chapter are examples of stories with interesting titles.

Short Stories in Lieu of Canon Novels

Short stories are a wonderful way to get off the "coverage treadmill" of tackling the canon through novels. To illustrate, let me take you into my classroom as we explore Hawthorne's "The Minister's Black Veil." In this "parable" Hawthorne explores sin and guilt among the Puritans, a theme consistent with that of his novel *The Scarlet Letter*. I asked the juniors with whom I worked to read this story in class; it was eight pages in our literature anthology. In support of their reading, I asked them to pay attention to the veil by marking references to it with sticky notes (which I supplied). This is a pattern repeated when we read any short story: most if not all of the reading is completed in class, I ask students to focus on something specific as they read, using some sort of tool or strategy, and then we use the information they've gathered as a catalyst for the class discussion.

We began our discussion of the story by focusing on the veil. We looked at veil references the students had marked. This allowed us to explore the story's plot as well as how the veil served as symbol (which the students defined as "something that has added meaning—stands for more than just itself"). In the case of this story, students found that the veil represents our need to hide our true selves. This need to veil ourselves had several layers. Students noted the need for a public face versus a private face. They also recognized that the veil could be an effort to show purity and cover up sins. One student explored the relationship of the veil to the role of the minister: the veil distanced the Reverend Hooper from his parishioners; they were not allowed to really know or see him, which allowed

67

him to have a status of mystery, perhaps even superiority. This analysis then led to a heated discussion of the veil as limitation with assertions that the veil was not about superiority but guilt. The veil allowed the minister to hide from the parishioners, but it also served to isolate him from them. They were never allowed to really see him. At this point I shared with the students Hawthorne's writing regarding isolation, "that saddest of all prisons, his own heart." Our discussion of the veil continued during the following class period. This then led to an in-class writing in which students explored how the quote, "I look around me, and, lo! on every visage a Black Veil" is the lesson or moral of the story.

From this two-day exploration of Hawthorne, students were introduced to Hawthorne as a writer who used symbolism to explore the issues of sin, guilt and isolation among the Puritans. If students wanted to know more, they were encouraged to read his well-regarded novel *The Scarlet Letter*. Here is where I would like to write that there was a waiting list for the library's copy of *The Scarlet Letter*, but this was not the case. What I can confirm is that students could identify and analyze symbolism within Hawthorne's writing.

Students in my English classes, even Honors English, read Nathaniel Hawthorne, Edgar Allan Poe, Mark Twain, Kate Chopin, Sherwood Anderson, John Steinbeck, Ernest Hemingway, F. Scott Fitzgerald, Bernard Malamud, Eudora Welty, William Faulkner, and Flannery O'Connor; they read each of these authors' short stories (see chart for stories that I used in place of novels from the canon).

SHORT STORIES IN PLACE OF NOVELS

AUTHOR	NOVEL	SHORT STORY SUBSTITUTION	WHAT TO TEACH
Nathaniel Hawthorne	The Scarlet Letter	"The Minister's Black Veil"	Parable Symbolism
Herman Melville	Moby Dick	"Bartleby the Scrivener"	Symbolism Allusion Theme
Kate Chopin	The Awakening	"The Story of an Hour"	Irony Theme
Willa Cather	My Antonia	"Wagner Matinee"	Setting: Contrast Figurative language
Jack London	The Call of the Wild	"To Build a Fire"	Conflict Theme
F. Scott Fitzgerald	The Great Gatsby	"Winter Dreams"	Theme Character
John Steinbeck	Of Mice and Men	"Flight"	Foreshadowing Naturalism
Ray Bradbury	Fahrenheit 451	"A Sound of Thunder"	Theme Paradox
William Faulkner	The Sound and the Fury	"Barn Burning"	Stream of consciousness Imagery
Thomas Wolfe	Look Homeward, Angel	"The Far and the Near"	Climax/Anticlimax Theme
Virginia Woolf	To the Lighthouse	* "The Mark on the Wall"	Stream of consciousness Poetic effect Feminine narrative
Ernest Hemingway	The Sun Also Rises	"Old Man at the Bridge"	Setting Character
Bernard Malamud	The Assistant	"A Summer's Reading"	Conflict Point of view

*Note: Two popular alternative rock groups, The Shins and Modest Mouse, drew their group names from Virginia Woolf's story "The Mark on the Wall."

Closing Thoughts on Short Stories

I recognize that short stories can serve as a bridge to studying novels, and I support their use for this purpose. But I included short stories in my literature workshop because short stories are a unique genre, as worthy of study as novels. "The short story demands contemplation and rewards interrogation, offering up its sweet secrets to those who probe it in earnest" (Hamilton and Katzke 1999, 1).

It's been my experience that students are willing to join me in the exploration of short stories. Their length makes short stories manageable, and although not every story we read is a hit with every student, I have found students are willing to dabble in a variety of short stories. I liken short stories to dishes on a literary buffet from which students are willing to taste things they would never order as full meals. Listed in the sidebar are short stories, some of which I have previously mentioned in this chapter, that students have been willing to publicly state they enjoy or at least appreciate. I have marked with an asterisk the stories on this list that I find lend themselves well to being read aloud. (Please note, as discussed in the first chapter, some of these stories may not be appropriate for your classroom or community.)

SHORT STORIES STUDENTS ENJOY

* "Here There Be Tygers"	Stephen King
"The Lottery"	Shirley Jackson
"Lamb to the Slaughter"	Roald Dahl
"The Way Up to Heaven"	Roald Dahl
"A Worn Path"	Eudora Welty
"Charles"	Shirley Jackson
"Checkouts"	Cynthia Rylant
* "How Did I Get Away with Killing One of the Biggest Lawyers in the State? It Was Easy."	Alice Walker
"Duel Identities"	David Lubar
"Final Cut"	Rich Wallace
"Tell Me Who You Hang Out With and I'll Tell You What You Are"	Eleanora E. Tate
"Autumn Rose"	Kevin Kyung
"First Love"	Gary Soto
"The Harringtons' Daughter"	Lois Lowry
"Squid Girl"	Todd Strasser
* "Angel and Aly"	Ron Koertge
"Noodle Soup for Nincompoops"	Ellen Wittlinger
* "Letter from the Fringe"	Joan Bauer

WORKS CITED

Anderson, Sherwood. 1999. "Sophistication." In *Winesburg, Ohio*. New York: ModernLibrary.

Armstrong, Jennifer, ed. 2004. *What a Song Can Do: 12 Riffs on the Power of Music*. New York: Laurel-Leaf.

Asimov, Isaac. 2004 "True Love." In *Robot Dreams*. New York: Ace Trade.

Baldwin, James. 2006. "Sonny's Blues." In *The Art of the Short Story: 52 Great Authors, Their Best Short Fiction, and Their Insights on Writing*, ed. Dana Gioia and R. S. Gwynn. New York: Pearson Longman.

Bambara, Toni Cade. 1996. "Raymond's Run." In *The Runner's Literary Companion:*

Great Stories and Poems about Running, ed. Garth Battista. New York: Penguin.

Bauer, Joan. 2001. "Letter from the Fringe." In *On the Fringe*, ed. Donald Gallo. New York: Dial Books.

Beattie, Ann. 1991. "Imagined Scenes." In *Distortions*. New York: Vintage.

Berriault, Gina. 1965. "The Stone Boy." In *The Mistress and Other Stories*. New York: E. P. Dutton.

Bradbury, Ray. 1980. "A Sound of Thunder." In *Stories of Ray Bradbury*. New York: Knopf.

Burke, Jim. 2000. *Reading Reminders: Tools, Tips, and Techniques*. Portsmouth, NH: Heinemann.

Carter, Alden R. 2001. "Satyagraha." In *On the Fringe*, ed. Don Gallo. New York: Speak.

Cather, Willa. 1994. *My Antonia*. New York: Signet Classics.

——.1997. "Wagner Matinee." In *The Portable American Realism Reader*, ed. James Nagel and Tom Quick. New York: Penguin Books.

Chin, Frank. 1994. "Yes, Young Daddy." In

Coming of Age in America: A Multicultural Anthology, ed. Mary Frosch. New York: New Press

Chopin, Kate. 1976. "The Story of an Hour." In *The Awakening and Selected Stories of Kate Chopin*. New York: Signet Classics.

Coles, Robert. 1989. *The Call of Stories: Teaching and the Moral Imagination*. Boston: Houghton Mifflin.

Collier, Eugenia. 1994. "Marigolds." *Coming of Age in America: A Multicultural Anthology*, ed. Mary Frosch. New York: New Press.

Collier, John. 1952. "The Chaser." In *Fifty Great Short Stories*, ed. Milton Crane. New York: Bantam Classic.

Crutcher, Chris. 1989. "The Other Pin." In *Athletic Shorts: Six Short Stories*. New York: Greenwillow Books.

Dahl, Roald. 1990. "Lamb to the Slaughter." In *The Best of Roald Dahl*. New York: Vintage.

——.1990. "The Landlady." In *The Best of Roald Dahl*. New York: Vintage.

——.1990. "The Way Up to Heaven." In *The Best of Roald Dahl*. New York: Vintage.

Faulkner, William. 1968. *Lion in the Garden: Interviews with William Faulkner 1926–1962*, ed. James B. Meriwether and Michael Millgate. New York: Random House.

——.2006. "Barn Burning." In *The Art of the Short Story: 52 Great Authors, Their Best Short Fiction, and Their Insights on Writing,* ed. Dana Gioia and R. S. Gwynn. New York: Pearson Longman.

Fitzgerald, F. Scott. 1995. *The Great Gatsby*. New York: Scribner.

——."Winter Dreams." In *Short Stories of F. Scott Fitzgerald*. New York: Scribner.

Gordon, Mary. 1991. "Separation." In *The Best American Short Stories: 1991*, ed. Alice Adams and Katrina Kenison. New York: Houghton Mifflin.

Hamilton, Carole L. and Peter Kratzke, eds. 1999. *Short Stories in the Classroom*. Urbana, IL: NCTE.

Harte, Bret. 1996. "The Outcasts of Poker Flats." In *Gold Rush*. Berkeley, CA: Heyday Books.

Hawthorne, Nathaniel. 1955. "The Minister's Black Veil." In *Fifty Great Short Stories*, ed. Milton Crane. New York: Bantam Classic.

——.1959. *The Scarlet Letter*. New York: New American Library.

Jackson, Shirley. 1948. "Charles." In *The Lottery and Other Stories*. New York: Noonday Press.

——. 1995. "The Little House." In *Come Along with Me*. New York: Penguin.

——.1948. "The Lottery." In *The Lottery and Other Stories*. New York: Noonday Press.

Kerr, M. E. 2001. "Great Expectations." In *On the Fringe*, ed. Don Gallo. New York: Speak.

King, Stephen. 1985. "Here There Be Tygers" In *Skeleton Crew*. New York: Putnam.

Koertge, Ron. 2003. "Angel and Aly." In *13: Thirteen Stories that Capture the Agony and Ecstasy of Being Thirteen*, ed. James Howe. New York: Antheneum Books for Young Readers.

Kyung, Kevin. 1990. "Autumn Rose." In *A Gathering of Flowers: Stories About Being Young in America*, ed. Joyce Carol Thomas. New York: Harper Trophy.

London, Jack. 1994. *The Call of the Wild*. New York: Aladdin Classics.

——.2006. "To Build a Fire." In *The Art of the Short Story: 52 Great Authors, Their Best Short Fiction, and Their Insights on Writing*, ed. Dana Gioia and R. S. Gwynn. New York: Pearson Longman.

Lowry, Lois. 1990. "The Harringtons' Daughter." In *A Gathering of Flowers: Stories About Being Young* in America, ed. Joyce Carol Thomas. New York: Harper Trophy.

Lubar, David. 2000. "Duel Identities." In *Lost & Found: Award-Winning Authors Sharing Real-Life Experiences Through Fiction*. New York: Forge.

Malamud, Bernard. 1998. "A Summer's Reading." In *The Complete Stories by Bernard Malamud*. New York: Farrar, Straus and Giroux.

Marston, Elsa. 2005. "Faces: A Story from Syria." In *Figs and Fate: Stories About Growing Up in the Arab World Today*. New York: George Braziller.

——. 2005. "The Hand of Fatima: A Story from Lebanon." In *Figs and Fate: Stories About Growing Up in the Arab World Today*. New York: George Braziller.

——. 2005. "In Line: A Story from Egypt." In *Figs and Fate: Stories About Growing Up in the Arab World Today*. New York: George Braziller.

——. 2005. "Santa Claus in Baghdad: A Story from Iraq." In *Figs and Fate: Stories About Growing Up in the Arab World Today*. New York: George Braziller.

Melville, Herman. 2003. *Moby Dick*. New York: Barnes and Noble Classics.

——.2006. "Bartleby the Scrivener: A Story of Wall-Street." In *The Art of the Short Story: 52 Great Authors, Their Best Short Fiction, and Their Insights on Writing*, ed. Dana Gioia and R. S. Gwynn. New York: Pearson Longman.

Myers, Walter Dean. 2000. "Big Joe's Funeral." In *145th Street: Short Stories*. New York: Dell Laurel-Leaf.

———. 2000. "The Streak." In *145th Street: Short Stories*. New York: Dell Laurel-Leaf.

O'Connor, Flannery. 1971. "The Life You Save May Be Your Own." In *The Complete Stories of Flannery O'Connor*. New York: Farrar, Straus and Giroux.

Olsen, Tillie. 1995. "I Stand Here Ironing." In *Points of View: An Anthology of Short Stories*. Rev. ed., ed. James Moffett and Kenneth McElheny. New York: Mentor.

Paley, Grace. 1985. "Samuel." In *Enormous Changes at the Last Minute*. New York: Farrar, Straus and Giroux.

Poe, Edgar Allan. 1984. "The Fall of the House of Usher." In *The Complete Stories and Poems of Edgar Allan Poe*. New York: Doubleday.

———. 1984. "The Pit and the Pendulum." In *The Complete Stories and Poems of Edgar Allan Poe*. New York: Doubleday.

———. 2006. "The Tale and Its Effect." In *The Art of the Short Story: 52 Great Authors, Their Best Short Fiction, and Their Insights on Writing*, ed. Dana Gioia and R. S. Gwynn. New York: Pearson Longman.

Porter, Katherine Anne. 1979. "He." In *The Collected Stories of Katherine Anne Porter*. New York: Harvest Books.

———. 1979. "The Jilting of Granny Weatherall." In *The Collected Stories of Katherine Anne Porter*. New York: Harvest Books.

Rylant, Cynthia. 1990. "Checkouts." In *A Couple of Kooks and Other Stories About Love*. New York: Orchard Books.

———. 1990. "Crush." In *A Couple of Kooks and Other Stories About Love*. New York: Orchard Books.

Saroyan, William. 1952. "The Summer of the Beautiful White Horse." In *Fifty Great Short Stories*, ed. Milton Crane. New York: Bantam Classic.

Soto, Gary. 1990. "First Love." In *A Gathering of Flowers: Stories About Being Young in America*. New York: Harper Trophy.

Steinbeck, John. 1976. "Flight." In *The Portable Steinbeck*, ed. Pascal Covici Jr. New York: Penguin.

———. 1993. *Of Mice and Men*. New York: Penguin.

Strasser, Todd. 2003. "Squid Girl." In *13: Thirteen Stories that Capture the Agony and Ecstasy of Being Thirteen*, ed. James Howe. New York: Atheneum Books for Young Readers.

Tate, Eleanora. 2000. "Tell Me Who You Hang Out With and I'll Tell You What You Are." In *Lost & Found: Award-Winning Authors Sharing Real-Life Experiences Through Fiction*. New York: Forge.

Thurber, James. 1952. "The Catbird Seat." In *Fifty Great Short Stories*, ed. Milton Crane. New York: Bantam Classic.

Updike, John. 2004. "Man and Daughter in the Cold." In *The Early Stories: 1953–1975*. New York: Ballantine Books.

Vonnegut, Kurt. 1998. "Harrison Bergeron." In *Welcome to the Monkey House*. New York: The Dial Press.

Walker, Alice. 1982. "How Did I Get Away with Killing One of the Biggest Lawyers in the State? It Was Easy." In *You Can't Keep a Good Woman Down*. New York: Harvest Books.

———2003. "Everyday Use." In *Love and Trouble: Stories of Black Women*. New York: Harvest Books.

74

Wallace, Rich. 2000. "Final Cut" In *Lost & Found: Award-Winning Authors Sharing Real-Life Experiences Through Fiction*. New York: Forge.

Welty, Eudora. 1982. "A Worn Path." In *The Collected Stories of Eudora Welty*. New York: Harvest Books.

Werlin, Nancy. 2001. "Shortcut." In *On the Fringe*. ed. Don Gallo. New York: Speak.

Wernli, Rick. 1990. "Colony." In *A Gathering of Flowers: Stories About Being Young in America,* ed. Joyce Carol Thomas. New York: Harper Trophy.

Wittlinger, Ellen. 2003. "Noodle Soup for Nincompoops." In *13: Thirteen Stories that Capture the Agony and Ecstasy of Being Thirteen*, ed. James Howe. New York: Atheneum Books for Young Readers.

Wolfe, Thomas. 1989. "The Far and the Near." In *The Complete Short Stories of Thomas Wolfe*. New York: Scribner.

Woolf, Virginia. 1989. "The Mark on the Wall." In *The Complete Shorter Fiction of Virginia Woolf,* 2nd ed. New York: Harvest Books.

RECOMMENDED RESOURCES IN SUPPORT OF TEACHING SHORT STORIES

Short Story Collections

Armstrong, Jennifer, ed. 2004. *What a Song Can Do: 12 Riffs on the Power of Music*. New York: Laurel-Leaf.

Crane, Milton, ed. 1952. *Fifty Great Short Stories*. New York: Bantam.

Crutcher, Chris. 1991. *Athletic Shorts: Six Short Stories*. New York: Greenwillow.

Ehrlich, Amy, ed. 1996. *When I Was Your Age: Original Stories About Growing Up*. Vol. 2. Cambridge, MA: Candlewick Press.

Frosch, Mary, ed. 1994. *Coming of Age in America: A Multicultural Anthology*. New York: The New Press.

Gallo, Donald R., ed. 2001. *On the Fringe*. New York: Speak.

Gioia, Dana, and R. S. Gwynn. 2006. *The Art of the Short Story: 52 Great Authors, Their Best Short Fiction, and Their Insights on Writing*. New York: Pearson Longman.

Halpern, Daniel, ed. 1999. *The Art of the Story: An International Anthology of Contemporary Short Stories*. New York: Penguin Books.

Howe, Irving, and Ilana Wiener Howe, eds. 1982. *Short Shorts: An Anthology of the Shortest Stories*. New York: Bantam Books.

Howe, James, ed. 2003. *13: Thirteen Stories that Capture the Agony and Ecstasy of Being Thirteen*. New York: Atheneum Books for Young Readers.

Jackson, Shirley. 1948. *The Lottery and Other Stories*. New York: Noonday Press.

Marston, Elsa. 2005. *Figs and Fate: Stories About Growing Up in the Arab World Today*. New York: George Braziller.

Moss, Steve, ed. 1995. *The World's Shortest Stories: Murder. Love. Horror. Suspense. All This and Much More in the Most Amazing Short Stories Ever Written—Each One Just Fifty-Five Words Long*. Philadelphia: Running Press.

Myers, Walter Dean. 2000. *145th Street: Short Stories*. New York: Laurel-Leaf.

Rochman, Hazel, and Darlene Z. McCampbell, eds. 1997. *Who Do You Think You Are: Stories of Friends and Enemies*. New York: Little, Brown.

Rylant, Cynthia. 1990. *A Couple of Kooks and Other Stories About Love.* New York: Orchard Books.

Smith, Patrick A., ed. 2002. *Thematic Guide to Popular Short Stories.* New York: Greenwood Press.

Weiss, M. Jerry, and Helen S. Weiss, eds. 2000. *Lost & Found: Award-Winning Authors Sharing Real-Life Experiences Through Fiction.* New York: Forge.

Books and Articles

Barchers, Suzanne I. 2005. *In Short: How to Teach the Young Adult Short Story.* Portsmouth, NH: Heinemann.

Bomer, Randy. 1995. "Fiction: Building a World of Possibilities." In *Time for Meaning: Crafting Literate Lives in Middle and High School.* Portsmouth, NH: Heinemann.

Coles, Robert. 1989. *The Call of Stories: Teaching and the Moral Imagination.* Boston: Houghton Mifflin.

Hamilton, Carole L., and Peter Kratzke, ed. 1999. *Short Stories in the Classroom.* Urbana, IL: NCTE.

Kaplan, Jeffrey S. 1997. "Laughing with Thurber and Young Adult Literature." In *Adolescent Literature as a Complement to the Classics.* Vol. 3, ed. Joan Kaywell. Norwood, MA: Christopher-Gordon.

Lattimer, Heather. 2003. "Short Story." In *Thinking Through Genre: Units of Study in Reading and Writing Workshops 4–12.* Portland, ME: Stenhouse.

CHAPTER 4

Essays

The essay can do anything a poem can do, and everything a short story can do—everything but fake it.

–ANNIE DILLARD

The limited use of essays in middle school and high school classrooms may be attributed to the fact that most of us who teach language arts are lovers of fiction in all its forms. But as Annie Dillard's quote indicates, essays have much to offer our students. Susan Orlean, editor of *The Best American Essays* (2005), celebrates the essay in noting, "What moves me most is an essay in which the writer turns something over and over in his or her head, and in examining it finds a bit of truth about human nature and life and the experience of inhabiting this planet" (xvii). Essays vary in their topics, structure, and writing style, but what links them together is the way an essay reflects the writer's unique perspective; essays allow us to examine the writer's thinking.

I have chosen to organize nonfiction writing into two genres: essays and memoir (see Chapter 5 for memoirs). Nonfiction writing that focuses on the author's personal story falls under memoir. I include nonfiction writing that focuses on issues extending beyond the author's personal story in this chapter. At times it was difficult to make a distinction because the categories blur. And I note that I am not alone in my efforts to categorize essays. According to Susan Orlean, in her efforts to solicit essays for *The Best American Essays*, she discovered there were "radically divergent ideas of what an essay was." In making her selections for the 2005 collection, she looked for essays that demonstrate "an awareness of craft and forcefulness of thought" (xiii).

It's my hope that this chapter will celebrate essays meeting this same criteria and demonstrate that the essay is first-class literature deserving of time and attention in middle school and high school classrooms for both content and craft. Essays provide an opportunity for students to debate what is fact and what is fiction. They offer an alternative to those students who don't embrace "stuff that isn't real." Essays can also be used to teach specific reading skills such as locating information, summarizing ideas, and making connections among concepts. Essays also serve as a model for the kind of writing we ask of students. Students can read, analyze, and discuss essays before they try to write their own.

Exploring Essays

Several months into teaching junior English for the first time, I came upon an excerpt from Ralph Waldo Emerson's essay "Self-Reliance" in our literature anthology. The teacher's guide suggested this essay could be used to explore the three kinds of essays: descriptive, narrative, and expository. I admit I was surprised to learn there were three kinds of essays, and I was not clear which of the three Emerson's "Self-Reliance" represented. I decided I would have students read the essay in class, see what they noticed, and go from there.

> *"Trust thyself: every heart vibrates to that iron string."*
> *"Nothing is at last sacred but the integrity of your own mind."*
> *"It is easy in the world to live after the world's opinion; it is easy in solitude to live after our own; but the great man is he who in the midst of the crowd keeps with perfect sweetness the independence of solitude."*
> *"But do your thing and I shall know you. Do your work and you shall reinforce yourself."*
> *"For nonconformity the world whips you with its displeasure."*

"A foolish consistency is the hobgoblin of little minds, adored by little statesmen and philosophers and divines."

Students noted the quotes listed above as lines that struck them in this essay. They wanted to know more about Ralph Waldo Emerson. As one boy commented, "This guy gets it." "Self-Reliance" was a way into essays for my students. They understood how Emerson's call for the maintenance of self despite societal pressures was reflective not only of Emerson's time but of the challenges today's adolescents face. Lively discussions about how expectations from parents, peers, and school conflicted with students' own struggle for self ensued. One young woman reported that she had quoted Emerson, "For nonconformity the world whips you with its displeasure," during an argument with her mom about what she was wearing to school.

I don't know which of the three kinds of essays Emerson's "Self-Reliance" represents. My students would tell you it is representative of all three: it tells a story, it is descriptive, and it presents information in a way that is persuasive. Most important, my students would tell you that Emerson's essay does what a good essay should do: it uses writing craft to show the author's thinking.

I debated how to organize this chapter, wondering if I should embrace the "types of essays: narrative, descriptive, and expository" mentioned in the literature anthology I was required to teach. I wondered about the role of persuasive essays—not mentioned in the literature anthology but a required writing genre in our state writing assessment. As I revisited the essays I taught as well as essays I was currently reading, I found myself focusing on essay topics rather than essay types. Thus I used topics to frame this chapter. Within each topic there are examples of narrative, descriptive, and expository essays as well as essays intended to persuade. I am struck by how often essays incorporate elements of all three types of essays. I made no effort to distinguish between formal and informal essays. These descriptors were used in literature anthologies, but I did not find them, nor any mention of essay types, in the essay collections I read. I would be remiss if I did not also note that I don't have any examples of the five-paragraph essay format that has become so prevalent in high school writing classes. I did find a five-paragraph essay in Maya Angelou's collection, *Wouldn't Take Nothing for My Journey Now* (1993), but it is clear this essay is five paragraphs because that's the number of paragraphs Angelou needed to make her point, not because she was following a formula. The other essays in this collection vary in length. I am confident that exposing students to essays as part of a literature workshop will support students in seeing beyond the five-paragraph formula, allowing them to discover that the essay, like other writing genres, is richly varied in form and writing craft.

My hope is that reading a wide variety of essays as part of our literature study will support the continued development of students' reading skills, push students' thinking regarding the subject or content of the essay, illustrate the power and importance of writing craft, and provide models for students' own essay writing.

Strategies that Support Essay Reading

As I described in the first chapter of this book, I was surprised when I realized I had to teach reading, not just assume all my students had reading skills they could apply to the literature we were reading. I have since discovered that essays are particularly useful for teaching and reinforcing reading skills. The following briefly describes three teaching strategies that focus on reading skills, followed by an exploration of essays based on their topics.

Teaching Strategy: Locating Information

I am a voracious reader of how-to essays. Our state writing assessment includes how-to essays in its definition of expository essays, so this gave me permission to include how-to essays in my classroom. Although my tendency is to bring in how-to essays as examples in support of writing expository essays, I also find that these essays reinforce reading skills, particularly locating information. Students learn not only to look for how authors draw attention to important information but also how to do things across a range of topics (see sidebar).

In support of reinforcing or developing students' ability to locate information while reading, I provide them with a short essay and ask them to read it on their own. As they read I ask them to mark with a highlighter pen any sentences or passages that provide information related to the how-to of the title.

I find that there is a wide range of essays providing how-to advice, so I can select essays in which the advice is in easy-to-find list form or I can select an essay that weaves the information into a narrative, which proves more challenging. I try to use more than one how-to essay to show students the range of organizational approaches and how these impact them as readers. I also try to pick how-to essays addressing a range of topics. My best sources for these essays are magazines, in particular *Real Simple*, which is rich with how-to advice. I have a passion for reading magazines, so I was thrilled to find a way to justify the time and money I spend on them. However, I have listed below some essays I found in books, recognizing that some have been reprinted from magazines.

HOW-TO ESSAYS

AUTHOR	SOURCE	TITLE	HOW-TO TOPIC
Philip Weiss	The Best American Essays: 1993	*"How to Get Out of a Locked Trunk"*	*Escaping a locked trunk*
Barbara Kingsolver	High Tide in Tucson	*Excerpt from "Be Careful What You Let In the Door" pp. 250–256*	*Drawing on emotion rather than event in writing*
Kitty Burns Florey	The Best American Essays: 2005	*"Sister Bernadette's Barking Dog"*	*The lost skill of sentence diagramming*
Cathleen Schine	The Best American Essays: 2005	*"Dog Trouble"*	*Coping with a difficult dog*
James Michener	The Writing Life: Writers on How they Think and Work	*"How to Identify and Nurture Young Writers"*	*Tips for being a writer and for supporting writers*
Ellen Degeneres	My Point . . . And I Do Have One	*"In the Kitchen with Ellen or As Tasty as Poison and Just as Deadly"*	*Making real Frenchy French toast*

Teaching Strategy: Synthesizing Ideas
What are the author's main points? What evidence or support did the author provide in support of his or her main points? Summarize the article in one or two sentences. What question(s) would you ask the author if you had a chance to interview him or her? These questions focus students' attention on synthesis. I use these questions, or variations of these questions, in discussing a variety of essays (see discussion in the next section regarding connections), but I find synthesis is especially crucial for analyzing persuasive essays. (See "Teaching Strategy: A Close Look at Essays Written to Persuade" later in this chapter.)

Teaching Strategy: Making Connections, with an Emphasis on Text to Text
E. B. White is a favorite essayist of mine, so I was thrilled to share his essay "Walden" with my juniors. We read it several weeks after reading excerpts from Thoreau's

Walden. I wanted students to admire the essay for its craft and humor, but I also wanted them to make connections between White's ideas and Thoreau's. (For more on text-to-text connections see *Strategies That Work: Teaching Comprehension to Enhance Understanding* by Stephanie Harvey and Anne Goudvis.)

In support of text-to-text connections, I asked students to use their literature logs (described in Chapter 2). These logs capture students' thoughts in response to previous and current reading. My goal was to focus students' attention first on the text read earlier. I asked students to write a short summary of that text. Here again the use of short texts supports this effort. I find that asking for a paragraph summary followed by a one-to-two-sentence summary works well. I invite volunteers to share their summaries so that we have the main ideas of the text in mind before we read the new text.

In support of summary writing I often provide a writing prompt or question. For example, in response to the excerpts from *Walden,* I asked students to respond to this question: "How would Thoreau explain what he learned during his time at the pond? Answer in a paragraph and then in a single sentence."

Students then share their summaries in small groups. Following this sharing, I ask students to turn to a new page in their literature logs and label it with the title of the new essay. I let them know I am going to read this new essay aloud but will stop periodically and ask them to write quick responses to questions. I provide students with a copy of the essay so that they can refer to it in writing their responses. I let them know that my purpose in using this stop-and-write approach is not to test their reading but to remind them of the reading strategies we have been using all year, which include asking questions as we read. Although I design prompts and questions that will focus students' attention on the new text, I am also using this writing-as-we-read strategy to support students in seeing connections between the two texts. I find the following prompts can be adapted to use with a variety of essays in support of text-to-text connections:

Briefly describe an image in the essay that strikes you.

So far this essay seems to be about . . .

I wonder . . .

I want to know more about . . .

What I find interesting so far is . . .

This is like the previous essay we read . . .

The author's message in this essay seems to be . . .

In using these prompts with the E. B. White essay and excerpts from Thoreau's *Walden* students noted the following connections:

Both authors described the physical surroundings of the pond in great detail.

Both authors focused on a close look: Thoreau looked at ants; White looked at dead animals on the side of the road: a snake and a turtle.

White contrasted the Concord of today with what he imagined Concord looked like in Thoreau's day.

White writes about the commercialization of Walden Pond but does so in a Thoreau-like style.

It would certainly not be practical to spend this kind of time reading and writing about essays every day. But I find that breaking the process of reading and writing in response to essays into increments supports students in seeing connections they might otherwise miss. The fact that the E. B. White essay is a complex parody imitating Thoreau's style strengthens the text-to-text connections. (For more on parody, see the discussion in the "Literary Craft in Essays" section of this chapter.)

Essays on Nature

I want students to understand and appreciate the power of writing about nature. In support of this we read essays on nature and do our own nature observation and writing. We read several examples of nature essays, noting the author's focus on small-scale or broader-scale observations. We also examine the author's emphasis on sensory details: how does the author help us, as readers, see, hear, feel, smell, and even taste what he or she is describing?

Typically I utilize the learning logs, detailed earlier, in support of this close reading, but this could also be taught as a single lesson or even a literature circle assignment, which would allow for the use of varied nature essays. Listed in the sidebar are examples of nature essays, their focus, and the sensory details they emphasize.

ESSAYS ON NATURE

AUTHOR	ESSAY TITLE AND SOURCE	OBSERVATION SCALE	SENSORY DETAILS
Henry David Thoreau	*"Brute Neighbors" in* Walden	*Small scale: ants*	*Sight*
Henry David Thoreau	*"Spring" in* Walden	*Large scale: the pond and surrounding area*	*Touch Sound Sight*
Annie Dillard	*"Heaven and Earth in Jest" in* Pilgrim at Tinker Creek	*Large scale: Tinker Creek and surrounding area Small scale: cat and frog*	*Sight Smell Sound Touch*
Kathleen Dean Moore	*"The John Day River" in* Riverwalking: Reflections on Moving Water	*Large scale: driving along and floating on the John Day River*	*Sight Sound Touch*
Paul Crenshaw	*"Storm Country" in* The Best American Essays: 2005	*Large scale: storms in western Arkansas*	*Sound Sight Touch*
John Muir	*"Stickeen" in* The Best American Essays of the Century	*Small scale: dog Large scale: Alaska*	*Sight Touch Smell*
Rachel Carson	*"The Marginal World" in* The Best American Essays of the Century	*Large scale: the shore Small scale: tide pools*	*Sight Sound*
Gretel Ehrlich	*"The Solace of Open Spaces" in* The Best American Essays of the Century	*Large scale: Wyoming*	*Sight Touch Sound*
David James Duncan	*"River Teeth: A Definition" in* River Teeth: Stories and Writing	*Small scale: a log in a stream*	*Sight*

Teaching Strategy: Observing Nature

84

After we have read several nature excerpts, I invite students to use their own skills of observation, to spend some time "poking around." I borrowed this term from Kathleen Dean Moore, author of *Riverwalking: Reflections on Moving Water* (1995), who writes in her essay "Winter Creek,"

> *The kind of poking around I am interested in advocating must be done outdoors. It is a matter of going into the land to pay close attention, to pry*

at things with the toe of a boot, to turn over rocks at the edge of a stream and
lift boards to look for snakes or the nests of silky deer mice, to kneel close to
search out the tiny bones mixed with fur in an animal's scat, to poke a cattail
down a gopher hole. (33)

Moore's quote is our starting place for a discussion about what we can observe, and where. I was fortunate to teach in a rural town, where many students had access to wooded areas that were made for poking around. But some of my students lived in town, so we discussed the value of observing in our own backyards.

The homework task was to poke around outside for at least twenty minutes. Students could choose to focus on a very small area or consider a broad area. The goal was to be specific, like the nature essays we had read. I asked students to focus on what they saw, heard, felt, smelled, and, only if safe, tasted. I encouraged them to take a notepad or sketch pad with them to capture their descriptions but let them know that their written reflection on their poking around would take place in class. I assigned this homework on a Thursday, and it was due the following Thursday so that students would have plenty of time to complete it. Each class day I checked in with students, inviting those who had done their observations to share their experiences to encourage those who had not yet poked around.

On the day the observations were due, I provided in-class writing time to respond to the following prompts:

1. Reflect on why you selected the observation site you chose to "poke around."

2. What did you see, hear, feel, smell, and (if applicable) taste?

3. What did you learn from this observation? In your reflection, refer to the nature essays we read and include quotes or ahas that support your observations.

After twenty to thirty minutes of in-class writing, students shared examples from their observations. I was stunned by their attention to detail, as the following examples illustrate:

"The trees' black, naked, knotty branches have lost all of their elasticity.
They loom into the bright, blue sky as if they wanted to prick or at least
tickle it."

"After a green, lavish summer life, the grass blades have now turned yellow, dry and rough."

"The panorama of the sky stretches above me like the wardrobe of a rich woman, rich midnight velvets and diamonds. Blue unto no blue under itself, the sky . . . is spattered and dabbled freely with multicolored stars, the 'gigantous' black silhouettes of pines tower above my head, like one-dimensional ink blots upon some artist's work of three-dimensional perfection."

In addition to powerful descriptions in their observations, students' in-class reflections are evidence that they connected their own experience with the nature essays we had read, particularly Thoreau's *Walden*. Claudia wrote in her nature observation about the ways nature adapts, describing a tree with barbed wire sticking out: "This wire must have scratched him for a long time, so he decided to make it a part of himself." She writes in her reflection, "All the things [in nature] adapt to the circumstances they live in and work together in a coordinated, brilliant balance. . . . Thoreau was aware of nature and tried to live as part of it. He balanced his life by simplifying it, going back to the rhythm of nature." She goes on to quote from Thoreau, "I wanted to live deep and suck out all the marrow of life."

This two-part assignment sets the stage for our continued exploration of essays. Students "own" essay writing in a new way. They understand that essays can be about what we observe as well as what we learn from our observations.

Essays About and in Response to Books and Literature

In the early 1990s the new superintendent of the school district where I taught high school English announced in his "state of the district" speech that computers would soon take the place of books. He spoke glowingly of students seated in front of computers reading the classics. I shifted uncomfortably in my auditorium seat. I was not ready to embrace computer in place of book. I knew the joy of opening a brand-new book and inhaling its scent. I knew the comfort I found curled up on a rainy afternoon with a book in my lap and a hot cup of tea nearby. I knew the power I felt marking favorite lines in books with highlighter pens or sticky notes. My house is filled with books I adore.

I wanted students to wrestle with the question of books versus computers. Anna Quindlen's essay "How Reading Changed My Life" (1999) provided rich fodder in support of our exploration. In her essay, Quindlen acknowledges the power of computers to support writing, noting "a laptop computer is a wondrous thing; it is inconceivable to me that I ever did without one, particularly in writing and revision" (168). But she goes on to report that " a computer is no substitute for a book" (168). She argues that we like books for more than their information or stories; we like books for their physical existence: "It is not simply that we need information, but that we want to savor it, carry it with us, feel the heft of it under our arm. We like the thing [book] itself" (170). Quindlen's essay is a starting point for an exploration of why books? Why read?

Teaching Strategy: Creating a List of Books That Matter

Whether it's Quindlen's essay or another, I want to get my students reading about books. This reading, followed by a discussion of books and reading, leads to the creation of a list: Books That Matter. I want students to think about books that matter to them. Fortunately there are a number of book lists available to use as models. Quindlen has "Three by Quindlen: Three Interesting Lists of Books" (1999) that build on her essay. Her lists are titled "Ten Big Thick Books That Could Take You a Whole Summer to Read (But Aren't Beach Books)," "The Ten Books One Would Save in a Fire (If One Could Save Only Ten)," and "Ten Nonfiction Books That Help Us Understand the World." I share these lists and other lists I have collected with students: best-seller lists from the newspaper and bookstores I have visited, lists from other teachers in the school, my own list of "Ten Books I Love." I am grateful to *O: The Oprah Magazine* for its monthly article in which a celebrity or author shares "Books That Made a Difference." I also commend to you the July 2006 issue of *O* that focuses on "Summer Reading," which includes not only lists of books but also essays about reading, including an essay by Toni Morrison and a delightful letter from Harper Lee about her own reading.

To support students' generation of book lists, I provide class time to work on lists and class-time visits to the school library. I invite students to share titles from their lists. Over the course of the school year, we revisit these lists, adding to them and creating new lists. We eventually create a class list entitled "Must Reads." One year we even created a mock bookshelf of "Must Reads." The wood shop teacher created a rack I could hang on the wall that looked like a bookshelf. Students then created book covers out of construction paper for their chosen

87

"Must Read" book to place on the shelf. Inside the paper book cover each student wrote why he or she recommended the book. It was wonderful to see students pulling the "books" off the shelf to read the recommendations.

During her first year of teaching, Lisa Root created a book recommendations system in which students created note cards of book recommendations; she asked that they create more than one card so that fellow students could take the cards. The book recommendation cards were slipped into a pocket chart from which students could remove them. Lisa was delighted to see students reading fellow students' recommendations, and she also appreciated how students monitored their own book recommendation cards. A culture of readers was being nurtured. And, yes, it's true, sometimes Lisa took recommendation cards so that students would need to make more recommendation cards. Lisa would tell you, as would I, that she is willing to do what it takes to get students excited about reading.

Listed at the end of this chapter are books on books that I have found helpful. I hope this list of resources will add to the book resources you already use.

Teaching Strategy: Book Reviews

It took me more years than it should have to include book reviews as part of my literature workshop. Reading published reviews supports the continued development of students as book connoisseurs, and it provides a model for writing literary essays. I am glad that there are now so many venues for book reviews. I have used book reviews I found in magazines, in the Sunday newspaper, and on Amazon.com. I have gotten in the habit of keeping a file of book reviews so that I can provide students with choices and have reviews of current best sellers and classics.

Teaching Strategy: Reviewing a Review

I introduce the review of a review with a whole-class focus on a review I have selected. I try to select a review of a current best seller, but I have also had success in using reviews written by authors with whom my students are familiar such as Ursula Le Guin's review of "The Dark Tower" by C. S. Lewis (see Le Guin 1989, 242).

I would be remiss if I didn't also note the success I have had with reviewing movie reviews. Ursula Le Guin reviewed the films *Close Encounters of the Third Kind* and *Star Wars* (1989, 245). She concludes that "*Star Wars* is all action and

Close Encounters is all emotion, and both are basically mindless" (247). It's fair to say her review gets students' attention. I ask them to list her criticisms of the films and note the examples or evidence she uses. We use this writing to examine the elements of a review. Students noted the following elements:

- The review clearly states the title(s) of what is being reviewed
- The review provides some description or summary of the book or film being reviewed.
- The reviewer states an opinion regarding the book or film and uses examples from the book or film to support this opinion.
- The review usually ends with a final recommendation to either read/see the book or film, read it or see it but be warned it has flaws, or don't read/see the book or film.

Students use this list of elements in reviewing a sample review. They then move from the review of the review to writing a review of their own about a book or movie of their choosing. We then spend time in class reviewing our own reviews. Students use the list of review elements in support of this work as well.

Entertainment Weekly magazine contains a wealth of reviews of movies, DVDs, television, music, and books. But it also contains a regular essay authored by Stephen King, entitled the "Pop of King," in which King reviews pop culture, including movies, books, television, and music. Recently King wrote about the Oscars, summer 2006 movies, and "Morning People," in which he touted CNN's morning news over the network morning shows. A number of adolescents, including my son, rave about King's work, and anything they read by choice grabs my attention. King's essays can be found on the *Entertainment Weekly* website (http://www.ew.com/ew/package/0,12938,472578_7_0_,00.html) and in the magazine's reviews.

ESSAYS ON BOOKS AND READING

AUTHOR	SOURCE	TITLE	FOCUS
Robert Frost	The Best American Essays of the Century	*"The Figure a Poem Makes"*	*The delight and wisdom of poetry*
Gertrude Stein	The Best American Essays of the Century	*"What Are Master-pieces and Why Are There So Few of Them?"*	*The creative process and writing a masterpiece*
Eudora Welty	The Best American Essays of the Century	*"A Sweet Devouring"*	*Devouring books*
Julia Alvarez	Something to Declare: Essays	*"First Muse"*	*Stories can save you*
Anatole Broyard	A Passion for Books	*"Lending Books"*	*The agony of loaning a book to a friend*

Essays About Writing

Writing is hard work. I think students need to know this. I want them to read about and understand the work of writing by reading essays about writing. In my own struggles to write, I have found comfort and inspiration in the words of people who share their insights about their own process of putting words on paper. It is not some magical process that just happens, at least it's not for most writers.

I once imagined myself living the life of a writer: light spilled across me perched at an antique desk, a sturdy coffee mug in hand, with book-lined shelves surrounding windows looking out on the enormous backyard of my huge house, paid for by the royalties from my award-winning books. The real picture, as I write this book, is I am sitting in my dining room, which does have very nice windows, and it is cloudy outside. Books are strewn across the table and stacked on the floor. The timer on the dryer just buzzed so I have towels to fold. I always do laundry when I write. Something about the sorting process helps me sort out what I am trying to say. I have just a few hours before my kids get home from school, which will end my writing day. A cup of lukewarm coffee is sitting on a coaster near me. I always choose a coffee blend in support of my writing project. My rule is that I can drink this good coffee only if I am writing. What I need to learn is how to drink the good coffee while it is still warm.

I write on a laptop. Next to the laptop is a legal pad on which I scribble notes to myself about quotes I want to add or places I need to add more details. The room in which I write is quiet; music distracts me. When I get stuck, I find it helpful to read about writing.

I particularly appreciate Donald Murray's advice regarding voice and writing:

> *Most important of all, voice. I do not begin to write until I hear the voice of the writing, and when that voice fades during drafting, rewriting/ replanning, or revising, I stop, make myself quiet, and listen until I hear again. The music of the writing, more than anything else, teaches me what I am learning about the subject to make those thoughts and feelings clear. And when the writing doesn't go well, the most effective tactic is to listen, quietly, carefully to the writing. If I listen closely enough the writing will tell me what to say and how to say it. As Jayne Anne Phillips says, "It's like being led by a whisper." (1991, 10)*

Like many of you, I shared writers' thoughts on writing with my students during writing workshop: Anne Lamott's *Bird by Bird* (1994) is a personal favorite. But I was fortunate to stumble across several collections in which authors wrote essays about writing—the challenges, the joys, the process, the hard work. I found myself informed by their insights and tricks of the trade, inspired by their craft and oddly comforted by the fact that so many of the authors whose words I savored admitted to struggle in putting those words on paper. I realized students needed to see these essays, for their message and for their craft as essays.

Teaching Strategy: The Writing Life
Before they read about the writing life of others, I wanted my students to spend some time reflecting on their own writing life. I shared my own essay, which expanded on the brief description I included above about my writing life, and then invited students to write about their writing life: what discoveries have you made about what supports you as writers? Think about the places you write, the paper you use, your writing instrument of choice.

One of my students wrote that she prefers pencil; she likes the feel of the lead on paper and the way the words she writes look soft. Another student wanted roller ball, black ink pens, the expensive kind. My own daughter prefers gel pens and

Hello Kitty notebook paper. Other students shared their frustration in having to handwrite; they prefer writing on computer. Many students spoke of their need for music while writing and the role of different songs in inspiring their writing. I also encouraged students to think about the content of their writing—what inspires them? I was surprised and delighted to learn that the pictures I tore out of old calendars and posted on the classroom walls were a frequent source of inspiration, particularly the Monet prints. I also asked students to focus on the process of writing: the work of revision, editing, putting words on paper even when the words don't feel right. I admitted to them that I don't do much prewriting on paper. All those webs and outlines I see other writers use intrigue me, but they don't help me. I need time to let myself think, to percolate as Tom Romano calls it (often my head is percolating as I sort laundry), and then I write on a laptop computer, typing as quickly as I can. My typing teacher, Mrs. Moore, would be very proud of me.

After we write about our own processes as writers, I invite students to share. We discover what makes us unique and what commonalities we all share. We then read an essay about writing. As we read, I ask students to note ahas about writing—what does this author say about writing? We focus on the same issues we explored in our own writing: place, equipment, inspiration, process. We share our ahas in a class discussion. We then reread the essay, focusing our attention on the essay's craft: how does the author convey his or her message?

I follow this whole-class read by asking students to choose from a variety of essays about writing. Using the same two-prong response, students first write in their literature logs about lessons learned from writers about writing and then note observations regarding the author's craft.

Next students work in groups to create writing lesson posters for the classroom. They make visual the strategies and the words used to convey the strategies. I am always heartened to see students including their own quotes on these posters. And as we post them in the room, my hope is that they will provide inspiration and support my goal to create a community of writers, a place where students see themselves as writers and discover what they can learn from other writers. I want them to understand that the hard work of writing can inform and inspire readers. I want them to find essays about writing that they can turn to when they need to be reminded why we write. I want my students to see writing as work worth doing.

As for what essay I choose to read as a class, it depends. I try to select an essay written by an author we have previously read, or an essay that will make us laugh, or an essay that addresses an issue I know students are struggling with in their own writing. I used this same criteria in creating a selection of essays about writing from which students choose. I have listed my recent favorite essays about writing in the sidebar.

ESSAYS ABOUT WRITING

AUTHOR	SOURCE	ESSAY TITLE	TOPIC
Nadine Gordimer	The Writing Life	"Being a Product of Your Dwelling Place"	Finding a subject or being found by a subject
Susan Minot	The Writing Life	"A Real-Life Education"	On not intending to become a writer
Ray Bradbury	The Writing Life	"Hunter of Metaphors"	Connecting writing and film
Julia Alvarez	The Writing Life	"On Finding a Latino Voice"	Voice inspired by William Carlos Wiliams
Julia Alvarez	Something to Declare	"Writing Matters"	Her process—and the work—of writing
Kent Haruf	Writers on Writing	"To See Your Story Clearly, Start by Pulling the Wool over Your Own Eyes"	Peculiar habits and methods of writing
Diane Johnson	Writers on Writing	"Pesky Themes Will Emerge When You're Not Looking"	Novels and themes
David Mamet	Writers on Writing	"The Humble Genre Novel, Sometimes Full of Genius"	The delight of genre novels
Sue Miller	Writers on Writing	"Virtual Reality: The Perils of Seeking a Novelist's Facts in Her Fiction"	The annoying question of the role of autobiography in one's fiction
Walter Mosley	Writers on Writing	"For Authors, Fragile Ideas Need Loving Every Day"	The importance of developing a daily habit of writing
Marge Piercy	Writers on Writing	"Life of Prose and Poetry: An Inspiring Combination"	Why she writes poetry and fiction
Annie Proulx	Writers on Writing	"Inspiration? Head Down the Back Road, and Stop for the Yard Sales"	Digging for inspiration in song, books, eavesdropping, and pamphlets you find as you travel
William Saroyan	Writers on Writing	"Starting with a Tree and Finally Getting to the Death of a Brother"	You write by writing

93

Essays About Issues and Politics

Essays designed to inform and persuade are part of our culture, and I want students to spend time reading and analyzing examples of these essays. My long-term goal is for students to make the reading of these essays a routine part of their reading lives. My short-term goal is for students to see how language can be used to convey a specific message.

Teaching Strategy: Reading to Hear the Message

To emphasize how we "hear the message" of an essay, I use a speech for our first whole-class reading. There are a number of speeches available. In selecting a speech to use I try to find one that allows students to hear and see the speaker on video. I begin our exploration by asking students to watch and listen for key themes in the speech's message. They are to note these themes in their literature logs. I then play the speech for them once. Students share their initial thoughts regarding theme identification with a peer.

We then watch and listen to the speech a second time, this time with a written copy of the speech. I invite students to add to their theme identification notes. Again they do a pair-share with their original partner.

I then ask each pair to select a quote that illustrates a key theme. I hand butcher paper and felt pens to select pairs and ask them to write their quote as a starting point for our class discussion.

The butcher paper quotes are posted in the front of the room. I reference these in asking questions about the speech and its message. We then use the quotes to examine the literary craft techniques used in the speech. In Martin Luther King Jr.'s speech students noted the way he repeats, "I have a dream." More important, they noted the way he used his voice to emphasize his words. Seeing and hearing this speech impacted my students more than I would have imagined. I could see they were invested in this message of dreams, so I stopped our discussion and invited students to list their dreams. The students then asked if they could share their dreams. When the bell rang at the end of class, none of the students moved until everyone had shared his or her dream.

Teaching Strategy: A Close Look at Essays Written to Persuade

I build on this exploration of hearing the message by asking students to read essays that address student issues. I find these essays in magazines and newspapers, particularly student newspapers. The essays we have explored address such topics as the school dress code, requiring school uniforms, raising the age for driving from sixteen to eighteen, standardized testing, the fairness of the SAT, college admissions procedures, grade inflation, and cafeteria food.

I keep a file folder of essays on hand, and the Web is also a rich resource (see sidebar list of essays in this section as well as the resource list at the end of this chapter). In addition, I invite students to bring in essays on topics that matter to them. I use a survey to glean student interest in essay topics. On the survey I list five to seven topics for which I have essays. I ask students to rank these topics based on their interest in reading more about them and then use this survey data to select a class essay topic and create essay literary circles.

For the class essay topic I select the most preferred topic and provide students with an essay on it. Ideally, it will be a topic on which I have two essays with differing points of view. I begin our class session by asking students to write on the essay topic themselves. In support of this writing I provide a prompt that encourages students to take a stand. For example, if the topic is school uniforms, I ask students to write in response to one of the following prompts:

> School uniforms are good for high school students.
>
> School uniforms are not what high school students need.

I then do a quick poll of the class as to which side of the issue they supported. In the case of school uniforms, most of the students write about why they do not support uniforms. I then ask students to spend five to seven minutes writing on the opposite side of this issue. The groans are audible. Typically when I check in with students, I find they have struggled to write on the topic from "the other side."

This is why we need to read essays that wrestle with topics that impact us. We need to consider the issue from a variety of viewpoints. The goal is not to change our minds, but to push our thinking.

Before I hand out the essays to be read, I ask students to generate a list of questions that will support their reading. We build on the reading strategies discussed in the first chapter of this book. Students have developed the following questions:

> What is the topic of the essay?

95

What is the author's stance or opinion on the issue?

What evidence does the author provide in support of his or her position?

If I were interviewing this author, what question(s) would I ask the author?

Now that I have read two essays with different viewpoints on this topic, how has my opinion changed?

Students write responses to these questions as they read the two essays. I then put students together in groups of four. I select these groups based on students' essay preference survey. The foursome will explore the class essays we have read in preparation for the literature circle reading the following day.

I ask the students as a foursome to share their responses to the questions on each essay and be prepared to defend to the class which of the two essays they read made the stronger case and why. As students share, I circulate and eavesdrop. My hope is that students will differ in their opinions as to which essay is more compelling.

I call on groups to present their preferred essay and their rationale for such. As our debate and discussion continues, I note on the board the reasons cited by each group. We then examine this list to see what elements we found compelling. Class lists usually include some of the following:

Grabber lead

Personal connections

Appeals to our emotions

Uses specific examples

Compares

Contrasts

Attacks the other side

Powerful conclusion

Passionate about the topic

The following day in class students regroup with their foursome from the previous day. Their task is to analyze a new essay or essays using the previous day's questions as well as the list of essay elements we generated in class. The questions and list are provided to each group along with essays on the topics in which they showed interest on their survey. I ask students to select a volunteer reader to read the essays aloud first, and then I indicate there will need to be quiet time for a second, silent reading. The initial reading is loud, but I find students lean forward and focus their attention on their group. The second, silent reading allows students to see the essay again. I have to be honest: this second reading also provides me with a few minutes of quiet time. It is amazing how loud a classroom can be when students are involved in group work.

Providing students with questions and elements to focus their attention, allowing them to work in groups, and focusing their efforts on essays that address a topic in which they are interested all support differentiation. Using a literature circle to read different essays on the same topic also supports reading ability. I tell students I am providing them with more than one essay, as we did in class the day before, to explore more than one point of view.

Each literature circle is then asked to present their essay(s) to the class. I ask them to use the questions and elements in support of their presentation as well as to select passages from the essay that illustrate the questions and elements. Listeners are required to note a "key learning about essays" they heard from each group. I have learned the hard way that if I don't build in a required listening component, some of my students are less than attentive during group presentations.

I also ask each student to complete a self-evaluation of his or her literature circle group and presentation. I use the self-evaluations and the student listening sheets to assign a grade for this activity.

ESSAYS ON ISSUES

AUTHOR	SOURCE	ESSAY TITLE	ISSUE
Wallace Stegner	Sports Illustrated: Fifty Years of Great Writing	*"We Are Destroying Our National Parks"*	*A call for conservation of our national parks*
Amy Tan	The Best American Essays: 1991	*"Mother Tongue"*	*Tan's opinion on the English language and its variations*
Zora Neale Hurston	The Best American Essays of the Century	*"How It Feels to Be Colored Me"*	*A reflection on being "colored"*
Mark Twain	The Best American Essays of the Century	*"Corn-Pone Opinions"*	*Our tendency to think like our neighbors rather than independently*
Gertrude Stein	The Best American Essays of the Century	*"What Are Master-pieces and Why Are There So Few of Them?"*	*An exploration of the creative process and masterpieces*
Martin Luther King Jr.	The Best American Essays of the Century	*"Letter from Birmingham Jail"*	*A plea for support of the civil rights movement efforts from white religious leadership*
Richard Rodriguez	The Best American Essays of the Century	*"Aria: A Memoir of a Bilingual Childhood"*	*A personal story that wrestles with the issues of individuality and assimilation in bilingual education*
Gerald Early	The Best American Essays of the Century	*"Life with Daughters: Watching the Miss America Pageant"*	*Struggles with issues raised by the Miss America pageant as a black family watches a black woman be named Miss America*
Jonathan Franzen	How to Be Alone: Essays	*Excerpt from "Imperial Bedroom" pp. 42–54*	*The challenge of ensuring a right to privacy*
Philip Roth	A Passion for Books	*"The Newark Public Library"*	*Why the public library should be saved*
Scott Turow	The Writing Life	*"Can Whites Write About Blacks?"*	*Should a white author try to write about blacks in his novels?*
Bill McKibben	The Writing Life	*"Speaking Up for the Environment"*	*Preventing drilling in the Arctic National Wildlife Refuge*

Essays About Sports

I live with a man who loves sports. He played them when he was growing up and well into adulthood until his knees and back let him know it was time to slow down. He watches sports: collegiate and pro. In addition to all the sports channels now available on cable, we purchase sports packages so he can watch more. My husband also reads about sports—not just the sports page, which often contains wonderful essays, but also books about sports. And although I have been known to yell for the Denver Broncos football team and enjoy my share of tennis viewing, it took my sports-addicted husband to help me find ways to support the sports fan students in my class.

Frank Deford provided my first experience with sports essays. My husband, Mike, handed me a Deford essay from *Sports Illustrated* entitled "The Best Against the Best at Their Best," the story of Tom Watson and Jack Nicklaus's pairing at the 1977 British Open at Turnberry (1987), and I became a fan. (I note that on the morning I wrote this, that particular 1977 golf game classic was being broadcast on the Golf Channel.) I admired Deford's eloquent word choice and his skill at weaving the humanity of sports with the skill and competition of sports. In this particular essay, Deford doesn't disclose the winner of the golf game until the very end of the essay. The story details the two golfers and highlights Watson's relationship with his Scottish caddie, Alfie.

Sports essays serve to connect students who are passionate about sports with writers who are passionate about sports. Students' interest in the essay's topic draws them in, and the quality of sports writing allows students to discover how to weave passion with words. As Terry McDowell writes in the introduction *to Sports Illustrated: Fifty Years of Great Sports Writing* (2003):

> *The classic SI piece, the so-called "Bonus" was designed to push writers beyond the stats and clichés. . . . It wasn't that SI didn't care about scores or that these pieces weren't fundamentally about winning and losing, which they were. But they were also about context, using sport as a prism to view a much wider world of experience and emotion. (6)*

99

Teaching Strategy: The Wide, Wide World of Sports Essays

I share McDowell's quote with students and ask them to select an essay from my file of sports essays, arranged according to the sport they highlight. I invite students to read two or three essays that intrigue them and select one to analyze in depth. I support their essay response by modeling my own response to Deford's essay on Watson and Nicklaus, described above. My goal is to show students how the essay highlights Watson and Nicklaus's golfing skill but how it is more than the details of their golf game. I first read the essay aloud and then place a copy of it on an overhead transparency so students can see the examples I use from the essay.

I let students know that they can write about the Deford essay or they can choose an essay from the file. I find that very few students choose the Deford essay, but those who do so use my essay as scaffolding in support of their own discoveries about the way this golf story illustrates " a much wider world of experience and emotion."

Listed in the sidebar are titles of sports essays. I do note my struggle to find gender balance in putting together this list. Sports essays about males written by males still dominate. In fact, in the *Sports Illustrated* collection of fifty years of sports writing, not one of the essays is written by a woman or about a woman. It's disheartening. So I did my best to track down and include sports essays by and about women. It's my hope that including sports essays in our classrooms may encourage girls as well as boys to write about sports.

ESSAYS ON SPORTS

AUTHOR	SOURCE OF ESSAY	ESSAY TITLE	SPORT HIGHLIGHTED IN ESSAY
William Faulkner	Sports Illustrated: Fifty Years of Great Writing	*"Kentucky: May: Saturday*	*Horseracing: the 1955 Kentucky Derby*
Frank Deford	Sports Illustrated: Fifty Years of Great Writing	*"The Best There Ever Was"*	*Football: a remembrance of Johnny Unitas*
Mark Rudman	The Best American Essays: 1991	*"Mosaic on Walking"*	*Walking*
David Owen	The Best American Sports Writing: 2001	*"The Chosen One"*	*Golf: focus on Tiger Woods*
Vahe Gregorian	The Best American Sports Writing: 2001	*"Olympics Dream Ends in Agony"*	*Wrestling: focus on USA wrestler Sammie Henson*
Beth Kephart	The Best American Sports Writing: 2001	*"Playing for Keeps"*	*Soccer: told from the perspective of a player's mom*
Floyd Skloot	The Best American Essays: 1993	*"Trivia Tea: Baseball as Balm"*	*Baseball and its healing powers*
Barbara Kingsolver	High Tide in Tucson	*"Semper Fi"*	*Sports team loyalty*

Essays About Family

I grew up with a golden retriever named Tawny. She was a member of our family, and her death of old age left me reeling. Thus I have always been drawn to essays that celebrate pets; these essays show how pets help us better understand life. I find that essays about pets—their antics and their losses—are a great way to connect students with text and to connect students with other students. We find community in pet stories.

Teaching Strategy: Exploring Family

Anna Quindlen's essay "Mr. Smith Goes to Heaven" (1993) is a favorite of mine. Her opening paragraph grabbed my attention:

> *Jason Oliver C. Smith, a big dumb guy who was tan, died March 30 of lung cancer and old age. He was thirteen years old and lived in New Jersey, Pennsylvania, and the back section of the minivan, behind the kids' seat. (121)*

The essay goes on to celebrate the life of Jason, the golden retriever who was known for eating coffee cake off the kitchen counter, liking babies, flushing quail and rabbits, his guilty expressions (particularly after rifling through the garbage), his longtime relationship with Pudgy (a fellow dog), and his antagonistic relationship with Daisy the cat. Clearly Jason Oliver C. Smith was well loved, except by Daisy.

This essay sets the stage for thinking about family. In the story of Jason, we glean details about Quindlen and her family. I invite students to write about a pet, focusing on the details of the pet in relationship with the family. If a student doesn't have a pet, I discuss their family with them and encourage them to focus on a specific detail around which they can build the description of their family.

David Sedaris's essay "Us and Them" (2004) also works well for exploring family. Sedaris describes the arrival of his neighbors, the Tomkeys, the night after Halloween:

> *The parents looked as they always had, but the son and daughter were dressed in costumes—she as a ballerina and he as some kind of rodent with terry-cloth ears and a tail made from what looked to be an extension cord. It seemed they had spent the previous evening isolated at a lake and had missed the opportunity to observe Halloween. "So, well, I guess we're trick-or-treating now, if that's okay," Mr. Tomkey said. (7–8)*

Sedaris and his sisters are sent to their rooms to select candy from their own Halloween stash to share with the Tomkey children. As David and his sister agonize over which of their candy they will reluctantly share, Mrs. Sedaris engages in small talk with the Tomkeys. Eventually, in frustration, Mrs. Sedaris storms David's room and selects candy from the pile he has spread on his bed, the pile from which he is currently grabbing and stuffing his favorites into his mouth. His mother is horrified by the sight. "'You should look at yourself,' she said. 'I mean really look at yourself'" (11). As the essay concludes, Sedaris describes how he moves from examining himself to blaming the situation on the Tomkeys and then escaping from any further thought by watching television. With descriptive detail and humor, we see Sedaris's family and the challenge of learning how to respond not just to family but family in relationship with others.

As is the case with pets, I find students have their own stories of family, holidays, and interesting neighbors. Again we use some quick writing about our own families that draws on the model of Sedaris's essay. Listed in the sidebar are more essays that focus on family.

ESSAYS ON FAMILY

AUTHOR	SOURCE OF ESSAY	ESSAY TITLE	ESSAY TOPIC
Dave Barry	Dave Barry Talks Back	*"Just Say No to Rugs"*	*Pets*
Dave Barry	Dave Barry Talks Back	*"The Web Badge of Courage"*	*Killing a spider*
Naomi Shihab Nye	In Short: A Collection of Creative Nonfiction	*"Mint Snowball"*	*Family recipe*
Rita Dove	In Short: A Collection of Creative Nonfiction	*"Loose Ends"*	*Daughter's refusal to tell stories of school*
Brenda Peterson	In Short: A Collection of Creative Nonfiction	*"Growing Up Game"*	*Going to college with 50 pounds of moose meat, a gift from Dad*
John Holman	In Short: A Collection of Creative Nonfiction	*"Cat-like"*	*Brother's cat*
Barbara Kingsolver	High Tide in Tucson	*"The Vibrations of Djoogbe"*	*Learning about life from the locals of Benin, West Africa*
Gerald Early	The Best American Essays of the Century	*"Life with Daughters: Watching the Miss America Pageant"*	*Struggles with issues raised by the Miss America pageant as a black family watches a black woman be named Miss America*

Essays About Finding Our Way in Life

Recently a colleague began her conversation with me by stating, "I don't mean to be disrespectful, but. . . ." And before she could continue I held up my hand and said, "I am going to stop you because if you have to preface your remarks with 'I don't mean to be disrespectful,' then you have already acknowledged that your remarks are going to be disrespectful. So, we can avoid this situation if you stop now." My colleague stared at me in stunned disbelief. So I went on to say, "Maya Angelou has a delightful essay on this very subject; I will get you a copy." And I walked away, feeling grateful for Maya Angelou's wise words:

Certain words excite and alarm me. . . . "Don't mind me, I'm brutally frank."
That is always a summons to arms. I recognize the timid sadist who would
like to throw a stone and hide her hand, or better, who would like not only to
wound but to be forgiven by the soon-to-be-injured even before the injury.
(1993, 117)

I am grateful for essays that provide me with advice for living. In addition to her essay on avoiding verbal attacks entitled "Brutality Is Definitely Not Acceptable," Angelou's collection *Wouldn't Take Nothing for My Journey Now* (1993) contains an essay that addresses the importance of manners in support of style. She writes, "Any person who has charm and some confidence can move in and through societies ranging from the most privileged to the most needy. Style allows the person to appear neither inferior in one location nor superior in the other" (28). I appreciate the juxtaposition of the style essay with Angelou's essay entitled "Getups," in which she comes to terms with the fact that her colorful outfits, which she acknowledges "brought surprise, to say the least, to the eyes of people who could not avoid noticing me" (53), were causing her young son embarrassment. Angelou responds to her son's query about whether she owns "pullover and cardigan sets, which were popular with white women" with a "No" (54), but she goes on to explain her decision to tone down her getups during her son's early years. "I learned to be a little more discreet to avoid causing him displeasure" (55). She then celebrates the return to her "eccentric way of dressing" when her son was older. "As he grew older and more confident, I gradually returned to what friends thought of as my eccentric way of dressing. I was happier when I chose and created my own fashions" (55).

Teaching Strategy: Essay as Advice

I want students to think about how essays can provide them with "life wisdom." In support of this objective, I select essays that address issues with which I think students can connect. This is where efforts to know my students well support my curriculum decisions. I have used the Angelou essays described previously and have listed additional essay choices in the sidebar.

Before we read advice essays, I share a story from my own experience that relates to the essay topic and then ask students to write about a similar experience to get them thinking about the situation addressed in the essay. I find Angelou's essay "Getups" works well because students understand Angelou's son's embarrassment over his mother's outfits. But students also appreciate Angelou's insights about why she wants to dress for herself. This essay builds on earlier discussions we've had in response to Emerson's essay "Self-Reliance."

I share my own story of my mother coming to pick up me up at elementary school in her brown leather, Western-style coat, complete with fringe. On her head she wore a brightly colored scarf of red, green, blue, and yellow (I think the pattern was colorful parrots) to cover the curlers in her hair. I slunk behind her, embarrassed by her colors and fringe, as we made our way down the dull school hallway. Over the years, I came to appreciate and even admire that brown leather coat with fringe, and when my mother bought a new leather coat with no fringe in a gorgeous shade of red, I asked to borrow it. My mother was a practical woman, which explains the scarf and curlers, but her brown leather coat with fringe was an indication not of practicality but of style. When I think about it now, I recognize my mother was ahead of her time.

Students laugh and nod as I tell this story. They begin writing their own stories of getups worn by parents, other family members, and, in the case of several students, their own getups. Clearly clothing choices resonate with students.

As we read Angelou's essay, I ask students to look for the "life wisdom" in the essay. What is Angelou telling us with her story? Students write in response to this question and share their response with a partner prior to our class discussion. I circulate as students share so I can check in and make note of differing viewpoints I want to be sure are heard by the whole class. The pair-share provides a time and space for all voices to be heard on the topic. I also find that the writing and pair-share encourage students to participate in the whole-group discussion so that more voices are heard. And I feel more comfortable calling on students because I know they have something to say.

ADVICE ESSAYS

AUTHOR	SOURCE	TITLE OF ESSAY	ADVICE GIVEN
Anne Morrow Lindbergh	Gift from the Sea	*"A Few Shells"*	*Make time to be quiet and savor simple pleasures*
Ellen Degeneres	The Funny Thing Is...	*"My Most Embarrassing Case Scenario"*	*Strategies for handling embarrassing situations*
David James Duncan	River Teeth: Stories and Writings	*"Rose Vegetables"*	*Witnessing death during a parade—and seeing how it's all cleaned up*
Ted Kooser	The Best American Essays: 2005	*"Small Rooms in Time"*	*Reflections on tragedy and being a young father*
Laurie Notaro	Autobiography of a Fat Bride	*"The Craft Toothbrush"*	*Finding humor in the struggle to adapt to married life*
Laurie Notaro	The Idiot Girls' Action-Adventure Club	*"On the Road"*	*The importance of properly inflated tires, and other car advice*
Jerry Seinfeld	SeinLanguage	*"Personal Maintenance"*	*Reflections on personal upkeep and outfits*

Literary Craft in Essays

As noted throughout this book, short texts provide opportunities to examine literary craft. In each chapter I have highlighted literary craft that I taught with respect to that genre of short text, recognizing that you could also use other genres. Parody and parallelism were two literary techniques we examined using essays.

Teaching Strategy: Playing with Parody

The word traveled quickly through the senior hall of the high school. "We're reading some really twisted stuff in Mrs. Campbell's English class." Any day that I have students providing an enthusiastic preview of the class for the next period I consider a good day. And we were reading really twisted stuff, specifically "A Modest Proposal" by Jonathan Swift. The fact it was a classic essay written hundreds of years ago came as a huge surprise to students. Swift writes:

> *I have been assured by a very knowing American of my acquaintance in*
> *London, that a young healthy child well-nursed, is, at a year old, a most*

delicious, nourishing, and wholesome food, whether stewed, roasted, baked, or boiled; and I make no doubt that it will equally serve in a fricasie, or a ragoust.

I did very little in the way of introduction to this essay. I wanted students to experience it without any prompting from me. As students followed along in the text, I read the essay aloud. I tried to keep my tone of voice the same throughout, a serious tone in keeping with the seriousness of the essay. As I read I observed students move from tolerance bordering on boredom to interest and then discomfort. As soon as I was done reading, the room was ripe with comments: "What's up with this guy?" "Is he really saying people should eat their children?" "This is gross."

The stage was set for an exploration of parody. I invited students to go back, reread, take a second and closer look. As they read I went to the board and wrote the word *parody*. It didn't take long for students to realize that Swift's essay was an example of parody. As students read their favorite "twisted" passages from the essay, I asked them to develop a definition of parody. One group defined the term as follows: a parody is writing that imitates other writing, serious literature, for the purpose of being funny or critical. This definition served us well as we savored (pun intended) Swift's proposal.

From Swift we went on to read other examples of parody, noting how the authors drew on the style of the subject or style of the literature they were attempting to parody. In addition to Swift's essay, we also read with delight E. B. White's "Walden" (see the description of this essay in the "Making Connections" teaching strategy section of this chapter and see the sidebar for more essays that illustrate parody).

I do feel compelled to share a cautionary tale with regard to parody. It is true that parody is an effort to be humorous or critical, but if one misses the mark, parody can have unintended results. One of my students learned this lesson the hard way when the essay he wrote for the state writing assessment, entitled "Why I Don't Have a Dog," was red-flagged for its "inappropriate content." I was required to meet with the student and a counselor to discuss his disturbing essay. I was pleased by the student's thoughtful explanation of how his essay was an example of parody. I certainly saw evidence of his efforts to mimic Swift in his graphic descriptions of how he disposed of his poor dog. I think the student said it best: "This parody stuff is tricky; if people don't see that you are trying to be funny, they could think you are really disturbed."

ESSAYS THAT ILLUSTRATE PARODY

AUTHOR	SOURCE	ESSAY TITLE
E. B. White	One Man's Meat	*"Walden"*
Jon Stewart	Naked Pictures of Famous People	*"The Devil and William Gates"* *Note: Uses some language that may be objectionable*
E. B. White	The Second Tree from the Corner	*"The Decline of Sport (A Preposterous Parable)"*
E. B. White	The Second Tree from the Corner	*"The Retort Transcendental"*
Dave Barry	Boogers Are My Beat	*"Supersize Your Fries with This Column"*
Ben Stiller	Feel This Book: An Essential Guide to Self-Empowerment, Spiritual Supremacy, and Sexual Satisfaction	*"The Peter (Piper) Principle"*
Janeane Garofalo	Feel This Book: An Essential Guide to Self-Empowerment, Spiritual Supremacy, and Sexual Satisfaction	*"Tomorrow, Tomorrow"*

Teaching Strategy: Pointing Out Parallelism

Literary technique can enhance the meaning of words. In the case of parallelism the expression of ideas using the same grammatical form emphasizes the ideas, adding a clarity and power that serves the *Declaration of Independence* and John Fitzgerald Kennedy in his inaugural address (www.bartleby.com/124/pres56.html). I point out parallelism to students using the *Declaration of Independence*. Jefferson and his coauthors describe the "repeated injuries and usurpations" of Great Britain's king as follows:

He has refused his assent to laws . . .

He has forbidden his Governors . . .

He has refused to pass . . .

He has called together . . .

He has dissolved . . .

He has refused . . .

He has endeavored . . .

He has obstructed . . .

In his inaugural address, Kennedy opens his speech with parallelism: "We observe today not a victory of party but a celebration of freedom—symbolizing an end as well as a beginning—signifying renewal as well as change." He goes on to use parallelism in his most famous passage:

> *And so, my fellow Americans: ask not what your country can do for you—ask what you can do for your country.*
> *My fellow citizens of the world: ask not what America will do for you, but what together we can do for the freedom of man.*

I don't spend a lot of time on parallelism, but I enjoy seeing the number of times students point it out to me in the reading we do as well as in their own writing.

Closing Thoughts on Essays

I close this chapter with a renewed appreciation for the essay. I want all of us, teachers and students, to agree that we will no longer view essays only as assignments one writes for school. Rather, we'll embrace James Moffett's explanation of essay in which he shares the etymology of *essay*, which comes from the term "essayer, to attempt" (1983, 171). Moffett goes on to define essay as "a candid blend of personal and universal" (171). E. B. White captures the spirit of essays that Moffett describes in noting, "Each new excursion of the essayist, each new 'attempt' differs from the last and takes him into new country" (1977, vii). I want students to read essays as attempts to capture the author's thinking with both truth and imaginative craft. It's my hope that exploring essays will open students' eyes to the rich and diverse possibilities of the genre for them, as readers and writers.

WORKS CITED

Alvarez, Julia. 1998. "First Muse." In *Something to Declare: Essays.* New York: Plume Books.

——.1998. "Writing Matters." In *Something to Declare: Essays.* New York: Plume Books.

——. 2003. "On Finding a Latino Voice." In *The Writing Life: Writers on How They Think and Work*, ed. Marie Arana. New York: Public Affairs.

Angelou, Maya. 1993. "Brutality Is Definitely Not Acceptable." In *Wouldn't Take Nothing for My Journey Now.* New York: Random House.

——. "Getups." In *Wouldn't Take Nothing for My Journey Now.* New York: Random House.

——. "Style." In *Wouldn't Take Nothing for My Journey Now.* New York: Random House.

Barry, Dave. 1991. "Just Say No to Rugs." In *Dave Barry Talks Back.* New York: Crown.

——. 1991. "The Web Badge of Courage." In *Dave Barry Talks Back.* New York: Crown.

——.2003. "Supersize Your Fries with This Column." In *Boogers Are My Beat.* New York: Crown.

Bradbury, Ray. 2003. "Hunter of Metaphors." In *The Writing Life: Writers on How They Think and Work,* ed. Marie Arana. New York: Public Affairs.

Broyard, Anatole. 1999. "Lending Books." In *A Passion for Books: A Book Lover's Treasury of Stories, Essays, Humor, Lore, and Lists on Collecting, Reading, Borrowing, Lending, Caring For, and Appreciating Books,* ed. Harold Rabinowitz and Rob Kaplan. New York: Three Rivers.

Carson, Rachel. 2000. "The Marginal World." In *The Best American Essays of the*

Century, ed. Joyce Carol Oates and Robert Atwan. Boston: Houghton Mifflin.

Crenshaw, Paul. 2005. "Storm Country." In *The Best American Essays: 2005,* ed. Susan Orlean. Boston: Houghton Mifflin.

Deford, Frank. 1987. "The Best Against the Best at Their Best." In *The World's Tallest Midget: The Best of Frank Deford.* Boston: Little, Brown.

——.2003. "The Best There Ever Was." In *Sports Illustrated: Fifty Years of Great Writing: 1954–2004,* ed. Rob Fleder. New York: Sports Illustrated Books.

Degeneres, Ellen. 1996. "In the Kitchen with Ellen or As Tasty as Poison and Just as Deadly." In *My Point . . . And I Do Have One.* New York: Bantam Books.

——.2003. " My Most Embarrassing Case Scenario." In *The Funny Thing Is . . .* New York: Simon and Schuster.

Dillard, Annie. 1974. "Heaven and Earth in Jest." In *Pilgrim at Tinker Creek.* New York: Harper and Row.

——. 1988. "Introduction." In *The Best American Essays: 1988,* ed. Annie Dillard. Boston: Houghton Mifflin.

Dove, Rita. 1996. "Loose Ends." In *In Short: A Collection of Creative Nonfiction*, ed. Judith Kitchen and Mary Paumier Jones. New York: W. W. Norton.

Duncan, David James. 1995. "River Teeth: A Definition." In *River Teeth: Stories and Writings.* New York: Bantam Books.

——. 1995. "Rose Vegetables." *In River Teeth: Stories and Writing.* New York: Bantam Books.

Early, Gerald. 2000. "Life with Daughters: Watching the Miss America Pageant." In *The Best American Essays of the Century*, ed. Joyce Carol Oates and Robert Atwan. Boston: Houghton Mifflin.

Ehrlich, Gretel. 2000. "The Solace of Open Spaces." In *The Best American Essays of the Century*, ed. Joyce Carol Oates and Robert Atwan. Boston: Houghton Mifflin.

Faulkner, William. 2003. "Kentucky: May: Saturday." In *Sports Illustrated: Fifty Years of Great Writing: 1954–2004*, ed. Rob Fleder. New York: Sports Illustrated Books.

Florey, Kitty Burns. 2005. "Sister Bernadette's Barking Dog." In *The Best American Essays: 2005*, ed. Susan Orlean. Boston: Houghton Mifflin.

Franzen, Jonathan. 2002. "Imperial Bedroom." In *How to Be Alone: Essays.* New York: Farrar, Straus and Giroux.

Frost, Robert. 2000. "The Figure a Poem Makes." In *The Best American Essays of the Century*, ed. Joyce Carol Oates and Robert Atwan. Boston: Houghton Mifflin.

Garofalo, Janeane. 1999. "Tomorrow, Tomorrow." In *Feel This Book: An Essential Guide to Self-Empowerment, Spiritual Supremacy, and Sexual Satisfaction*, Ben Stiller and Janeane Garofalo. New York: Ballantine Books.

Gordimer, Nadine. 2003. "Being a Product of Your Dwelling Place." In *The Writing Life: Writers on How They Think and Work,* ed. Marie Arana. New York: Public Affairs.

Gregorian, Vahe. 2001. "Olympics Dream Ends in Agony." In *The Best American Sports Writing: 2001*, ed. Bud Collins. Boston: Houghton Mifflin.

Haruf, Kent. 2001. "To See Your Story Clearly, Start by Pulling the Wool over Your Own Eyes." In *Writers on Writing: Collected Essays from the* New York Times. New York: Times Books.

Harvey, Stephanie, and Anne Goudvis. 2000. *Strategies That Work: Teaching Comprehension to Enhance Understanding.* Portland, ME: Stenhouse.

Holman, John. 1996. "Cat-like." In *In Short: A Collection of Creative Nonfiction*, ed.

Judith Kitchen and Mary Paumier Jones. New York: W. W. Norton.

Hurston, Zora Neale. 2000. "How It Feels to Be Colored Me." In *The Best American Essays of the Century*, ed. Joyce Carol Oates and Robert Atwan. Boston: Houghton Mifflin.

Johnson, Diane. 2001. "Pesky Themes Will Emerge When You're Not Looking." In *Writers on Writing: Collected Essays from the* New York Times. New York: Times Books.

Kephart, Beth. 2001. "Playing for Keeps." In *The Best American Sports Writing: 2001*, ed. Bud Collins. Boston: Houghton Mifflin.

King, Martin Luther, Jr. 2000. "Letter from Birmingham Jail." In *The Best American Essays of the Century*, ed. Joyce Carol Oates and Robert Atwan. Boston: Houghton Mifflin.

King, Stephen. 2006. "Pop of King." In *Entertainment Weekly* (http://www.ew.com/ew).

Kingsolver, Barbara. 1995. "Be Careful What You Let in the Door." In *High Tide in Tucson: Essays from Now or Never.* New York: HarperCollins.

———.1995. "Semper Fi." In *High Tide in Tucson: Essays from Now or Never.* New York: HarperCollins.

———.1995. "The Vibrations of Djoogbe." In *High Tide in Tucson: Essays from Now or Never.* New York: HarperCollins.

Kooser, Ted. 2005. "Small Rooms in Time." In *The Best American Essays: 2005*, ed. Susan Orlean. Boston: Houghton Mifflin.

111

Lamott, Anne. 1994. *Bird by Bird: Some Instructions on Writing and Life*. New York: Pantheon Books.

Le Guin, Ursula K. 1989. "Close Encounters, Star Wars, and the Tertium Quid." In *Dancing at the Edge of the World: Thoughts on Words, Women, Places*. New York: Harper and Row.

———. "'The Dark Tower,' by C. S. Lewis." In *Dancing at the Edge of the World: Thoughts on Words, Women, Places*. New York: Harper and Row.

Lindbergh, Anne Morrow. 1955. "A Few Shells." In *Gift from the Sea*. New York: Pantheon.

McDowell, Terry. 2003. "Introduction." In *Sports Illustrated: Fifty Years of Great Writing: 1954–2004*, ed. Rob Fleder. New York: Sports Illustrated Books.

McKibben, Bill. 2003. "Speaking Up for the Environment." In *The Writing Life: Writers on How They Think and Work*, ed. Marie Arana. New York: Public Affairs.

Mamet, David. 2001. "The Humble Genre Novel, Sometimes Full of Genius." In *Writers on Writing: Collected Essays from the* New York Times. New York: Times Books.

Michener, James. 2003. "How to Identify and Nurture Young Writers." In *The Writing Life: Writers on How They Think and Work*, ed. Marie Arana. New York: Public Affairs.

Miller, Sue. 2001. "Virtual Reality: The Perils of Seeking a Novelist's Facts in Her Fiction." In *Writers on Writing: Collected Essays from* the New York Times. New York: Times Books.

Minot, Susan. 2003. "A Real-Life Education." In *The Writing Life: Writers on How They Think and Work,* ed. Marie Arana. New York: Public Affairs.

Moffett, James. 1983. "On Essaying." In *Fforum: Essays on Theory and Practice in the Teaching of Writing*, ed. Patricia L. Stock. Upper Montclair, NJ: Boynton/Cook.

Moore, Kathleen Dean. 1995. "The John Day River." In *Riverwalking: Reflections on Moving Water*. New York: Harvest.

———. 1995. "Winter Creek." In *Riverwalking: Reflections on Moving Water*. New York: Harvest.

Mosley, Walter. 2001. "For Authors, Fragile Ideas Need Loving Every Day." In *Writers on Writing: Collected Essays from the* New York Times. New York: Times Books.

Muir, John. 2000. "Stickeen." In *The Best American Essays of the Century*, ed. Joyce Carol Oates and Robert Atwan. Boston: Houghton Mifflin.

Murray, Donald. 1991. "Getting Under the Lightning." In *The Heinemann Reader: Literacy in Process*, ed. Brenda Miller Power and Ruth Hubbard. Portsmouth, NH: Heinemann.

Notaro, Laurie. 2002. "On the Road." In *The Idiot Girls' Action-Adventure Club: True Tales from a Magnificent and Clumsy Life*. New York: Villard Books.

———. 2003. "The Craft Toothbrush." In *Autobiography of a Fat Bride: True Tales of a Pretend Adulthood*. New York: Villard Books.

Nye, Naomi Shihab. 1996. "Mint Snowball." In *In Short: A Collection of Creative Nonfiction*, ed. Judith Kitchen and Mary Paumier Jones. New York: W. W. Norton.

Orlean, Susan, ed. 2005. "Introduction." In *The Best American Essays: 2005*. Boston: Houghton Mifflin.

Owen, David. 2001. "The Chosen One." In *The Best American Sports Writing: 2001*, ed. Bud Collins. Boston: Houghton Mifflin.

Peterson, Brenda. 1996. "Growing Up Game." In *In Short: A Collection of Creative Nonfiction*, ed. Judith Kitchen and Mary Paumier Jones. New York: W. W. Norton.

Piercy, Marge. 2001. "Life of Prose and Poetry: An Inspiring Combination." In *Writers on Writing: Collected Essays from the* New York Times. New York: Times Books

Proulx, Annie. 2001. "Inspiration? Head Down the Back Road, and Stop for the Yard Sales." In *Writers on Writing: Collected Essays from the* New York Times. New York: Times Books.

Quindlen, Anna. 1993. "Mr. Smith Goes to Heaven." In *Thinking Out Loud: On the Personal, the Political, the Public, and the Private*. New York: Random House.

———. 1999. "How Reading Changed My Life." In *A Passion for Books: A Book Lover's Treasury of Stories, Essays, Humor, Lore, and Lists on Collecting, Reading, Borrowing, Lending, Caring For, and Appreciating Books*, ed. Harold Rabinowitz and Rob Kaplan. New York: Three Rivers.

———. 1999. "Three by Quindlen: Three Interesting Lists of Books." In *A Passion for Books: A Book Lover's Treasury of Stories, Essays, Humor, Lore, and Lists on Collecting, Reading, Borrowing, Lending, Caring For, and Appreciating Books*, ed. Harold Rabinowitz and Rob Kaplan. New York: Three Rivers.

Rodriguez, Richard. 2000. "Aria: A Memoir of a Bilingual Childhood." In *The Best American Essays of the Century*, ed. Joyce Carol Oates and Robert Atwan. Boston: Houghton Mifflin.

Roth, Phillip. 1999. "The Newark Public Library." In *A Passion for Books: A Book Lover's Treasury of Stories, Essays, Humor, Lore, and Lists on Collecting, Reading, Borrowing, Lending, Caring For, and Appreciating Books*, ed. Harold Rabinowitz and Rob Kaplan. New York: Three Rivers.

Rudman, Mark. 1991. "Mosaic on Walking." In *The Best American Essays: 1991*, ed. Joyce Carol Oates. New York: Ticknor and Fields.

Saroyan, William. 2001. "Starting with a Tree and Finally Getting to the Death of a Brother." In *Writers on Writing: Collected Essays from the* New York Times. New York: Times Books.

Schine, Cathleen. 2005. "Dog Trouble." In *The Best American Essays: 2005*, ed. Susan Orlean. New York: Houghton Mifflin.

Sedaris, David. 2004. "Us and Them." In *Dress Your Family in Corduroy and Denim*. New York: Back Bay Books.

Seinfeld, Jerry. 1993. "Personal Maintenance." In *SeinLanguage*. New York: Bantam Books.

Skloot, Floyd. 1993. "Trivia Tea: Baseball as Balm." In *The Best American Essays: 1993*, ed. Joseph Epstein and Robert Atwan. New York: Ticknor and Fields.

Stegner, Wallace. 2003. "We Are Destroying Our National Parks." In *Sports Illustrated: Fifty Years of Great Writing: 1954–2004*, ed. Rob Fleder. New York: Sports Illustrated Books.

Stein, Gertrude. 2000. "What Are Masterpieces and Why Are There So Few of Them?" In *The Best American Essays of the Century*, ed. Joyce Carol Oates and Robert Atwan. Boston: Houghton Mifflin.

Stewart, Jon. 1998. "The Devil and William Gates." In *Naked Pictures of Famous People*. New York: Perennial.

Stiller, Ben. 1999. "The Peter (Piper) Principle." In *Feel This Book: An Essential Guide to Self-Empowerment, Spiritual Supremacy, and Sexual Satisfaction*, Ben Stiller and Janeane Garofalo. New York: Ballantine Books.

Tan, Amy. 1991. "Mother Tongue." In *The Best*

113

American Essays: 1991, ed. Joyce Carol Oates. New York: Ticknor and Fields.

Thoreau, Henry David. 1995. *Walden*. New ed. New York: Houghton Mifflin.

Turow, Scott. 2003. "Can Whites Write About Blacks?" In *The Writing Life: Writers on How They Think and Work,* ed. Marie Arana. New York: Public Affairs.

Twain, Mark. 2000. "Corn-Pone Opinions." In *The Best American Essays of the Century,* ed. Joyce Carol Oates. Boston: Houghton Mifflin.

Weiss, Philip. 1993. "How to Get Out of a Locked Trunk." In *The Best American Essays: 1993*, ed. Joseph Epstein and Robert Atwan. New York: Ticknor and Fields.

Welty, Eudora. 2000. "A Sweet Devouring." In *The Best American Essays of the Century,* ed. Joyce Carol Oates. Boston: Houghton Mifflin.

White, E. B. 1944. "Walden." In *One Man's Meat.* New York: Harper and Row.

——.1953. "The Decline of Sport (A Preposterous Parable)." In *The Second Tree from the Corner.* New York: Harper and Brothers.

——.1953. "The Retort Transcendental." In *The Second Tree from the Corner.* New York: Harper and Brothers.

——.1977. "Introduction." In *Essays of E. B. White.* New York: Harper and Row.

RECOMMENDED RESOURCES IN SUPPORT OF TEACHING ESSAYS

Essay Collections

Alvarez, Julia. 1998. *Something to Declare: Essays.* New York: Plume Books.

Angelou, Maya. 1993. *Wouldn't Take Nothing for My Journey Now.* New York: Random House.

Arana, Marie. ed. 2003. *The Writing Life: Writers on How They Think and Work.* New York: Public Affairs.

Barry, Dave. 1991. *Dave Barry Talks Back.* New York: Crown.

Duncan, David James. 1995. *River Teeth: Stories and Writings.* New York: Bantam Books.

Kingsolver, Barbara. 1995. *High Tide in Tucson: Essays from Now or Never.* New York: HarperCollins.

Moore, Kathleen Dean. 1995. *Riverwalking: Reflections on Moving Water.* New York: Harvest Book.

Oates, Joyce Carol, and Robert Atwan, eds. 2002. *The Best American Essays of the Century.* New York: Houghton Mifflin.

Orlean, Susan, ed. 2005. *The Best American Essays: 2005.* Boston: Houghton Mifflin.

Rabinowitz, Harold, and Rob Kaplan. 1999. *A Passion for Books: A Book Lover's Treasury of Stories, Essays, Humor, Lore, and Lists on Collecting, Reading, Borrowing, Lending, Caring For, and Appreciating Books.* New York: Three Rivers.

Writers on Writing: Collected Essays from the New York Times. 2001. New York: Times Books.

Books

Bomer, Randy. 1995. "Making Sense of Nonfiction." In *Time for Meaning: Crafting Literate Lives in Middle and High School.* Portsmouth, NH: Heinemann.

Burke, Jim. 2000. *Reading Reminders: Tools, Tips, and Techniques.* Portsmouth, NH: Heinemann.

Christensen, Linda. 2000. "Essay with an Attitude." In *Reading, Writing, and Rising Up: Teaching about Social Justice and the Power of the Written Word.* Milwaukee, WI: Rethinking Schools.

Lattimer, Heather. 2003. "Editorial." In *Thinking Through Genre: Units of Study in Reading and Writing Workshops 4–12.* Portland, ME: Stenhouse.

——. 2003. "Response to Literature." In *Thinking Through Genre: Units of Study inReading and Writing Workshops 4–12.* Portland, ME: Stenhouse.

Romano, Tom. 1987. "Writing Amid Literature Part One: Other Than Essays." In *Clearing the Way: Working with Teenage Writers.* Portsmouth, NH: Heinemann.

——.1987. "Writing Amid Literature Part Two: Restoring a Reputation." In *Clearing the Way: Working with Teenage Writers.* Portsmouth, NH: Heinemann.

——. 2004. *Crafting Authentic Voice.* Portsmouth, NH: Heinemann.

Seinfeld, Jerry. 1993. *SeinLanguage.* New York: Bantam Books.

Tovani, Cris. 2000. *I Read It, but I Don't Get It: Comprehension Strategies for Adolescent Readers.* Portland, ME: Stenhouse.

——.2004. *Do I Really Have to Teach Reading? Content Comprehension, Grades 6–12.* Portland, ME: Stenhouse.

CHAPTER 5

Memoir

*For some time—I think since I was a child—I have been
possessed of the desire to put down the stuff of my life."*

–LORRAINE HANSBERRY

It's been my experience that memoir is a genre that appeals to adolescents.
Memoirs grab readers and draw them in. The "stuff of one's life" is fascinating,
particularly to adolescents who are in the work of figuring out their own life
stuff. As one of my former freshman students once said in response to reading
an excerpt from Annie Dillard's *An American Childhood*, "It's amazing how her
life is so much like mine. I like knowing I am not the only one who feels this way
about her family."

William Zinsser tells us that memoir is "how we try to make sense of how we
are, who we once were, and what values and heritage shaped us" (1998, 6). Good
memoirs require "integrity of intention" and "careful act of construction" (6). For
purposes of this chapter, memoir includes works of nonfiction that explore events
in the author's life. In some cases these events are life-changing epiphanies. In

others they are the everyday routines that make up the "stuff of life." Exploring an author's memoir, his or her story, invites us to examine our own stories, to look for links and connections as well as those experiences that are uniquely our own.

In addition to its content appeal, memoir serves the goal of using short texts in the classroom. Memoir excerpts are the perfect short text genre since any great memoir has small, stand-alone moments so vivid and compelling they don't require much, if any, contextual explanation. Other strengths of memoir as a short text genre include the following:

1. Read-alouds: A wealth of short text memoirs are available and lend themselves to being read aloud.

2. Accessibility: The accessible language in most memoirs supports a range of reading abilities.

3. Vivid material: Memoir material has an immediacy for students, connecting their lives to those in books.

4. Quick writes: Memoir topics lend themselves to quick write extensions.

5. Discussion: Memoirs encourage classroom discussion.

This chapter begins with a favorite memoir as a starting place and then explores thematic categories of memoirs, from what memoir is to memoirs about lessons from childhood, family, reading, writing, and vocation. It then moves into an exploration of writing craft in support of memoir. In making my memoir selections, I looked to autobiography, personal narrative, and memoirs that authors have labeled as memoir. I have attempted to select from a wide range of authors and topics in hopes I will capture the attention, interest, and diversity of today's middle school and high school students. The good news is that a wealth of wonderful memoirs, many of them humorous, are available. As Zinsser notes, this is the "age of memoir. . . . Everyone has a story to tell, and everyone is telling it" (1998, 3).

A Starting Place for Memoir: Candy

As an entry into memoir, I offer one of my favorite memoirs, a love story entitled *Candy and Me* by Hilary Liftin. This delightful collection of candy memories recounts the author's obsession with candy. Teachers, graduate students, high

school students, and middle school students will find a chapter that speaks to
their own experience with sweet confections. For me, it's Snickers bars, a candy
that perfectly blends chocolate, peanuts, nougat, and caramel. Liftin shares
the story of how Snickers was the candy bar that "ate like a meal" during a high
school graduation camping trip. She captures the decadence of childhood and the
independence of adulthood in her story of a two-week diet of Snickers bars while
camping. Each chapter of her book is devoted to candy or other sweet treats such
as frosting. It's a delightful, even delicious, read with a wealth of teaching possibilities. I find it particularly helpful for building community.

A couple of years ago I was working with a new group of graduate students.
Each of them was studying to be a secondary English/language arts teacher. They
were impressive writers; their collective wisdom of literature was nothing short
of stunning. But they were not a community of learners. Although we shared
our writing efforts, discussions of literature, and texts on pedagogical content
knowledge, there was a polite distance in the room. After several weeks, in des-
peration I brought in Liftin's book and an assortment of candy; the fact that it
was early October made the candy assortment not only doable but also reasonable since candy was on sale. As students arrived, an assortment of candy sat in
colorful arrays on their shared tables. A buzz of conversation I had not heard
before filled the room. I began by explaining that for today's writing workshop we
would explore our own memories of candy. I read aloud the excerpt from Liftin
on Snickers bars and then held up a Snickers bar from the candy display. I then
read a second selection from Liftin, "The Assortment," in which she shares her
passion for creating candy cornucopias as gifts. I invited students to try writing
a story from their own lives about candy.

As our writing began I could hear pens scratching and wrappers crinkling
as students sampled the assortment I had provided. After ten minutes of writing, I asked students to share a line or two. I began by sharing my own story
of succumbing to the sheer joy of eating a PayDay candy bar, followed by the
wrath of my mother and my orthodontist when I broke my braces wires eating the caramel and peanutty goodness. As students shared their own stories
of Milky Ways, circus peanuts, Skittles, and even a secret addiction to canned
frosting, knowing nods, laughter, and even groans (particularly with respect to
circus peanuts) filled the room. The polite distance began to fade as we bonded
over shared stories of sugar. Interestingly, several of these students developed

their candy stories into powerful memoirs, which were published in our class literary magazine.

These same graduate students took their experience with reading and writing about candy into their own middle school and high school classrooms. They were pleased to discover the power of candy memoirs to bring a community of learners together. To date, I have not had the candy memoir writing lesson fail. This past spring a student teacher who was being challenged by a group of resistant seventh-grade readers and writers found this shared candy memoir writing was the turning point for her students. It brought the students together as a community of writers. It became the foundation on which she continued to build relationships with students. And, yes, she did bring an assortment of candy to support the activity and was pleased to see it inspired rather than distracted students.

Teaching Strategy: What Is Memoir?

I begin an exploration of memoir by sharing short memoir excerpts and asking students to begin defining this genre. Over the course of our memoir study, we return to our definition and refine it. I also ask students to note quotes that strike them. I want students' understanding and appreciation of memoir to unfold.

In choosing the two memoir excerpts listed here I focused on stories of childhood because I find such stories resonate with students. I appreciate how these memoir excerpts help students identify the following with regard to memoir:

- The point of view is first-person: I.
- The writer uses description to show the reader what is happening.
- The writer shares his or her thoughts and feelings about the incident and the other characters involved.
- The writer uses dialogue.
- The writer includes a lesson, a reason why the story is important.

In a short excerpt from *Two or Three Things I Know for Sure* (1995) Dorothy Allison shares the story of a school assignment from a struggling substitute teacher. Her task is to create a family tree. The teacher suggests that students "interview relatives" and "check family Bibles for the names of previous generations." When Dorothy queries her mother and aunt Dot, per the teacher's instructions, she is greeted with "pure exasperation."

*"This girl ain't from around here. Is she?" From the other side of the table
Aunt Dot gave Mama a quick grin over her coffee cup. . . .
"That brand-new teacher ain't gonna last out the month. Around here
parentage is even more dangerous than politics." (1995, 10)*

I read this excerpt aloud to students. I ask them to think about the following
questions as they listen: Who is telling this story? What do we learn about the
narrator from her story? What do we learn about her teacher? What do we learn
about her family? What is the lesson learned? This excerpt is an example of memoir: how would you define memoir based on this example?

I follow this lesson by reading the opening section of the chapter "Bawlbaby"
in *King of the Mild Frontier* (2003) from Chris Crutcher's "ill-advised autobiography." I ask students to listen and consider questions similar to those we explored
in response to the Dorothy Allison excerpt: Who is telling this story? What do we
learn about the narrator from his story? What do we learn about his brother? His
parents? What is the lesson learned? This excerpt is an example of memoir: how
would you define memoir based on this example?

Teaching Strategy: Defining Memoir
After we have explored these two excerpts, I ask students to work with a partner
to define memoir: What distinguishes this genre from other genres? What examples from the two excerpts would they use to illustrate memoir? From their
pair-share conversations, we develop a class definition of memoir and write it on
a large sheet of butcher paper. Beneath the definition we write lines or passages
we think illustrate memoir at its best. As our exploration of memoir continues,
we add lines. I want students to become comfortable with picking quotes, and I
want them to be surrounded by these examples of great memoir writing.

This introduction to memoir reflects the big-picture focus of the unit. I
want to draw students' attention to the power of memoir to help us better understand our own lives by examining an author's story. I also want students to
find their own stories and draw on the craft they see in memoirs to support their
storytelling.

A starting place is to look at the theme or focus of memoir. Zinsser observes
that "memoir narrows the lens, focusing on a time in the writer's life that was
unusually vivid, such as childhood or adolescence, or that was framed by war or

travel or public service or some other special circumstances" (1998, 15). As noted previously, I find that adolescents relate well to stories of childhood so I build on the memoirs about childhood described in the "What Is Memoir?" section with more stories of childhood.

Lessons from Childhood

In Portland, Oregon, where I live and teach, we get very little snow. So when we do get snow, it is cause for celebration. I am always on the lookout for memoirs that connect snow and childhood, which is why Annie Dillard's excerpt from *An American Childhood* caught my eye.

In December when my students and I were watching the sky in hopes it would snow, I read aloud from Part 1 of Annie Dillard's richly descriptive memoir. The excerpt I chose was the story of throwing snowballs at cars. "A soft snowball hit the driver's windshield right before the driver's face. It made a smashed star with a hump in the middle" (Dillard 1987, 46). The driver of the car pulled over and chased Dillard and her snowball-throwing friends. As I read aloud I watched knowing smiles spread across the faces of my freshman students, and I saw them lean forward as the driver chased Annie and friends block after block. Finally, the driver caught Annie and her friend Mikey—the others involved in snowball throwing managed to escape.

Teaching Strategy: Memoir as Inspiration for Memoir

I followed the reading with an invitation to "write your own memory of snow." The room was silent except for the sounds of pens and pencils trying to keep up with the flood of words. A class read-around of three to five lines from each draft led to students' begging to have more time to work on this memory writing. For several students, Dillard's excerpt inspired memoirs that ended up in our class literary magazine. As one freshman writer noted, her description of the "snowball hitting the car was just perfect; I could see it and feel it."

We followed this writing with a discussion of Dillard's choice to include this incident in the book. Students noted how the snowball fight drew them in with its description and action. I then reread the final paragraphs of the incident. Dillard notes the driver's first remark, once he caught his breath and could speak. "'You stupid kids.' He began perfunctorily." And she notes that she and Mikey "listened perfunctorily indeed." She goes on to describe that the lesson of this incident was

121

not in the lecture; it was in the chase. She admired the driver for his passion in not giving up until he caught them. She also admired her own passion, noting, "If in that snowy backyard the driver of the black Buick had cut off our heads, Mikey and mine, I would have died happy, for nothing has required so much of me since as being chased all over Pittsburgh in the middle of winter" (48–49).

In writing about her memoir, Dillard says that the book is about two things: "a child's interior life—vivid, superstitious, and timeless—and a child's growing awareness of the world" (1998, 144). I admire it for this reason, and I reference another Dillard excerpt that can be used in support of memoir study in the sidebar along with other memoirs that explore childhood and its lessons.

MEMOIRS OF CHILDHOOD

TITLE	AUTHOR	RECOMMENDED EXCERPT
An American Childhood	*Annie Dillard*	*Imagination and car lights, pp. 20–23*
Living Up the Street	*Gary Soto*	*"Being Mean"*
Bad Boy: A Memoir	*Walter Dean Myers*	*"Let's Hear It for the First Grade"*
Guys Write for Guys Read	*David Bauer*	*"My Entire Football Career"*
When I Was Your Age	*Howard Norman*	*"Bus Problems"*
When I Was Your Age	*Michael J. Rosen*	*"Pegasus for a Summer"*
When I Was Your Age	*Karen Hesse*	*"Waiting for Midnight"*
Always Running	*Luis J. Rodriguez*	*School excerpt, pp. 25–27*
Marshfield Dreams: When I Was a Kid	*Ralph Fletcher*	*"Friends"*
Marshfield Dreams: When I Was a Kid	*Ralph Fletcher*	*"The Sound in the Wall"*
Marshfield Dreams: When I Was a Kid	*Ralph Fletcher*	*"War"*

Family

The distinction between the "Lessons from Childhood" section and this section is subtle. The memoirs in this section are often told from the point of view of childhood, but they emphasize family interactions, how parents and siblings shape our childhoods and the lessons we learn.

Teaching Strategy: Text-Self Connection

Before we read an excerpt from Bebe Moore Campbell's memoir, *Sweet Summer: Growing Up With and Without My Dad* (1989), I ask students to think about a family member or friend who stands out in their memory. I draw on Campbell's story of summer and share my own description of my beloved grandmother. I tell the story of her perfect size-10 body, always dressed impeccably, with her bubble hairdo that didn't move, how she navigated her large, new Cadillac through the streets of Madison, Wisconsin. I want students to picture my grandmother and see how her emphasis on appearances made me pay attention to detail and helped me learn how to push back against a world that is too quick to judge based on looks.

I provide a copy of the Campbell excerpt and a highlighter pen for each student. As I read aloud I ask students to follow along and highlight sections that help them picture Campbell's father.

In her powerful and poetic account of growing up, Campbell details summers spent with her paraplegic father. Chapter 2 captures the tension of waiting for her daddy to show up in his big, green Pontiac. Campbell details the struggle of reconnecting with each other after time apart. "We sat there silently, searching desperately for a road that would lead us back to where he had left off on our last visit" (36).

She goes on to describe the casual conversation between Daddy and Campbell's mother and grandmother, followed by the adventure of driving to Daddy's, which includes a number of stops along the way to visit relatives and friends. With each detail Daddy, as seen through Campbell's little-girl eyes, comes to life. In particular, she shares the story of fixing a flat tire at night. She can hear the crickets as her father reaches for his wheelchair, hops into the seat, rolls to the trunk, and takes out "the jack, a spare, and a flashlight." She goes on to describe what she sees as her dad, in his wheelchair, changes the tire. "I could see his thick arms, his muscles flexing in the moonlight. Sweat was dripping behind his ears." In five minutes her daddy has completed the task and is back in the car. Campbell shares her surprise at his ability to change the tire all by himself, noting the car he waved on, refusing any help. She writes, "I was halfway grown before I realized it was my father's determination to see himself as strong and capable that had him changing tires in the night. He wanted me to see him that way too" (40).

After the reading, students share their highlighted sections with a peer. I then ask them to revisit their own writing and add details that help us see the family member they are describing and show us why this person is important to them.

We follow with a discussion of Campbell's realization that her father needed to see himself as "strong and capable." As we read additional memoirs about family, we looked for the ahas that are woven into stories of family.

MEMOIRS THAT EMPHASIZE FAMILY

BOOK TITLE	AUTHOR	EXCERPT	FAMILY RELATIONSHIP THAT IS EMPHASIZED
The Woman Warrior	Maxine Hong Kingston	"At the Western Place"	Grown sisters reuniting after years apart—one lived in China and the other in America
Why I'm Like This	Cynthia Kaplan	"Jack Has a Thermos"	A father's love of gadgets told by his daughter
When I Was Your Age	Kyoko Mori	"Learning to Swim"	Mother and daughter
When I Was Your Age	Joseph Bruchac	"The Snapping Turtle"	Grandson and grandparents
Marshfield Dreams: When I Was a Kid	Ralph Fletcher	"Kids"	Siblings and a bad night with the babysitter
Marshfield Dreams: When I Was a Kid	Ralph Fletcher	"Jimmy"	Adventures with a brother
Marshfield Dreams: When I Was a Kid	Ralph Fletcher	"Daily Life"	Family cleaning rituals
The Idiot Girls' Action-Adventure Club	Laurie Notaro	"It Smells Like Doody in Here"	An unfortunate family camping trip
Chinese Cinderella	Adeline Yen Mah	"PLT"	Father, siblings, and pet
River Teeth: Stories and Writings	David James Duncan	"Red Coats"	Young boy is temporarily separated from his family while walking downtown

Reading One's Life and the World

I am so appreciative of the number of memoirs that tout the power of reading. It's like double coupons at the grocery store: memoirs about reading highlight the power and craft of memoir while hammering home the message that books have a powerful influence in our lives.

In the small, rural town where I taught, leaving town for college or other reasons was fraught with tension. As much as high school juniors with whom I worked wanted to leave, they were torn about the message their leaving sent. Although they could not always name what their town and their families meant to them, they felt it. An excerpt from Richard Rodriguez's autobiography, *Hunger of Memory* (1982) served as a way for us to explore the power of reading and education to take you away, but also to reconnect you. It hit home for students on a number of levels.

I particularly appreciate the section where Rodriguez explores his fourth-grade reading program. In this memoir he shares his fascination for books, adult books such as *Great Expectations*, *Moby Dick*, and *The Pearl*, to name a few. In his distinctive style of varied sentence lengths, questions, parenthetical remarks, and repetition, he shows how books and reading became his refuge and his method for expanding his world—but at a price. "I'd feel a mysterious comfort then, reading in the dawn quiet—the blue-gray silence interrupted by the occasional churning of the refrigerator motor" (62). But as Rodriguez drew praise for his efforts, his book learning, he also grew away from his parents. He notes his mother's wondering concern: "'What do you see in your books?' (Was reading a hobby like her knitting? Was so much reading even healthy for a boy? Was it the sign of 'brains'? Or was it just a convenient excuse for not helping around the house on Saturday mornings)" (62). Rodriguez acknowledged that as he grew more academic, he also recognized his efforts to "remake" himself and that it took education for him to see this and its impact; "If because of my schooling, I had grown culturally separated from my parents, my education, finally [after several years] had given me ways of speaking and caring about that fact" (72).

Teaching Strategy: Reading Time Line

As students read this excerpt from *Hunger of Memory* I asked them to note passages where reading brought Rodriguez comfort and passages where reading brought him challenge. They then did an in-class quick write in which they summarized Rodriguez's ahas with regard to reading: what did he discover and how do his discoveries compare/contrast with your own experiences as a reader?

These passages were then used to support the creation of a reading time line. Students highlighted their experiences as readers, including memorable books. I hesitated the first time I asked students to create a time line. I was aware that

125

for many students reading had not been a powerful influence in their lives. But I was surprised and delighted to find that all of my students could create a reading time line. In the process they discovered, as did I, that reading and certain books were important to them. I would be remiss if I did not note how many of them celebrated reading experiences that happened outside of school: the discovery of comic books, reading how-to manuals to support hobbies, reading Stephen King books late at night with a flashlight. Our brief foray into our own stories of reading created a framework for exploring memoirs about the influence of reading.

MEMOIRS ABOUT READING

AUTHOR	BOOK	EXCERPT
Cynthia Ozick	Modern American Memoirs	*"A Drugstore in Winter" from* Art and Ardor
Jack Gantos	Hole in My Life	*"Kings Court"*
Annie Dillard	An American Childhood	*"Part 1" pp. 78–85*
Barbara Kingsolver	High Tide in Tucson: Esssays from Now or Never	*Excerpt from "How Mr. Dewey Decimal Saved My Life," pp. 50–53*

Memoirs About Writing

Reading memoirs about reading leads naturally into reading memoirs about writing. I delight in writers' stories of how they discovered their passion for writing. But I also recognize that not all of my students shared my passion for putting words on paper. So I was pleased to discover Pulitzer Prize–winning columnist Russell Baker's practical analysis of choosing the writer's life in his memoir *Growing Up* (1982). He notes that his mother's suggestion that he be a writer triggered the following response:

> *I clasped the idea to my heart. . . . I loved stories and thought that making up stories must surely be almost as much fun as reading them . . . what really gladdened my heart, was the ease of the writer's life. Writers did not trudge through the town peddling from canvas bags, defending themselves against angry dogs, being rejected by surly strangers. . . . So far as I could make out, what writers did couldn't even be classified as work. (16–17)*

Teaching Strategy: A Writer's Notebook

Students chuckled nervously at this characterization of the writer's life. I asked them to hold it in their heads, checking it against the other memoirs we would read and their own experience as writers.

We then turned our attention to reading a series of memoirs about writing (selected from the list in the sidebar). I created class sets of excerpts with multiple copies of each excerpt that were numbered and placed in labeled folders. The first time I did this activity was time consuming, so I provided choice-reading time for only one day. Over time, as my class sets of memoirs expanded, I increased the numbers of days we spent on memoir choice-reading.

Creating memoir text sets allowed me to select excerpts that varied in length, vocabulary, and writing style. If I have students with a wide range of reading abilities, I sometimes assign certain excerpts under the guise that I want at least one reader for each text. Another option is to work with students during the selection process so that I can steer students to particular excerpts. However, it's been my experience that providing a variety of texts and encouraging choice supports readers of all abilities with very little intervention on my part. This idea is an adaptation of Cris Tovani's text sets; see her book *Do I Really Have to Teach Reading? Content Comprehension, Grades 6–12* (2004, 43–49).

As they read selected memoir excerpts, I asked students to note in their literature logs lines they admired and writing strategies they discovered and to compare and contrast what they read with Baker's view of the writer's life (see Chapter 2 for more on literature logs). I also asked them to write five observations a day for a week. I borrowed and adapted this observation writing idea from Georgia Heard's book *Writing Toward Home: Tales and Lessons to Find Your Way* (1995). Heard proposes that as writers "we must become what we see. That's why our unmediated observations of the world become the foundation for writing" (67–68). I shared with students several of Heard's observations from the book and offered them her words in support of this assignment:

> *Take a walk and write what you notice, describe the sounds you hear in or outside your house or apartment. Write these sketches quickly and with no judgment, no editorializing. The more accurately you can observe your world and capture it in words the more concrete your writing will become. (68)*

We began each literature workshop with a pair-share of students' observation sketches and a discovery they made from reading a memoir about writing. This decision to focus the exploration of memoirs about writing on self-selected memoir excerpts and students' own writing was in keeping with my own discoveries about writing from reading memoirs. In her memoir *Long Quiet Highway: Waking Up in America* (1993) Natalie Goldberg writes about seeking out authors, in her case Raymond Carver and Victor Richard Hugo. She notes that these authors were a " salve for my personal grief . . . because they had wrestled through lonesome, alienated, ordinary beginnings and managed to find a way through writing to make their lives glow" (22). I want my students to find authors that serve as their "salve" and to discover how to make their own lives "glow."

MEMOIRS ABOUT WRITING

AUTHOR	TITLE	SUGGESTED EXCERPT
Zoe Trope	Please Don't Kill the Freshman: A Memoir	*"10.14," p. 24*
Natalie Goldberg	Long Quiet Highway: Waking Up in America	*"Writing Practice," pp. 43–46 Note: May want to delete LSD comparison*
Georgia Heard	Writing Toward Home: Tales and Lessons to Find Your Way	*"A Conversation with Myself"*
Georgia Heard	Writing Toward Home: Tales and Lessons to Find Your Way	*"First Memory"*
Russell Baker	Growing Up	*Learning about writing from Elliot Coleman, pp. 253–255*
Stephen King	On Writing: A Memoir of the Craft	*"20," sports writing and revision, pp. 55–58 Note: Profanity in the opening paragraph*
Walter Dean Myers	Bad Boy: A Memoir	*"A Writer Observes"*
Walter Dean Myers	Bad Boy: A Memoir	*"The Typist"*
Ralph Fletcher	Marshfield Dreams: When I Was a Kid	*"First Pen"*

128

Passion for One's Work

Teaching Strategy: Writing and Interviewing About Hobbies and Passions

Before we read memoir excerpts about passion and vocation, I asked students to write about the things they love to do; thinking about their hobbies and passions is a first step in connecting students' stories with this type of memoir. Students referred to this quick write as they reflected on what they learned from authors' memoirs.

One of the memoirs I used to explore passion and vocation is from Agnes De Mille's autobiography, *Dance to the Piper*. I discovered this work in the literature anthology I was required to use for junior English. Although not all of my students appreciated De Mille's descriptions of ballet, and some balked at her admonitions about discipline, this memoir excerpt was a way into a discussion of finding our life's passion, learning to recognize and honor the "wheels turning within our own hearts."

"No trumpets sound when the important decisions of our life are made.... The wheels turn within our hearts for years and suddenly everything meshes and we are lifted into the next level of progress" (77). De Mille writes about her epiphany that she was born to be a dancer, a discovery that comes when her sister's love interest, seventeen-year-old Douglas Montgomery, watches her dance and with "tears of excitement in his eyes" tells her, "You've got a calling. You've got a duty. ... You're a great dancer" (77). For De Mille, these were the words she "had waited all [her] life to hear" (77).

As a follow-up, I asked students to conduct interviews with adults about their career choices, to explore how we come to find our "voice of vocation." In support of these interviews, I share a short excerpt from Parker Palmer's book, *Let Your Life Speak: Listening for the Voice of Vocation* (2000*)*. Parker explains that we need to look at the clues from our lives, including our childhood interests, to find our true selves. He writes, "The deepest vocational question is not 'What ought I to do with my life?' It is the more elemental and demanding 'Who am I? What is my nature?'" (15). I recognize this is heady stuff for adolescents, but I know they are already wrestling with the question: who am I? So asking this of others is well timed. Students learned much from these interviews, and I heard from interview participants that they valued the experience as well.

The good news is that so many public figures, including sports heroes, are writing memoirs, so there is a wide variety of memoir choices.

MEMOIRS ABOUT PASSION/VOCATION

AUTHOR	TITLE	PASSION/VOCATION
Henry David Thoreau	Walden	*Observation of nature*
Annie Dillard	Pilgrim at Tinker Creek	*Observation of nature*
Arthur Ashe with Frank DeFord	Arthur Ashe: Portrait in Motion	*Tennis*
Pat Conroy	My Losing Season	*College basketball*
Frank McCourt	Teacher Man	*Teaching*
E. R. Braithwaite	To Sir with Love	*Teaching*
Linda Ellerbee	"And So It Goes": Adventures in Television	*Television news*
Anderson Cooper	Dispatches from the Edge: A Memoir of War	*Journalism and television*

Writing Craft and Memoir

In *Inventing the Truth: The Art and Craft of Memoir* (1998) William Zinsser, along with nine well-known memoir authors, writes about the challenges and pleasures of this genre. Zinsser notes, "Memoir writers must manufacture a text, imposing order on a jumble of half-remembered events" (6). I want students to pay close attention to the craft authors use to construct memoir. I begin with an exploration of finding the subject of memoir in the small moment because to me this is the essence of memoir. I also draw students' attention to leads that draw the reader in, the use of descriptive detail, figurative language, exploration of character, dialogue, and the power of place (setting).

130

FINDING THE SUBJECT: THE SMALL MOMENT

In his book *On Writing: A Memoir of Craft* (2000), Stephen King shares snapshots from his life in an effort to tell his story of how "one writer was *formed*. Not how one writer was *made*" (18). He goes on to state that he doesn't believe writers possess special talents. Rather, "I believe large numbers of people have at least some talent as writers and storytellers, and that those talents can be strengthened and sharpened" (18). I concur with Mr. King. One of my primary goals in teaching memoir is to show students how writers bring the stuff of their lives to an audience through the snapshot writing of memoir.

Teaching Strategy: Small Moment Snapshots

In "Memory #2" from *On Writing* Stephen King captures a snapshot of his babysitter, Eula-Beulah (2000, 19–21). King shows his gift for bringing to life a small moment through detail. The fact it is laugh-out-loud funny is an added bonus. I appreciate that King and his brother admired Eula-Beulah for her "dangerous sense of humor," which included farting on King while he was pinned to the couch. I recognize that some might not consider this excerpt the kind of literature we want students to experience. But I find this excerpt resonates with students, inspiring them to tell their own stories of humorous and at times humiliating moments with babysitters, siblings, and friends. After reading King's snapshot I share the story of my older brother, Craig, pinning me to the lawn. I can feel the grass scratching through my T-shirt as I squirm to get away. Above me, Craig's face is intently focused on me. He smiles with glee as I first hear the hacking cough and then glimpse the stream of spit forming in his mouth. It glistens in the sun as it begins to drop toward my face. I want to close my eyes, but they remain riveted as I twist my head from side to side like I am watching a tennis match. Just before the spit fully drops, he flicks it back into his mouth. I hear him cackle as he releases me from the pin. As I scramble to safety, I am sure I called him the kinds of names younger sisters throw at older brothers, but I don't remember any of them now. However, the rest of the story is burned into my memory. It's not surprising that to this day I avoid lying on the lawn and staring at the sky.

In addition to triggering students' stories, this excerpt highlights the power of writing about a single event. I read the King excerpt again, asking students to listen for the details he includes that enable us to picture what he describes.

I hand out blank five-by-seven-inch note cards and ask students to picture the details they hear in an excerpt from Alice Walker's *Living the Word* (1988, 101–103). Walker writes "word photographs" of her trip to China. I share a "picture" in which Walker describes her first glimpse of Beijing in the taxi ride from the airport. In the second excerpt I share, she focuses her eye on her traveling wardrobe. I read the two excerpts aloud once and then ask students to reread

131

each, noting the pictures she paints. On their note card I ask them to capture one of the pictures in images, words, or a combination of both.

This focus on detailing a snapshot memory then moves us into a discussion of writing our own memories, focusing on the details of a single incident.

GRABBER LEADS

Teaching Strategy: Analyzing Characteristics of Grabber Leads

As I discussed in Chapter 3 on short stories, I want students to recognize the importance of writing a lead that draws readers in. I want them to recognize that grabber leads are possible in nonfiction; in fact, they are essential. As JoAnn Portalupi and Ralph Fletcher note in their book *Nonfiction Craft Lessons: Teaching Information Writing K–8* (2001), nonfiction writers "draw on a wealth of fictional writing strategies (a sense of character, detail, suspense, and so on) to make their writing come alive" (88). I focus students' attention on the use of fictional writing strategies by taking a close look at memoirs with grabber leads.

An example of a narrative lead that introduces character through detail and sets up the tension for the rest of the story is the opening chapter of Maya Angelou's powerful autobiography *I Know Why the Caged Bird Sings* (1969). This lead grabs me, and I find it grabs my students. I read it aloud and, if possible, provide students with a copy of the text to follow along. Providing a text copy allows students who need more support with reading to hear and see the text. Copied text also allows for rereading the text to note the author's craft. Angelou starts with dialogue, or, to be more specific, monologue:

> *"What you looking at me for?*
> *I didn't come to stay..." (3)*

Maya, then known as Marguerite, struggles to remember the poem she is reciting. But she also foreshadows the rest of her story in noting, "Whether I could remember the rest of the poem or not was immaterial. The truth of the statement was like a wadded-up handkerchief, sopping wet in my fists" (3).

After noting Angelou's use of a simile we move on to analyze how this opening chapter shows us Maya's struggle to find her dignity. We look at descriptive details of Maya: her initial description of her lavender dress and how this contrasts with her discovery in the light of day that her dress is really just a "plain ugly cut-down from a white woman's once-was-purple throwaway" (4) and the contrast of Maya's physical appearance with her dream of waking up with long, blonde hair in place of her "kinky mass" and "light-blue eyes" that could hypnotize. Her dream image stands in stark contrast to the Marguerite struggling to recite a poem in the front of the church; the Marguerite who stumbles out of the church and runs home, crying and then peeing in anger and frustration. Angelou wraps up this narrative lead with a prophetic comment that sets the tone for the remainder of her story: "If growing up is painful for the Southern Black Girl, being aware of her displacement is the rust on the razor that threatens the throat. It is an unnecessary insult" (6).

From this exploration of Angelou's lead, we revisit other memoirs we have read, noting the characteristics of their leads. Listed in the sidebar are memoir leads students considered grabbers.

GRABBER LEADS

AUTHOR	TITLE	SENTENCE(S) FROM LEAD
Norma Fox Mazer	*"In the Blink of an Eye" in* When I Was Your Age	*"In the gutter, a lit cigarette butt catches my eye. I swoop for it, stick it in my mouth, and take a puff"* (15).
Michael J. Rosen	*"Pegasus for a Summer" in* When I Was Your Age	*"This is a true story about a horse. It's a mostly true story about the horse's rider, me" (108).*
Mary Karr	Cherry	*"Violet Durkey has a hamster and a miniature turtle who lives in a shallow plastic bowl under a palm tree with snap-on fronds, and an albino rabbit named Snuffles with pink ears from Easter; it's the hamster I am thinking about here" (17).*
Gary Soto	*"Being Mean" in* Living Up the Street	*"We were terrible kids, I think. My brother, sister, and I felt a general meanness begin to surface from our tiny souls while living on Braly Street, which was in the middle of industrial Fresno" (1).*

DESCRIPTIVE DETAIL

133

The five senses are what descriptive writing is all about. I want students to see, hear, taste, smell, and touch what the memoir author is describing. To get them thinking, I share examples of memoirs that home in on descriptive details. I want students to see how detail brings the memoir into focus: the action, the people, and the place.

Teaching Strategy: Detailing Detail

I ask students to listen to a memoir excerpt with graphic visual details. As they listen, I ask them to write down words or images that help them "see" what the author is describing. I find the excerpt "Diner" in *A Girl Named Zippy: Growing Up Small in Moreland, Indiana* (2001) by Haven Kimmel works well. This witty, descriptive, compelling memoir is filled with well-depicted scenes of childhood that make me laugh. I appreciate how Kimmel, who earned the nickname Zippy because of her propensity for zipping around the house, writes in the voice of her childhood as she tries to make sense of the adult world.

"Diner" illustrates how one event from childhood can be brought to life through rich description. Students appreciate the graphic details of the aftereffects of Zippy's decision to quench her hunger by eating an entire bag of carrots. She describes her painful walk to the diner: "I was stooped over like the emphysemic old man my grandma was married to" (169). She goes on to describe her discomfort as she sits on a stool in the diner: her stomach somersaulting and ultimately spewing forth its carrot luncheon neatly into a water glass where both she and her mother can admire it as "one of the most interesting sights we'd ever beheld" (170).

FIGURATIVE LANGUAGE

I build on our exploration of descriptive detail by looking closely at the use of figurative language. Memoirs with a poetic feel appeal to me. I want students to see how simile and metaphor work in prose and in poetry. To highlight this, I hand students two colors of highlighter pens. We review the definitions of simile, a comparison using *like* or *as* between two unlike things, and metaphor, a comparison of two unlike things that have something in common. I ask students to use one color to mark similes and one to mark metaphors. If we are reading an excerpt in a textbook, I ask students to use two different colors of sticky flags.

134

Teaching Strategy: Highlighting Similes and Metaphors

A memoir excerpt that works well for highlighting figurative language is in the chapter entitled "The Kitchen" in Alfred Kazin's *A Walker in the City* (1951, 66–71). I admire the way Kazin brings the kitchen of his childhood to life in his memoir. In this excerpt Kazin writes, "The kitchen was the great machine that set our lives running; it whirred down a little only on Saturdays and holy days" (67). In support of students' examination of this memoir, I read this excerpt aloud first. I ask students to listen for words that are new to them, and we spend some time talking about these words before students reread the excerpt with attention to simile and metaphor. When they reread the excerpt, I ask them to circle or mark the new words and we then define them as a class before we share our marked examples of similes and metaphors.

Although this excerpt is a challenging read, with Yiddish words that need to be translated, I appreciate how it shows that Kazin's Jewish culture is not so different from other cultures. We can all find common ground in the kitchen.

MEMOIRS WITH FIGURATIVE LANGUAGE

AUTHOR	TITLE	FIGURATIVE LANGUAGE EXCERPT
Richard Wright	*Excerpt from Chapter 1 in* Black Boy: A Record of Childhood and Youth, *pp. 7–8*	*Detailed descriptions of moments of living that reveal "their coded meanings"*
Mary Karr	*Excerpt from* Cherry, *pp. 80–82*	*Description of seventh grade rich with similes*
Laurie Notaro	*"More Bread, Please" in* The Idiot Girls' Action-Adventure Club	*Detailed description of a dinner roll frenzy in a trendy L.A. restaurant*

DETAILS TO SUPPORT CHARACTER

In her book *An American Childhood* (1987) Annie Dillard homes in on the small detail of her parents' and grandparents' "limp, coarse skin" (24). She details hands and faces, contrasting her own "fluid, pliant fingers" with adults' "misshapen, knuckly hands loose in their skin likes bones in bags" (24). She lifts a hair from her father's arm and studies "the puckered tepee of skin it pulled with it" (26). She describes the feel of her parents shinbones' at the beach: "The bones were flat and curved, like the slats in a Venetian blind," and then notes, "loose under their shinbones, as in a hammock, hung the relaxed flesh of their calves. You could push and swing this like a baby in a sling" (26).

I read the Dillard excerpt aloud and ask students to spend a few minutes writing a description of their own hands, focusing on the small details. I then ask them to observe and describe a family member. I stress the importance of focusing on details, like Dillard does. We discuss her less than respectful tone in this excerpt and then analyze how it emphasizes a child's view of aging. I ask them to find their own tone in their descriptive writing and be prepared to explain it to the small group with whom they will be sharing their writing. I do note that with some groups of students I have had to discuss the need for "school-appropriate" descriptions.

CHARACTER DETAIL

AUTHOR	TITLE	CHARACTER EXCERPT
Mary Karr	Cherry	*Her friend Violet in Chapter 1, pp. 17–20*
Eleanor Munro	Modern American Memoirs	*Grandfather in "Memoirs of a Modernist's Daughter," pp. 19–21*
Reynolds Price	Modern American Memoirs	*Uncle Mac in "Clear Pictures," pp. 172–177*
Bailey White	Mama Makes Up Her Mind and Other Dangers of Southern Living	*Mama in "Roseys," pp. 3–5*
Bailey White	Mama Makes Up Her Mind and Other Dangers of Southern Living	*Aunt Belle in "Alligator," pp. 92–94*
Bailey White	Mama Makes Up Her Mind and Other Dangers of Southern Living	*Mr. Harris, the substitute teacher, in "One-Eared Intellectual," pp. 197–199*
Laurie Notaro	The Idiot Girls' Action-Adventure Club	*Grandmother in "Extreme Clean Sports"*

DIALOGUE

Dialogue is another way authors bring detail to their memoirs and show us character. I find that students struggle with dialogue in their own writing. As an entry into dialogue I ask students to eavesdrop on a conversation, keeping in mind the need to be sensitive to privacy issues. I borrowed this idea from Leslea Newman's book *Writing from the Heart* (1993). Although this book focuses on fiction writing exercises for women, I have found it to be a wonderful resource for girls and boys that also supports memoir.

The eavesdropping assignment's goal is to have students capture dialogue, not pry into others' personal business. I encourage them to select public places and note conversations of folks they don't know if possible. This is a homework assignment that has a 100 percent turn-in rate every time! I even had a parent submit a note saying how much he learned about dialogue while helping his daughter capture the conversation of an angry couple at the table next to them in a pizza parlor. One of my favorite conversations was that of a salesclerk and potential customer that a student jotted down while sitting in the dressing room next door. This student did end up making a purchase, so I trust the store did not mind that she combined her homework assignment with her shopping.

Students share their eavesdropping dialogue with a partner. I then ask them to jot down what they know about each "character" based on the conversation. This leads to a whole-group discussion about how dialogue contributes to character development.

I build on the eavesdropping assignment by asking students to capture a conversation they have had recently with a friend or family member. This writing sets the stage for our exploration of dialogue in memoir.

I find that Norma Fox Mazer's memoir, "In the Blink of an Eye" (1999), captures students' attention because it focuses on a conversation between sisters. Students relate to the tension in the conversation and discuss how this conversation helps us see the author and her relationship with her sister. A side benefit is how this excerpt illustrates paragraphing in support of dialogue; I ask students to notice how new paragraphs for each speaker allow us to know who is speaking without using "she said." Students are then invited to return to the friend/family conversations they had previously written with attention to paragraphing.

DIALOGUE IN MEMOIR

AUTHOR	TITLE	DIALOGUE EXCERPT
Richard Wright	*Excerpt from* Black Boy: A Record of Childhood and Youth, *pp. 91–93*	*Angry confrontation between Richard and his aunt Addie, who was his classroom teacher*
Bailey White	Mama Makes Up Her Mind and Other Dangers of Southern Living	*Conversation in a car on the way to a wedding in "The Lips of a Stranger," pp. 118–123*
Laurie Notaro	The Idiot Girls' Action-Adventure Club	*Conversation with friend, AAA, and police officer regarding car tires and strange car noises in "On the Road"*
Bebe Moore Campbell	*Excerpt from* Sweet Summer: Growing Up With and Without My Dad, *pp. 45–51*	*Bebe's conversation with grandmother and then father about killing and eating chicken*
Haven Kimmel	*Excerpt from* A Girl Named Zippy	*Conversation between Zippy and her big sister about a neighbor girl with disabilities in "Professionals," pp. 120–124*

137

DETAILS TO SUPPORT PLACE

I have never been to Italy, but I feel like I have been there in my mind thanks to the rich picture Frances Mayes paints of her home in *Under the Tuscan Sun* (1996):

> *The fonts in all the churches are dry. I run my fingers through the dusty*
> *scallops of marble; not a drop for my hot forehead. The Tuscan July heat*
> *is invasive to the body but not to the stone churches that hold on to the*
> *dampness of winter, releasing a gray coolness slowly throughout the summer.*
> *. . . A lid seems to descend on our voices, or a large damp hand. (258)*

I want students to see how descriptive detail allows us as readers to see, hear, and feel the place of the memoir. And place matters.

Georgia Heard writes, "Home is what can be recalled without effort—so that sometimes we think, oh, that can't be important. Memories are the blueprint of home. A memoir is built from those blueprints" (1995, 2). I want students to reflect on their own memories of home before we look closely at how authors show us their homes through descriptive detail.

Teaching Strategy: Graphing Home

We begin our exploration of home with graph paper (another opportunity to visit the office supply store). I ask students to think about a place from their childhood: their house, a friend's house, a relative's house. I want them to capture the details of this place on graph paper with words, images, maps, symbols—whatever helps them focus on details. I find that graph paper supports students' exploration of place because it looks different from the lined paper we typically use; it is a new place to write about place.

After students have "graphed" their place, we read an excerpt about place. I hand them a new sheet of graph paper and ask them to note details from the excerpt. There are so many memoirs that can be used for this teaching technique. I like to use a short excerpt from Harry Crews's memoir, *A Childhood: The Biography of a Place* in *Modern American Memoirs* (Dillard and Conley 1995). As the following quote illustrates, Crews focuses on the details of place.

> *I awoke in the middle of morning in early summer from the place I'd been*
> *sleeping in the curving roots of a giant oak tree in front of a large white*

house. Off to the right, beyond the dirt road, my goats were trailing along in the ditch, grazing in the tough wire grass that grew there. (1)

Listed in the sidebar are other memoir excerpts that focus on place.

MEMOIRS OF PLACE

AUTHOR	TITLE	EXCERPT	PLACE
Jane Yolen	When I Was Your Age	*"The Long Closet"*	*Grandparents' closet*
Annie Dillard	An American Childhood	*Part 1, pp. 20–23*	*Hometown: Pittsburgh*
Barry Lopez	Modern American Memoirs	*"IV Southern California, 1988," in "Replacing Memory"*	*Whittier, California*
Jill Ker Conway	The Road from Coorain	*"Childhood," pp. 31–33*	*Home: Coorain in New South Wales, Australia*
Mary Karr	The Liars' Club	*Antelope excerpt from Chapter 11, pp. 212–216*	*Town of Antelope and details of house she lived in. Note: Excerpt contains references to vampires*

Closing Thoughts on Memoir

I would like to think students appreciate their own life stories more after reading memoir. What I know for sure is that they have nodded in recognition, laughed, and even teared up as we explored the stuff of memoirs.

WORKS CITED

Allison, Dorothy. 1995. *Two or Three Things I Know for Sure*. New York: Plume.

Angelou, Maya. 1969. *I Know Why the Caged Bird Sings*. New York: Random House.

Ashe, Arthur, and Frank Deford. 1976. *Arthur Ashe: Portrait in Motion*. New York: Ballantine Books.

Baker, Russell. 1982. *Growing Up*. New York: Congdon and Weed.

Bauer, David. 2005. "My Entire Football Career." In *Guys Write for Guys Read*, ed. Jon Scieszka. New York: Viking.

Braithwaite, E. R. 1977. *To Sir, with Love*. New York: Jove/Penguin Putnam.

Bruchac, Joseph. 1999. "The Snapping Turtle." In *When I Was Your Age, Volume Two: Original Stories About Growing Up*, ed. Amy Ehrlich. Cambridge, MA: Candlewick Press.

Campbell, Bebe Moore. 1989. *Sweet Summer: Growing Up With and Without My Dad*. New York: Ballantine Books.

Conroy, Pat. 2003. *My Losing Season*. New York: Dial.

Conway, Jill Ker. 1989. *The Road from Coorain: Recollections of a Harsh and Beautiful Journey into Adulthood*. New York: Alfred A. Knopf.

Cooper, Anderson. 2006. *Dispatches from the Edge: A Memoir of War, Disasters, and Survival*. New York: HarperCollins.

Crutcher, Chris. 2003. "Bawlbaby." In *King of the Mild Frontier: An Ill-Advised Autobiography*. New York: Greenwillow Books.

De Mille, Agnes. 1952. *Dance to the Piper*. Boston: Little, Brown.

Dillard, Annie. 1974. *Pilgrim at Tinker Creek*. New York: Harper and Row.

———. 1987. *An American Childhood*. New York: HarperPerennial.

———.1998. "To Fashion a Text." In *Inventing the Truth: The Art and Craft of Memoir*, ed. William Zinsser. Boston: Mariner Books.

Dillard, Annie, and Cort Conley. 1995. *Modern American Memoirs*. New York: HarperPerennial.

Duncan, David James. 1995. "Red Coats." In *River Teeth: Stories and Writings*. New York: Bantam Books.

Ellerbee, Linda. 1986. *"And So It Goes": Adventures in Television*. New York: Putnam.

Fletcher, Ralph. 2005. *Marshfield Dreams: When I Was a Kid*. New York: Henry Holt.

Gantos, Jack. 2002. "King's Court." In *Hole in My Life*. New York: Farrar, Straus and Giroux.

Goldberg, Natalie. 1994. *Long Quiet Highway: Waking Up in America*. New York: Bantam.

Heard, Georgia. 1995. *Writing Toward Home: Tales and Lessons to Find Your Way*. Portsmouth, NH: Heinemann.

Hesse, Karen. 1999. "Waiting for Midnight." In *When I Was Your Age, Volume Two: Original Stories About Growing Up*, ed. Amy Ehrlich. Cambridge, MA: Candlewick Press.

Kaplan, Cynthia. 2002. *Why I'm Like This: True Stories*. New York: Perennial.

Karr, Mary. 1995. *The Liars' Club: A Memoir*. New York: Viking.

———. 2000. *Cherry: A Memoir*. New York: Penguin Group.

Kazin, Alfred. 1951. *A Walker in the City*. New York: MJF Books.

140

Kimmel, Haven. 2001. *A Girl Named Zippy: Growing Up Small in Moreland, Indiana*. New York: Broadway Books.

King, Stephen. 2000. *On Writing: A Memoir of the Craft*. New York: Scribner.

Kingsolver, Barbara. 1995. "How Mr. Dewey Decimal Saved My Life." In *High Tide in Tucson: Essays from Now or Never*. New York: HarperCollins.

Kingston, Maxine Hong. 1989. "At the Western Place," pp. 119–160. In *The Woman Warrior: Memoirs of a Childhood Among Ghosts*. New York: Vintage International.

Liftin, Hilary. 2003. *Candy and Me: A Love Story*. New York: Free Press.

Lopez, Barry. 1995. "Replacing Memory." In *Modern American Memoirs*. New York: HarperPerennial.

Mah, Adeline Yen. 1997. "Family Ugliness Should Never Be Aired in Public," pp. 54–57. In *Falling Leaves: The True Story of an Unwanted Chinese Daughter*. New York: John Wiley and Sons.

——.1999. "PLT." In *Chinese Cinderella: The True Story of an Unwanted Daughter*. New York: Dell Laurel-Leaf.

Mayes, Frances. 1996. *Under the Tuscan Sun: At Home in Italy*. New York: Broadway Books.

Mazer, Norma Fox. 1999. "In the Blink of an Eye." In *When I Was Your Age, Volume Two: Original Stories About Growing Up*, ed. Amy Ehrlich. Cambridge, MA: Candlewick Press.

McCourt, Frank. 2006. *Teacher Man: A Memoir*. New York: Scribner.

Mori, Kyoko. 1999. "Learning to Swim." In *When I Was Your Age, Volume Two: Original Stories About Growing Up*, ed. Amy Ehrlich. Cambridge, MA: Candlewick Press.

Munro, Eleanor. 1995. "Memoirs of a Modernist's Daughter." In *Modern American Memoirs*, ed. Annie Diliard and Cort Conley. New York: HarperCollins.

Myers, Walter Dean. 2001. *Bad Boy: A Memoir*. New York: HarperTempest.

Newman, Leslea. 1993. *Writing from the Heart: Inspiration and Exercises for Women Who Want to Write*. Freedom, CA: The Crossing Press.

Norman, Howard. 1999. "Bus Problems." In *When I Was Your Age: Volume Two: Original Stories about Growing Up*, ed. Amy Ehrlich. Cambridge, MA: Candlewick Press.

Notaro, Laurie. 2002. " Extreme Clean Sports." In *The Idiot Girls' Action-Adventure Club*. New York: Villard Books.

——.2002. "It Smells Like Doody in Here." In *The Idiot Girls' Action-Adventure Club*. New York: Villard Books.

——.2002. "More Bread, Please." In *The Idiot Girls' Action-Adventure Club*. New York: Villard Books.

——.2002. "On the Road." In *The Idiot Girls' Action-Adventure Club*. New York: Villard Books.

Ozick, Cynthia. 1995. "A Drugstore in Winter." In *Modern American Memoirs*. New York: HarperPerennial.

Palmer, Parker. 2000. *Let Your Life Speak: Listening for the Voice of Vocation*. San Francisco: Jossey-Bass.

Portalupi, Joann, and Ralph Fletcher. 2001. *Nonfiction Craft Lessons: Teaching Information Writing K–8*. Portland, ME: Stenhouse.

Price, Reynolds. 1995. "Clear Pictures." In *Modern American Essays*, ed. Annie Dilliard and Cort Conley. New York: HarperCollins.

Rodriguez, Luis J. *Always Running: La Vida Loca: Gang Days in LA*. New York: Touchstone.

Rodriguez, Richard. 1982. *Hunger of Memory: The Education of Richard Rodriguez: An Autobiography*. New York: Bantam Books.

Rosen, Michael J. 1999. "Pegasus for a Summer." In *When I Was Your Age, Volume Two: Original Stories About Growing Up*, ed. Amy Ehrlich. Cambridge, MA: Candlewick Press.

Soto, Gary. 1985. "Being Mean." In *Living Up the Street: Narrative Recollections*. New York: Bantam Doubleday Dell Books.

Thoreau, Henry David. 1995. *Walden*. New ed. New York: Houghton Mifflin.

Tovani, Cris. 2004. *Do I Really Have to Teach Reading? Content Comprehension, Grades 6–12*. Portland, ME: Stenhouse.

Trope, Zoe. 2003. "10.14." In *Please Don't Kill the Freshman: A Memoir*. New York: Harper Tempest.

Walker, Alice. 1988. *Living By the Word: Selected Writings 1973–1987*. New York: Harcourt, Brace, Jovanovich.

White, Bailey. 1993. *Mama Makes Up Her Mind and Other Dangers of Southern Living*. New York: Vintage Books.

Wright, Richard. 1937. *Black Boy: A Record of Childhood and Youth*. New York: Harper and Brothers.

Yolen, Jane. 1999. "The Long Closet." In *When I Was Your Age, Volume Two: Original Stories About Growing Up*, ed. Amy Ehrlich. Cambridge. MA: Candlewick Press.

Zinsser William, ed. 1998. *Inventing the Truth: The Art and Craft of Memoir*. Boston: Houghton Mifflin.

142

SUPPORT OF TEACHING MEMOIR

Memoirs and Memoir Collections

Allison, Dorothy. 1995. *Two or Three Things I Know for Sure*. New York: Plume.

Angelou, Maya. 1969. *I Know Why the Caged Bird Sings*. New York: Random House.

Dillard, Annie. 1987. *An American Childhood*. New York: HarperPerennial.

Dillard, Annie, and Cort Conley. 1995. *Modern American Memoirs*. New York: HarperPerennial.

Ehrlich, Amy, ed. 1999. *When I Was Your Age, Volume Two: Original Stories About Growing Up*, Cambridge, MA: Candlewick Press.

Kimmel, Haven. 2001. *A Girl Named Zippy: Growing Up Small in Moreland, Indiana*. New York: Broadway Books.

Liftin, Hilary. 2003. *Candy and Me: A Love Story*. New York: Free Press.

Myers, Walter Dean. 2001. *Bad Boy: A Memoir*. New York: HarperTempest.

Notaro, Laurie. 2002. *The Idiot Girls' Action-Adventure Club: True Tales from a Magnificent and Clumsy Life*. New York: Villard Books.

Soto, Gary. 1985. *Living Up the Street*. New York: Laurel-Leaf.

White, Bailey. 1993. *Mama Makes Up Her Mind and Other Dangers of Southern Living*. New York: Vintage Books.

RECOMMENDED RESOURCES IN

Books

Atwell, Nancie. 1998. "Call Home the Child: Memoir." In *In the Middle: New Understandings About Reading, Writing, and Learning.* Portsmouth, NH: Heinemann.

Bomer, Randy. 1995. "Making Something of Our Lives: Reading and Writing Memoir." In *Time for Meaning: Crafting Literate Lives in Middle and High School.* Portsmouth, NH: Heinemann.

Heard, Georgia. 1995. *Writing Toward Home: Tales and Lessons to Find Your Way.* Portsmouth, NH: Heinemann.

King, Stephen. 2000. *On Writing: A Memoir of the Craft.* New York: Scribner.

Lattimer, Heather. 2003. *Thinking Through Genre: Units of Study in Reading and Writing Workshops 4–12.* Portland, ME: Stenhouse.

Portalupi, Joann, and Ralph Fletcher. 2001. *Nonfiction Craft Lessons: Teaching Information Writing K–8.* Portland, ME: Stenhouse.

Zinsser, William, ed. 1998. *Inventing the Truth: The Art and Craft of Memoir.* New York: Houghton Mifflin.

CHAPTER 6

Poetry

Poetry is a river; many voices travel in it; poem after poem moves along in the exciting crests and falls of the river waves.

–MARY OLIVER

love poetry. I treasure my collection of poetry books, and I am always on the lookout for more poetry. I send poems I have discovered to friends and family. I consider a poem printed on pretty paper a heartfelt gift. I even like to write poetry. Poetry speaks to me; it helps me make sense of the complexities of my life.

But this was not how my high school students reacted when I introduced poetry to them. As I entered my freshman classroom I was giddy with anticipation. It was poetry time. I announced with enthusiasm that we would be immersed in poetry for the next several weeks, and before I had even finished my sentence an audible groan filled the air. I checked the faces to see if I had misheard but even my barometer-student's smile was gone. I had my work cut out for me.

Rather than plunge ahead with my lesson plan, I stopped and checked in with students. I invited them to write for a few minutes about poetry: What did they remember about poetry that made it challenging, even worthy of the groan I had just heard? And what, if anything, had they experienced that made them think poetry might have some value?

That afternoon as I read through their writing I found myself cringing; many of their criticisms reflected things I had done in an effort to teach poetry:

- Requiring students to memorize poems
- Using poems I had selected and loved and being resistant or even resentful when students did not love the poem
- Suggesting there was one "interpretation" of a poem
- Focusing too much on the craft of poetry, particularly types of poems and rhyme schemes

As one student wrote, "Poetry is something that English teachers love and most kids hate. I don't know anyone who reads poetry anywhere other than school."

I wanted my students to discover that poetry is something to be read and enjoyed in and out of school. In her collection of essays about teaching, *Side by Side* (1991), Nancie Atwell tells the story of walking in the woods with her young daughter, who responded to Atwell's question, "I wonder who owns this land?" by reciting Robert Frost's poem, "Stopping by Woods on a Snowy Evening":

Stopping by Woods on a Snowy Evening

Whose woods these are I think I know.
His house is in the village, though;
He will not see me stopping here
To watch his woods fill up with snow.

My little horse must think it queer
To stop without a farmhouse near
Between the woods and frozen lake
The darkest evening of the year.

He gives his harness bells a shake
To ask if there is some mistake.

The only other sound's the sweep
Of easy wind and downy flake.

The woods are lovely, dark, and deep,
But I have promises to keep,
And miles to go before I sleep
And miles to go before I sleep.

(Frost 1973, 204)

Atwell celebrates this moment as a reflection of why poetry is important in her daughter's life:

> *Poetry won't keep her safe. It won't ensure her a happy life or heal her pain or make her rich. But it will give voice to the experiences of her life. This seems enough to ask of it.*
>
> *"You will find poetry nowhere unless you bring some of it with you." To which might be added that if you do bring some of it with you, you will find it everywhere.*
>
> *(Atwell 1991, 98)*

I read this section of Atwell's essay to my class the following day. I then told the story of requiring middle school students to memorize this very poem, "Stopping by Woods on a Snowy Evening." Listening to twenty-seven students recite this poem in one class period made me wonder why I had made this choice. And then I told the story of Brandon. Brandon was a quiet seventh grader. He came to me the day before the poem recitations were to begin and explained he could not recite the poem to the class because he had a heart condition. I was stunned. I asked him to tell me more about his heart condition. He explained that although he could not get a note from his doctor, he really did have a heart condition and being required to stand in front of the class and recite the poem just might kill him. I nodded and wisely paused before responding, "Brandon, I appreciate you sharing this with me. I don't want to jeopardize your health. Do you think your heart could tolerate you reciting the poem just to me at lunch tomorrow?" Brandon agreed to this plan.

The next day at lunch Brandon came in and recited the poem. His quiet voice was compelling, particularly during the last two lines, which he whispered with closed eyes: "And miles to go before I sleep/And miles to go before I sleep." I leapt up and hugged him (it's true that sometimes I do hug my students). Brandon was

146

so pleased by his effort that he agreed to recite to the class; apparently his heart condition could handle it. He was even more compelling as he stood, hands behind his back, clutching the chalk-tray on the blackboard, looking out over the heads of his fellow students, until the final lines, which he again whispered, eyes closed. Spontaneous applause filled the room as Brandon took his shy smile back to his seat.

I looked at my current class of freshmen and said, "I am not telling you this story to defend my 'memorize a poem' assignment. I cannot defend it, despite Brandon's success. I am telling you this story because this poem by Frost has special meaning for me. It reminds me of this moment with Brandon. It reminds me that my job as a teacher is not to make you memorize poetry or create heart conditions to get out of memorizing poetry; it is to help you discover what poetry means for you. I want poetry to give voice to your lives."

Teaching Strategy: Finding Poetry Everywhere
I followed with their first poetry assignment: "Your task is to find the poetry that is already in your life. Perhaps it is in a book of favorite poems from your childhood, or in the woods behind your house, or in a hobby or sport that you feel passionately about. Find poetry and bring it to class tomorrow. Be prepared to share what you found and how it represents poetry to you. I cannot wait to see what you discover."

In support of their efforts, I modeled my own example of poetry in my life by sharing with them my well-worn copy of Emily Dickinson poems. I read aloud one of my favorites, "This Is My Letter to the World."

This is my letter to the World
That never wrote to me—
The simple News that Nature told—
With tender Majesty

Her Message is committed
To Hands I cannot See—
For Lover of Her—Sweet—countrymen—
Judge tenderly—of Me.
                    (Dickinson 2001, 1)

I went on to tell the story of how I admired Emily for capturing her thoughts on paper—not for an audience, for herself. I then held up my own spiral notebook of attempted poetry and shared how this notebook is hidden in my sock drawer, away from the prying eyes of family. It is writing I do just for me. I opened the notebook and shared with students that I write poetry about the little things in life as a way of making sense of the big issues. I have a poem about Ben and Jerry's ice cream, sliding down the stairs of my house in a blue nylon sleeping bag, swimming laps, the challenge of summer birthdays, and being a daughter and a mom. I remind students that poetry gives voice to my life, and theirs.

I wanted students to ponder the role of poetry in their lives, so I gave them several days to think about this assignment. Each day in class I shared another example of poetry's role in my life: I read Robert Frost's poem "The Road Not Taken" and told them the story of how this poem hung over my desk in college, as a reminder to me that I had not taken the safe route of going to college in state with most of my friends. I share a photograph of my former cat, Emily, and tell why I named her after my favorite poet, Emily Dickinson. I read a poem I wrote about watching ice-skaters at the mall with my daughter.

The day the assignment was finally due, I was anxious for my final period freshman class to begin and nervous that I had set students up to ridicule my out-there assignment. This was not a class known for its completion of homework assignments, and they had already indicated their dislike for poetry. As students entered I could feel the energy level in the room rise. Cheryl clutched a tattered book of poems to her chest. Frank proudly clung to a well-worn copy of Shel Silverstein's *Where the Sidewalk Ends*. Suzy went to the bookshelf in the back of my room and grabbed my copy of Emily Dickinson. I watched as she scanned the table of contents, a smile breaking across her face when she found the poem she was looking for. Joe looked sheepish, and I was ready for his excuse about why he hadn't done the homework.

Before students shared, I asked them to write about what they had done to find poetry everywhere and what they were prepared to share. After seven or eight minutes of quiet writing—and it really was quiet writing—I asked for volunteers to share their discoveries. A sea of hands greeted me. I really do think every student had his or her hand in the air. I can confirm that every student shared his or her "poetry everywhere" example.

Joe explained how basketball is poetry in his life; it requires form and creativity, and when the "ball swishes through the basket it is a thing of beauty." Cheryl shared her collection of children's poems, which her dad read to her when she was a little girl. Frank held up his copy of Shel Silverstein and the class erupted by calling out their favorites from this book. Frank read his favorite to the class, and when he finished, we applauded and then begged him to read one or two more. Suzy stood up to read her favorite poem, which began with the line "I am Nobody, who are you?" by Emily Dickinson. And then she turned to me and said, "I am so glad you had her book; I read this poem a long time ago and when you gave us this assignment I looked everywhere for it. It was fun to find it and read it again. I hope we can read some of her other poems." Lindsay played a favorite song and shared how its lyrics bring her comfort. (I must note that I asked students to show me before class the lyrics of any song they planned to share with the class.) Jason held up a picture of his favorite basketball player, Michael Jordan, and described in vivid detail how Jordan's playing is poetic. Sarah read a poem she had written about her cat, Mr. Snuggles. Lisa held up photos she had taken of the forest near her house and told us she was working on a poem but wasn't quite ready to share. Chris read his favorite cowboy poem. The energy in the room was palpable as students shared the poetry of their lives.

I know this sounds too idyllic to be real; it felt that way too. But every year that I did this opener to poetry with freshmen, it worked. And it worked well with graduate students who were studying to be language arts teachers. It's an entry to poetry that helps dispel some of the practices we have used to squelch poetry's appeal.

And poetry has appeal for adolescents. My own experience and the experiences of the preservice teachers with whom I now work can confirm this. Crystal tells the story of her seventh-grade students coming into class on the second Friday after she began "Poetry Friday," which involved her reading a poem aloud to the class, followed by a brief discussion. Students arrived asking if it was "Poetry Friday" and cheered when they learned it was. Laura shares the story of James, a seventh grader, who was the last to leave the room after class, and as he put his chair on the desk announced, "Today was really fun." When Laura asked him which part of class, which had focused on poetry, he replied, "The whole class—and finding new things to write for my clock poem." This is James who announced on the first day of poetry exploration, "No offense, but I'm not really

149

a poetry person." During the final poetry slam, James read his poem "Six Ways of Looking at Clocks" along with two other poems. James discovered what I continue to discover: poetry speaks to adolescents in ways that other genres do not.

This chapter will explore strategies for incorporating poetry into our classrooms, including poems to read aloud, strategies for reading poetry, and ways to explore the craft of poetry that support students' poetry reading and writing.

Reading Poetry Aloud

In addition to linking poetry to students' lives, we need to open their ears and eyes to poetry. We need to read poetry aloud.

TIPS FOR READING POETRY ALOUD

1. Read poetry, seek it out, savor it, and start keeping a folder of poems you love.

2. Make poetry visible. Post it in your room; invite students to bring in poems they love.

3. Practice reading before you read a poem aloud to the class.

4. Invite students to join you in reading poems aloud; choral readings are great!

5. Be open to reading a poem and just letting the words hang in the air. It is not required that every poem you read be discussed.

In selecting poems to read aloud I look for poems that I think will connect with my students. I look for poems that celebrate language or paint vivid pictures. I look for poems that emphasize the sounds of words. I look for poems that encourage students to savor poetry. Listed in the sidebar are poems that have met all or some of these criteria and have received favorable reviews from students as good read-alouds.

POEMS TO READ ALOUD

"Introduction to Poetry" by Billy Collins
"The History Teacher" by Billy Collins
"You Reading This, Be Ready" by William Stafford
"The Secret" by Denise Levertov
"Did I Miss Anything?" by Tom Wayman

"The Art of Disappearing" by Naomi Shihab Nye

"What a Relief" by Barbara Drake

"Poetry Is the Art of Not Succeeding" by Joe Salerno

"Vacation" by Rita Dove

"The Rider" by Naomi Shihab Nye

"Hate Poem" by Julie Sheehan

"Selecting a Reader" by Ted Kooser

Strategies for Reading Poetry

Poets give poetry readings. Years ago I read an interview with Maya Angelou in which she commented, "Poetry is music written for the human voice. And until you actually speak it or someone speaks it, it has not come into its own" (Angelou 1996, 11). I want students to speak poetry, so every poem we read in class is read aloud at least twice. I want students to hear the poem more than once, but I also want them to see the poem, so I do what I can to get copies made. I am well aware of the challenges of limited copy budgets. I found making a class copy of the poem and collecting it back after each class to reuse is one option. I was always grateful when students begged to keep their copy. I also found writing poems on large sheets of butcher paper to post on the wall worked well. These poems can then be left up for students to reread over and over.

If I am bringing a poem to the class, I am always the first to read it to the students because I have had the opportunity to practice reading the poem.

For the second reading, I use a variety of strategies:

- If I am confident in the class's read-aloud abilities, I ask for a volunteer reader.
- If we are still developing read-aloud skills, I may ask a student a day in advance to prepare to read the poem.
- Some poems lend themselves well to choral reading so we read the poem as a class.

151

As part of our poetry study, I talk with students about reading poetry aloud. We look at the way poets use white space, line breaks, stanzas, and punctuation to guide poetry reading. I provide copies of Billy Collins's tips for reading poetry aloud from his website, Poetry 180.

Teaching Strategy: Reading Poetry Aloud

Billy Collins, a favorite poet of mine, has created a wonderful website, http://www.loc.gov/poetry/180. His delightful poem "Introduction to Poetry," which can be found on the website, sets just the right tone for our poetry exploration, and it works well for talking about how to read a poem.

Introduction to Poetry

I ask them to take a poem
and hold it up to the light
like a color slide

or press an ear against its hive.

I say drop a mouse into the poem
and watch him probe his way out,

or walk inside the poem's room
and feel the walls for a light switch.

I want them to waterski
across the surface of a poem
waving at the author's name on the shore.

But all they want to do
is tie the poem to a chair with rope
and torture a confession out of it.

They begin beating it with a hose
to find out what it really means.
(Collins 2001, 16)

I hand out the poem and tell students I am going to read it twice. The first time I read it without attention to punctuation and the way it is arranged on the page. I then read it a second time with attention to the arrangement and punctuation.

I ask students to comment on the two readings by exploring questions such as:

- How were the two readings different?
- What do you notice about the way the lines are arranged on the page? How did this arrangement affect my second reading?
- Punctuation: what does he use and how does it guide the reader?

After working with Collins's poem, we look at several others, focusing our attention on the ways poets use line breaks, white space, stanzas, and punctuation. I want students to understand that there is a pause, albeit a brief one, at the end of each line. For those of you who wonder if there is a pause at the end of lines, Georgia Heard provides us with a definitive answer: pause at each line break. Her source for this answer is twofold. First, when she reads the poems she has written, she pauses at the line breaks. Second, she tells the story of listening to Gwendolyn Brooks read her own poem "We Real Cool: The Pool Player/Seven at the Golden Shovel." Brooks paused at the line breaks. Often they were long pauses, and her pauses created a rhythm that sounded like jazz (1989, 55–56).

I want students to see how line breaks, as well as commas and periods, dictate pauses. Listed in the sidebar are poems that work well for developing read-aloud skills.

POEMS TO SUPPORT READ-ALOUD SKILLS DEVELOPMENT
"How to Eat a Poem" by Eve Merriam
"Wild Geese" by Mary Oliver
"The Trouble with Reading" by William Stafford
"Kindness" by Naomi Shihab Nye
"Now I Become Myself" by May Sarton
"Family Dog" by Jeffrey Harrison
"The Art of Disappearing" by Naomi Shihab Nye
"Our Other Sister" by Jeffrey Harrison
"The Poet's Obligation" by Pablo Neruda
"About Long Days" by Anthony Ostroff
"Poetry" by Billy Collins

Teaching Strategy: "Found Poem" of Favorite Lines

In support of giving poetry voice, I invite students to create an in-class "found poem" by sharing favorite lines, lines that strike them, from a poem we are exploring in class. We begin by my reading the poem. For the second reading I ask students to mark lines that strike them. After the second reading I explain that we are going to create our own poem using lines from the poem we have just read. Our found poem will come to life when students share the lines they have marked in "popcorn" fashion (by calling them out when they think the time is right). I encourage students to listen to the lines being read and jump in when their line feels right. It is permissible to read lines more than once, creating our own repetition.

This brief oral activity supports students in reading poetry aloud by starting with just one line. It encourages students to listen to poetry, adding their line to our oral found poem. I want students to fill the room with the poem's language. To trust their own choices in putting lines together in a new way. To celebrate lines they admire by reading them more than once. To create a new poem that exists only for them.

In selecting poems for this activity, I pick poems I admire for their powerful imagery and word choice. A particular favorite of mine for this activity is Marge Piercy's poem "To Be of Use." Most of the poems listed in this chapter would work well for this activity.

Teaching Strategy: Snapping the Beat

Georgia Heard's book *For the Good of the Earth and Sun: Teaching Poetry* (1989) is one of my favorite resources. I got the idea of snapping to the beat of a poem from her. She describes her experience of reading poetry aloud to kindergartners and first graders. Without any prompting, these young students sway and snap to the rhythms of the poems they hear. Heard notes, "They know the music of the poem because they feel it in their bodies" (1). I want middle school and high school students to "know the music" of poetry too, so I force the issue.

At the beginning of class I ask students to push their desks to the side of the classroom so we can create an open space in the middle. I then ask them to find a spot in the open space. It's fair to say they are now a bit intrigued. I share with them Heard's story of working with young children and poetry and I ask them to reach back to those days when they were willing to let themselves move to the music of poetry. I invite them to join me in snapping and, if they are so inclined, swaying to the music of Gwendolyn Brooks's poem "We Real Cool." I share with them that the first time I tried this I felt silly, but silly can be good. I read the poem aloud once, and on the second reading, we snap and sway. I snap and sway with them. I read the poem aloud several more times and the snapping and swaying continues; typically it increases as students let themselves feel the jazz rhythm of this poem. We then move to several more poems (see sidebar for suggested poems).

After this activity, we sit on the floor in the open space we have created and talk about poetry. We look at Brooks's poem and note how the poem's arrangement on the page creates the rhythm. In end-of-term course evaluations, a number of students mentioned this lesson—how it helped them to rediscover poetry and how they appreciated being given permission to be silly.

POEMS FOR SNAPPING AND SWAYING

"Jazz Fantasia" by Carl Sandburg
"I Hear America Singing" by Walt Whitman
"Loud Music" by Stephen Dobyns

Teaching Strategy: Poetry Set to Music
I build on the snapping and swaying lesson by sharing examples of poems that have been set to music. The Alan Parson Project did an album in the 1970s of Edgar Allan Poe literature set to music. Their rendition of "The Raven" is worth tracking down a record player. I also used T. S. Eliot's cat poems and the Broadway musical *Cats*. My students particularly enjoyed "Gus, the Theatre Cat."

Teaching Strategy: Conversing with Poetry Through Dialogue Journals and Discussion
After these initial explorations of poetry, I invite students to "converse" with poetry in writing and in a group discussion. In selecting a poem for our "conversation" I look for a poem that I admire for its word choice and content. I want it to be a poem that encourages students to find personal and world connections. Naomi Shihab Nye's poem "Kindness" meets my criteria and serves students well (see the sidebar for other poem suggestions).

155

We begin our conversation with a copy of the poem, which I read aloud. I then invite a student volunteer to read the poem a second time. (As noted previously, I often ask students before class if they would be willing to be the second reader so they have some time to practice.) After the second read, we write. I use an interactive dialogue journal for this writing.

In the first column of their journal page, I ask students to list two lines from the poem that strike them. In the second column, they write why they chose these lines. I model this for them by sharing my own line choices, noting what I admire about the language of the lines as well as my personal connection with the lines. After they have written about their lines, they exchange papers with a peer, who then responds to the line responses in Column 3. If I am concerned about how students will respond to each other, I collect the dialogue journals and distribute them so I can control the process. More typically, I ask students to pass their dialogue journal to the student behind them. (Note: if they pass to the sides I find students are more likely to interact with their peer respondent, which is not my goal. I want a written conversation.) Before students respond to their peers, I model the response process. This modeling process can be a way to support students who might find this activity challenging. I call on a student to share the lines and response she has in front of her. That way I can support this student directly while modeling for the class. I stress that the goal of this dialogue response is to comment on what is written on the page.

After six to eight minutes of response time, students return the dialogue journals to the original authors. In Column 4, I ask students to comment on the response as well as address the question, what does this poem make you think about?

This initial writing sets the foundation for a class discussion about the poem. I call on students to share the lines they selected and comment on what they learned from writing and receiving response to their writing. This serves to keep our conversation grounded in the poem's language. This is not to say that students are not encouraged to make connections with the poem, but I ask them to link their connections directly to the lines of the poem.

I collect the dialogue journals and skim them, looking for patterns in their line choice and response that I can build on in our continued poetry exploration. I generally don't grade the dialogue journals, but I assign participation points for the good-faith completion of the assignment.

POEMS TO SUPPORT CONVERSATION

"Wild Geese" by Mary Oliver
"You Reading This, Be Ready" by William Stafford
"Our Other Sister" by Jeffrey Harrison
"Hate Poem" by Julie Sheehan
"The Hand" by Mary Ruefle
"The Summer Day" by Mary Oliver
"Summer I Was Sixteen" by Geraldine Connolly
"Dream Deferred" by Langston Hughes
"Imperfection" by Elizabeth Carlson
"Courage" by Anne Sexton
"Saturday at the Canal" by Gary Soto

Exploring the Craft of Poetry

When I think about poetry, I am struck by the fact that its craft is so complex. My goal is to honor the craft, but not at the expense of savoring the poem's overall effect. In an effort to meet the challenge of this task, I think about poetry craft as follows: "The language of the poem is the language of particulars. Without it poetry might still be wise, but it would surely be pallid," writes poet Mary Oliver (1994, 92). One of my objectives for studying poetry is to focus students' attention on this "language of particulars."

IMAGERY: "THE LANGUAGE OF PARTICULARS"

Years ago I had the privilege of taking a poetry workshop from Peter Sears. He shared with us a technique he called "poetry corruption" in which he deleted words from published poems and invited us to supply our own word choice. We then discussed our chosen words before we looked at the poet's word choice. Homing in on individual words in the poem allowed us to appreciate the importance of word choice.

157

Teaching Strategy: Poetry Corruption

Georgia Heard uses this strategy, without the name "poetry corruption," in her book on teaching poetry, *For the Good of the Earth and Sun* (1989). She writes, "Poets work long and hard choosing the right words for a poem—original words that evoke a vivid image, words whose sounds are right." She goes on to share how she uses an excerpt from Robert Lowell's "Mr. Edwards and the Spider" with words eliminated to focus students' attention on word choice (70).

In choosing poems to use for poetry corruption I focus on short lines. Peter Sears's poem "Accident" has worked well for me. I have the luxury of having his drafts of the poem, which I share with students after we have "corrupted" it. But there are a number of poems that work well for this. Denise Levertov's "A Day Begins" has been a big hit with students, particularly middle school students. Its opening image of a "headless squirrel" is unexpected and stands in contrast to the later description of "ethereal irises."

This focus on individual word choice serves as scaffolding for our continued exploration of imagery, with a focus on figurative language.

Teaching Strategy: Paying Attention to the "Language of Particulars"

In *A Poetry Handbook* (1994*)*, Mary Oliver uses Elizabeth Bishop's richly detailed poem "The Fish" to illustrate imagery. This poem was a favorite of my students, so I also commend it to you.

I begin, as always, by reading the poem aloud. After the first read I ask students to listen and look for images: what pictures does Bishop paint in this poem? I read it a second time. I then provide students with either highlighter pens or sticky note arrows and ask them to mark lines that show the fish.

Next I gather students in groups. I ask each group to pick an image from the poem that they think is particularly powerful and write it on the board. I don't know why students like writing on the board; I just know they do. We then use these lines as the starting point for looking at imagery, including metaphor and simile.

We examine each example, noting how the use of "particulars" adds to the image. I use colored chalk to underline sections of lines that illustrate simile and metaphor and invite students to define these terms.

I then instruct students to return to their groups and have each group find additional examples of imagery, including metaphor and simile, in the poem. In an effort to avoid duplication of examples, I divide the poem into sections and assign each group a section. Each group shares its examples, and these are added to the definitions of imagery, simile, and metaphor, which we hang on the classroom wall.

To support students in this activity, I select the groups so that I can ensure I have a mix of student abilities in each group. I also circulate during the time students are marking the poem and check in with students regarding the lines they marked.

We build on this examination of imagery by looking at a variety of poems that are rich in imagery, what Mary Oliver calls the "texture—the poet gives the reader a plentitude of details" (1994, 94). For each of the poems we read, I ask students to find examples of imagery, and we add these to our posters so students are surrounded by "language of particulars."

POEMS RICH IN IMAGERY

"Hope Is the Thing with Feathers" by Emily Dickinson
"Chicago" by Carl Sandburg
"The Love Song of J. Alfred Prufrock" by T. S. Eliot
"Traveling Through Dark" by William Stafford
"Tulips" by Mark Halperin
"Last Shot" by Jon Veinberg
"Fast Break" by Edward Hirsch
"Gouge, Adze, Rasp, Hammer" by Chris Forhan
"Her Head" by Joan Murray
"Forgiving Buckner" by John Hodgen
"Mother to Son" by Langston Hughes
"Seven Preludes to Silence" by Richard Shelton
"Young" by Anne Sexton
"Lighting Up Time" by Patrick Taylor

SOUND

I begin our exploration of sound by asking students to think about words they admire because of the way the words sound. I tell the story of my daughter, at the age of three, lying on the stairs in our house singing the word *unexpectedly* over and over. It was the only word from the song in the movie *Beauty and the Beast* that she remembered. She loved the sound of it.

Teaching Strategy: Chanting Favorite Words

The writing prompt for the day asks students to make a list of words they love based on their sound. I share a few examples from my own list, which I began drafting the night before class so I would have some examples: *lavender, snow-flake, bumblebee, mauve, luminous.* We spend five to six minutes writing our lists, and then I ask students to pick a word from their list and write it on the board. I begin by writing a new word from the list I wrote in class.

I then get a yardstick and point to each word. We read the word aloud as a class, and I ask the student who supplied it to share why they love its sound. After discussing each word, I tell students we are going to fill the classroom with the sounds of their words. We'll create a found poem with our list by calling out the words as I point to them. Before we begin I ask if there are any words we need to check on regarding pronunciation.

And the poem begins; I point to words and students call them out in a choral reading. I point randomly, looking for interesting patterns. Students' voices grow louder as they begin to delight in the sounds of words.

Next we turn our attention to a poem that I love for its sound, Jane Kenyon's "Let Evening Come." *A Note Slipped Under the Door: Teaching from Poems We Love* (Flynn and McPhillips 2000) devotes an entire chapter to working with Kenyon's poem and how it uses sound. I commend this book and this chapter to you.

We read the Kenyon poem and others, focusing our attention on sounds: hard letters, soft letters, assonance, alliteration, rhyme, and repetition. Listed in the sidebar are poems that illustrate these sound devices. I also want to draw students' attention to onomatopoeia (what a great word). I relish the opportunity to teach students this term as we continue to explore the ways poets use sound in poetry.

Teaching Strategy: Onomatopoeia Through Concept Attainment

To teach onomatopoeia, I utilize a teaching strategy I learned when I was earning my master's: concept attainment. As a quick review, the idea of concept attainment is that examples of the concept are shared along with examples that don't represent the concept. Students look for patterns in the examples to determine the concept.

When students arrive for class I have already divided the front blackboard into halves. Each half is labeled: one half is "Yes" and one half is "No." I explain to students that we will be exploring a poetry term today by looking at examples and nonexamples of the term. Their task is to take out a sheet of paper and, as they look at the examples, write down what they notice about them, looking for patterns or clues that link the Yes examples and that distinguish these examples from the No examples.

I have written examples on brightly colored construction paper. I hold up the first example, "Pow," and tell students this word is an example of the poetry term so it is placed on the Yes section of the board. I then hold up the second example, "Explode," and let students know this is not an example of the term so it is placed under No. I follow with two more examples: "Dad," which is a No, and "Pop," which is a Yes. I ask students to write down what they notice about the Yes and No examples. Our lists of examples continue but as I share examples I invite students to guess if the example is a Yes or No. After two or three more examples, I again ask students to write down their thoughts about the examples. I continue to share examples until I hear the majority of students correctly identifying the examples. I then ask students to write down the Yes examples' key characteristics. From this writing, we develop a class definition for the Yes examples. Students shared the following: "All the 'yes' examples are words that describe a noise and the word itself sounds like the noise it is describing." Yes!

I then share with students that this literary technique is called *onomatopoeia*, a word that literally means "name making." I find that students usually giggle as I talk about onomatopoeia; it is a funny-sounding word. As one student said, "It sounds like a disease that you should take a purple pill for—not a poetry term." We then look at poems that illustrate onomatopoeia. Eve Merriam's "Cheers" is a great example. I also share some lines from Edgar Allan Poe's "The Bells":

From the jingling and the tingling of the bells.
To the rhyming and the chiming of the bells!
In the clamor and the clangor of the bells!
To the moaning and the groaning of the bells.

161

Other poems that demonstrate onomatopoeia are listed in the sidebar.

POEMS THAT ILLUSTRATE SOUND DEVICES

POET	POEM	SOUND DEVICE
Carl Sandburg	"Jazz Fantasia"	Onomatopoeia
Gwendolyn Brooks	"We Real Cool"	Rhyme Repetition
Walt Whitman	"I Sit and Look Out"	Repetition
Emily Dickinson	"Fame Is a Fickle Food"	Alliteration
Paul Laurence Dunbar	"We Wear the Mask"	Rhyme Repetition
Edgar Allan Poe	"The Raven"	Rhyme Repetition Alliteration
Robert Frost	"Stopping by Woods on a Snowy Evening"	Soft letter sounds Rhyme Repetition
Naomi Shihab Nye	"Elevator"	Alliteration Onomatopoeia
Robert Burlingame	"small poems"	Hard and soft letter sounds Alliteration
Linda Pastan	"Elegy"	Hard letter sounds "s" sounds Alliteration
Mary Oliver	"Winter"	Alliteration Hard and soft letter sounds
Miller Williams	"Love Poem with Toast"	Repetition
Marilyn Annucci	"Wrecked World"	Alliteration
Dick Allen	"Time to Hear Ourselves Think"	Onomatopoeia
Mary Oliver	"Learning About the Indians"	Onomatopoeia Alliteration
Jane Kenyon	"The Blue Bowl"	Onomatopoeia
Theodore Roethke	"The Bat"	Rhyme
Charles Harper Webb	"The Time We Cherry-Bombed the Toilet at the River Oaks"	Onomatopoeia Hard sounds Descriptive language in support of sound
Barbara Kingsolver	"Beating Time"	Rhyme Hard letter sounds Repetition

STRUCTURE/FORMAT

Poems have a design—lines, breaks, white space, and stanzas. I want students to examine how poets design poems. Although we may look at examples of poetry forms such as sonnet, haiku, sestina, and cinquain, these explorations are secondary (see the resource list at the end of this chapter for books that address these forms). My primary goal is to focus students' attention on how poets use structure to enhance their poems. In particular, I focus on line breaks. As Mary Oliver notes, "Poets today, who do not often write in the given forms, such as sonnets, need to understand what effects are created by the turning of the line at any of various possible points—within (and thus breaking) a logical phrase, or only at the conclusion of sentences, or only at the ends of logical units, etc." (1994, 35).

Teaching Strategy: Turning Lines

We begin by looking at poems I have rewritten into paragraph form. After reading the rewritten poem in paragraph format, we then look at the poem as the poet wrote it, paying particular attention to line breaks. I find Mary Oliver's poem "Alligator Poem" works well for an exploration of line breaks in that it tells a story when written as a paragraph but as a poem the line breaks focus the reader's attention on descriptive images and highlight the intensity of the encounter with the alligator.

Georgia Heard discusses the power of line breaks and white space in Chapter 4 of her book *For the Good of the Earth and Sun* (1989, 59). She focuses on William Carlos Williams's poem about a cat entitled "Poem." I have had success using this poem and the poems listed in the sidebar.

POEMS THAT ILLUSTRATE THE "TURNING OF LINES"

"Poppies" by Mary Oliver
"Silver Star" by William Stafford
"Traveling Through the Dark" by William Stafford
"Emily Dickinson's To-Do List" by Andrea Carlisle
"Sonnet" by Billy Collins
 "A New Poet" by Linda Pastan
"This Is Just to Say" by William Carlos Williams

163

Poetry Connections: Supporting Students as They Read and Write Poetry

I want students to build on their "finding poetry everywhere" experience by continuing to examine the myriad ways poetry is part of their daily lives. In support of this, I offer the following teaching strategies.

Teaching Strategy: Poetry in Film

There are a number of films that portray the power of poetry. A favorite film of mine is *Dead Poets Society,* which has several poetry scenes, including the tearing out of the textbook section that describes "graphing poetry" to determine its greatness. In *10 Things I Hate About You,* which is based on Shakespeare's *Taming of the Shrew,* Julia Stiles, who plays the main character, shares her poem about lost love in English class, surprising the entire class with her vulnerability. (This clip is available at YouTube.com. Type in the film title *10 Things I Hate About You* and look for the clip with the photo of Julia Stiles standing in the classroom.) My son, John, shared with me that his writing workshop teacher, David Frick, used a clip from the film *Before Sunrise* to illustrate poetry. In the clip, a guy comes up to Ethan Hawke and Julie Delpy, the actors who star in the film, and says if they give him a word, he can write a poem about it. They provide him with the word *milkshake* and on the spot, a poem is born. My son appreciates how this clip shows a poem can be written about anything. (The clip from *Before Sunrise* is also available at YouTube.com. Type in the film title *Before Sunrise* and scroll down for the clip titled "Delusion Angel.")

Teaching Strategy: Music Video as Poetry Analysis

A class of juniors and I were immersed in reading Emily Dickinson's poem "Because I Could Not Stop for Death." As we wrestled with the images in the first stanza, of Death and Immortality in the carriage, I asked, "So, if you were making a video of this poem, what would Death and Immortality be wearing?" A lively conversation ensued that resulted in the on-spot assignment of sketching out or storyboarding a music video of Dickinson's poem. In the process, students brought the poem's images to life: school recess, fields of gazing grain, the narrator of the poem in a flowing "gossamer gown" with a "tulle" scarf. (I see Stevie Nicks singing "Landslide" every time I read this poem.) As groups shared their ideas for costuming, setting, and the music that would accompany the reading of the poem, Dickinson's poem took on new meaning.

Our exploration of Dickinson's poetry, including the music video, preceded our study of Walt Whitman, so we had already begun discussions of reading strategies and poetry's craft. I studied Whitman in college and remembered intense discussions of his use of free verse and how his poems addressed issues of sexuality. So when I saw a section on Whitman's poetry in the anthology I was required to use for junior English, I was not sure how to invite students into his work.

Teaching Strategy: Live the Lines

I decided we would just dive in rather than spending time talking about Whitman, and I chose to use an excerpt from Whitman's "Song of Myself, Section 1." I wanted to see what questions students would ask about him after they read some of his work.

From Song of Myself

1

I celebrate myself and sing myself,
And what I assume you shall assume,
For every atom belonging to me as good belongs to you.

I loaf and invite my soul,
I lean and loaf at my ease observing a spear of summer grass.

My tongue, every atom of my blood, form'd from this soil, this air,
Born here of parents born here from parents the same, and their parents the
same,
I, now, thirty-seven years old in perfect health begin,
Hoping to cease not till death.

Creeds and schools in abeyance,
Retiring back a while sufficed at what they are, but never forgotten,
I harbor for good or bad, I permit to speak at every hazard,
Nature without check with original energy. . . .

We began by reading the poem together. I read the poem aloud and students followed along. I then invited a volunteer to read the poem again so we could hear

165

it in another voice. I asked students to read the poem a third time and mark and jot down lines that struck them—lines that intrigued them, resonated with them, or confused them. We began our discussion with these student-identified lines.

"I loaf and invite my soul" was a line identified by a number of students. "What does it mean?" they asked.

I responded with a question: "What do you think it means?"

Silence filled the room. I waited; more seconds ticked by. I invited students to look at the next line in the poem, "I lean and loaf at my ease observing a spear of summer grass." Does this line provide you with any insight about what Whitman means by "loaf and invite my soul"?

Again the room was silent; heads were down, avoiding eye contact. I was surprised by their resistance to even venture a guess about this line. So I decided that rather than my telling them what I thought the line meant, I would invite students to experience Whitman's line. Their homework was to live the line—to "loaf and invite" their souls and to come to class prepared to write about what they did and how their experience gave meaning to the line.

It's fair to say students' response was less than enthusiastic. They began peppering me with questions, which I deflected with the response, "It's up to you to decide what you think 'loaf and invite' your soul means. I will be trying this with you and we'll talk tomorrow." And then the bell rang.

That night as I prepared for class I wasn't sure I knew what it meant to "loaf and invite" my soul. It seemed to me that being alone in some place quiet was key, so I curled up in an armchair in my bedroom, away from my family. I closed my eyes and took deep breaths. After a few minutes of settling, I turned my attention to the window. Although it was dark, the moon illuminated the lawn. I observed the shape of the bushes just outside the window, the shadows cast by the large walnut tree near the deck, and the sparkle of stars in the sky. I could feel myself relaxing as I continued to take in the sights that existed just outside my window. It was as if I was seeing them for the first time. Whitman's lines popped into my head: "I loaf and invite my soul/I lean and loaf at my ease observing a spear of summer grass." I felt at ease as I leaned and loafed at my bedroom window, observing the backyard.

The next day in class I asked students to write about their efforts to "loaf and invite" their souls by responding to the following questions:

- Describe what you did to "loaf and invite" your soul.
- What did you learn/discover?
- What do you think Walt Whitman means by this line?
- How could/do you "celebrate" yourself?

I expected to be peppered with questions and disclaimers about why they hadn't done this assignment, but the room was silent except for the sound of pens scratching words on paper.

After ten to twelve minutes of writing, I invited students to share what they had done to "loaf and invite" their souls. They shared stories of quiet observation; several noted how the almost-full moon helped them "observe the night." One student shared that he fell asleep. Students in the class challenged him, concluding that "to loaf and invite" your soul you had to be conscious, not asleep. I was stunned when he asked me if he could redo the assignment.

Students' in-class writing in response to my questions was compelling reading. I was heartened by their good-faith efforts to "loaf and invite" their souls and how this experience supported their analysis of the poem's lines.

Scott wrote: "I laid on my bed and relaxed. I thought of how to invite my soul. I invited my soul to be free, free from the worries of the day, and the pressure of trying to just get by." He went on to write, "I invited my soul as if talking to myself, on the inside . . . To rest, to wonder and think."

Jennifer shared her experience of staring out her bedroom window at the "stars and almost full moon." She went on to describe how she thought about her future and the career options she could pursue. And she concluded her in-class writing by noting, "I think I invited my soul because life seemed a lot more clear and I felt a certain bond and closeness with myself, like I took time to really think about myself instead of others. It was like becoming friends with a stranger."

This "loaf and invite" assignment opened a door into this poem. Students were no longer hesitant to dive into Whitman's poem. They concluded that "loaf and invite" meant to be willing to step back, slow down, and really listen to one's inner voice. They also noted how nature supported their efforts, seeing the connection between their own experiences and Whitman's "lean and loaf at my ease observing a spear of summer grass."

Teaching Strategy: Poem as Mentor/Inspiration

We worked our way through the rest of the poem, and students continued to explain Whitman's words by connecting the poem to their own lives. I invited students to build on their "loaf and invite" experience and our discussion and use Whitman's "song" as a mentor poem for their own "song." I asked them to draft a "Song of Myself" using as much or as little of Whitman's format and word choice as they wanted. I provided class time for this writing and joined them in the effort. My poem, "Song of a Weary English Teacher," used lines from Whitman's poem and contrasted my own busy life with his "loaf and ease."

> *"I loaf and invite my soul"*
> *Loaf? With two meetings and three stacks of papers to grade?*
> *Loaf? With lessons to plan and Xeroxing awaiting?*
> *Oh, my soul sends its regrets till June.*

Just before class ended I asked volunteers to share lines from their draft poems. Almost every student read.

Students were given the choice to continue working on their songs of self using Whitman's poem as their inspiration or to try their hand at using another mentor poem, drawing on Whitman or Dickinson. The assignment was framed as follows:

Using Emily Dickinson or Walt Whitman as your inspiration/mentor, write your own poem. Some suggestions:

"Your Letter to the World"

"Song of Your Self"

"I Hear [name of your school/town] Singing"

"Hope Is"

The majority of students chose to take their "Song of Self" poems to final draft. The results were delightful. Jennifer began her poem with

> *I celebrate and share myself*
> *With a world that is lost and cold*
> *I am opening my soul*
> *For all to see everything that is truly me.*

Trish also utilized Whitman's lines in singing her song of a soccer player:

I run and become one with my soul
I run and kick at my ease
Observing your every move.

My moves, every structure
Of my skills, form'd from
this turf, this atmosphere . . .

I, now, 16 years of age begin,
Hoping to play until I can
No more.

Whitman was no longer an intimidating poet who looked like Santa Claus and wrote free verse poetry; he was Walt. Students had lived his words and discovered how his words and structure could support them in finding their own voices as poets.

Final Thoughts on Poetry

It's my hope that students will discover, or rediscover, poetry's value in their lives. I was fortunate to have a student speak to this goal years later when I ran into her while shopping. I was standing in a checkout line at the local Target store when the woman in front of me turned and said with surprise, "Oh, it's you." I did not recognize her but noted she had a cart containing two small children and was carrying a baby. She went on, "I don't know if you remember me but you were my freshman English teacher." I smiled and nodded while searching her face and my memory banks to see if I could place her. And then to my surprise and delight she added, "And, Mrs. Campbell, because of you, I love poetry." My eyes welled with tears as I gave her a quick hug. "Thank you so much for sharing this with me. I am thrilled to know you love poetry."

I recognize this student doesn't represent all my students, but her words serve as a reminder to me that I have the opportunity to create a classroom where students can learn to love poetry, or at least like it. And it's my hope that this chapter will build on the ways you are already doing the important work of helping students discover how poetry gives voice to their lives.

169

WORKS CITED

Allen, Dick. 2003. "April 16: 'Time to Hear Ourselves Think.'" In *Poetry Daily: 366 Poems from the World's Most Popular Poetry Website*, ed. Diane Boller, Don Selby, and Chryss Yost. Naperville, IL: Sourcebook.

Angelou, Maya. 1996. "Yes, You Can Be a Poet." *react*, Jan. 29–Feb. 4.

Annucci, Marilyn. 2003. "March 14: 'Wrecked World.'" In *Poetry Daily: 366 Poems from the World's Most Popular Poetry Website*, ed. Diane Boller, Don Selby, and Chryss Yost. Naperville, IL: Sourcebook.

Atwell, Nancie. 1991. "Finding Poetry Everywhere." In *Side by Side: Essays on Teaching to Learn*. Portsmouth, NH: Heinemann.

Bishop, Elizabeth. 1983. "The Fish." In *The Complete Poems: 1927–1979*. New York: Farrar, Straus and Giroux.

Brooks, Gwendolyn. 2005. "We Real Cool." In *The Essential Gwendolyn Brooks*, ed. Elizabeth Alexander. New York: The Library of America.

Burlingame, Robert. 1996. "small poems." In *I Feel a Little Jumpy Around You: Paired Poems by Men and Women*, ed. Naomi Shihab Nye and Paul B. Janeczko. New York: Aladdin.

Carlisle, Andrea. 1996. "Emily Dickinson's To-Do List." In *I Feel a Little Jumpy Around You: Paired Poems by Men and Women*, ed. Naomi Shihab Nye and Paul B. Janeczko. New York: Aladdin.

Carlson, Elizabeth. 2003. "Imperfection." In *Teaching with Fire: Poetry that Sustains the Courage to Teach*, ed. Sam M. Intrator and Megan Scribner. San Francisco: Jossey-Bass.

Collins, Billy. 2001. "The History Teacher." In *Sailing Around the Room: New and Selected Poems*. New York: Random House.

——. 2001. "Introduction to Poetry." In *Sailing Around the Room: New and Selected Poems*. New York: Random House.

——. "Sonnet." In *Sailing Around the Room: New and Selected Poems*. New York: Random House.

——. 2002. "Poetry." In *Nine Horses*. New York: Random House.

*Connolly, Geraldine. 1998. "The Summer I Was Sixteen." In *Province of Fire*. Oak Ridge, TN: Iris Press.

Dickinson, Emily. 2000. "Fame Is a Fickle Food." In *Emily Dickinson's Poems*, ed. Johanna Brownell. Edison, NJ: Castle Books.

——. 2000. "Hope Is the Thing with Feathers." In *Emily Dickinson's Poems*, ed. Johanna Brownell. Edison, NJ: Castle Books.

——. 2000. "This Is My Letter to the World." In *Emily Dickinson's Poems*, ed. Johanna Brownell. Edison, NJ: Castle Books.

* Dobyns, Stephen. 1988. "Loud Music." In *Cemetery Nights*. London: Penguin.

Dove, Rita. 1999. "Vacation." In *The New Breadloaf Anthology of Contemporary American Poetry*, ed. Michael Collier and Stanley Plumly. Hanover, NH: Middlebury College Press.

Drake, Barbara. 1978. "What a Relief." In *Love at the Egyptian Theatre: Poems by Barbara Drake*. East Lansing, MI: Red Cedar Press.

Dunbar, Paul Laurence. 1993. "We Wear the Mask." In *The Collected Poetry of Paul Lawrence Dunbar*, ed. Joanne Braxton. Charlottesville: University Press of Virginia.

Eliot, T. S. 1939. "Gus." In *Old Possum's Book of Practical Cats*. New York: Harcourt Brace Jovanovich.

———.1973. "The Love Song of J. Alfred Prufrock." In *The Norton Anthology of Modern Poetry*, ed. Richard Ellman and Robert O'Clair. New York: Norton.

Flynn, Nick, and Shirley McPhillips. 2000. *A Note Slipped Under the Door: Teaching from Poems We Love*. York, ME: Stenhouse.

Forhan, Chris. 2000. "Gouge, Adze, Rasp, Hammer." *New England Review* 21: 4.

Frost, Robert. 1973. "Stopping by Woods on a Snowy Evening." In *The Norton Anthology of Modern Poetry*, ed. Richard Ellman and Robert O'Clair. New York: Norton.

———.1973. "The Road Not Taken." In *The Norton Anthology of Modern Poetry*, ed. Richard Ellman and Robert O'Clair. New York: Norton.

Halperin, Mark. 2003. "February 12: 'Tulips.'" In *Poetry Daily: 366 Poems from the World's Most Popular Poetry Website,* ed. Diane Boller, Don Selby, and Chryss Yost. Naperville, IL: Sourcebook.

Harrison, Jeffrey. 1999. "Family Dog." In *The New Breadloaf Anthology of Contemporary American Poetry*, ed. Michael Collier and Stanley Plumly. Hanover, NH: Middlebury College Press.

*———.2001. "Our Other Sister: For Ellen." In *Feeding the Fire*. Louisville, KY: Sarabande Books.

Heard, Georgia. 1989. *For the Good of the Earth and Sun: Teaching Poetry*. Portsmouth, NH: Heinemann.

Hirsch, Edward. 1990. "Fast Break: In Memory of Dennis Turner, 1914–1984." In *Wild Gratitude*. New York: Knopf.

* Hodgen, John. 2000. "Forgiving Buckner." *FIELD: Contemporary Poetry and Poetics,* 62, Spring.

Hughes, Langston. 2003. "Dream Deferred." In *Teaching with Fire: Poetry That Sustains the Courage to Teach*, ed. Sam M. Intrator and Megan Scribner. San Francisco: Jossey-Bass.

———. "Mother to Son." In *Teaching with Fire: Poetry That Sustains the Courage to Teach*, ed. Sam M. Intrator and Megan Scribner. San Francisco: Jossey-Bass.

*Kenyon, Jane. 1996. "The Blue Bowl." In *Otherwise: New and Selected Poems*. St. Paul, MN: Graywolf Press.

Kingsolver, Barbara. 2003. "Beating Time." In *Teaching with Fire: Poetry That Sustains the Courage to Teach*, ed. Sam M. Intrator and Megan Scribner. San Francisco: Jossey-Bass.

*Kooser, Ted. 1980. "Selecting a Reader." In *Sure Signs*. Pittsburgh, PA: University of Pittsburgh Press.

Levertov, Denise. 1983. "A Day Begins." In *Denise Levertov Poems 1960–1967*. New York: New Directions.

———.1983. "The Secret." In *Denise Levertov Poems 1960–1967*. New York: New Directions.

Merriam, Eve. 1967. "Cheers." In *Reflections on a Gift of Watermelon Pickle*, ed. Stephen Dunning. New York: HarperTeen,

———. 2006. "How to Eat a Poem." In *How to Eat a Poem: A Smorgasbord of Tasty and Delicious Poems for Young Readers*, ed. American Poetry and Literacy Project and the Academy of American Poets. New York: Dover.

Murray, Joan. 1999. "Her Head." In *Looking for the Parade*. New York: W. W. Norton.

171

Neruda, Pablo. 2003. "The Poet's Obligation." In *Teaching with Fire: Poetry That Sustains the Courage to Teach*, ed. Sam M. Intrator and Megan Scribner. San Francisco: Jossey-Bass.

Nye, Naomi Shihab. 1995. "The Art of Disappearing." In *Words Under the Words: Selected Poems*. Portland, OR: Far Corner Books.

———. 1995. "Kindness." In *Words Under the Words: Selected Poems*. Portland, OR: Far Corner Books.

———. 1996. "Elevator." In *I Feel a Little Jumpy Around You: Paired Poems by Men and Women*, ed. Naomi Shihab Nye and Paul B. Janeczko. New York: Aladdin.

———. 1998. "The Rider." In *Fuel: Poems by Naomi Shihab Nye*. Rochester, NY: Boa Editions.

Oliver, Mary. 1992. "Alligator Poem." In *New and Selected Poems*. Boston: Beacon Press.

———. 1992. "Learning About the Indians." In *New and Selected Poems*. Boston: Beacon Press.

———. 1992. "Poppies." In *New and Selected Poems*. Boston: Beacon Press.

*———. 1992. "The Summer Day." In *New and Selected Poems*. Boston: Beacon Press.

———. 1992. "Wild Geese. " In *New and Selected Poems*. Boston: Beacon Press.

———. 1992. "Winter." In *New and Selected Poems*. Boston: Beacon Press.

———. 1994. *A Poetry Handbook: A Prose Guide to Understanding Poetry*. San Francisco: Harvest Original.

Ostroff, Anthony. 1975. "About Long Days." In *Modern Poetry of Western America*, ed. Clinton F. Larson and William Stafford. Provo, UT: Brigham Young University Press.

* Pastan, Linda. 1991. "A New Poet." In *Heroes in Disguise*. New York: W. W. Norton.

———. 1996. "Elegy." In *I Feel a Little Jumpy Around You: Paired Poems by Men and Women*, ed. Naomi Shihab Nye and Paul B. Janeczko. New York: Aladdin.

Piercy, Marge. 2003. "To Be of Use." In *Teaching with Fire: Poetry That Sustains the Courage to Teach*, ed. Sam M. Intrator and Megan Scribner. San Francisco: Jossey-Bass.

Poe, Edgar Allan. 1984. "The Bells." In *The Complete Stories and Poems of Edgar Allan Poe*. New York: Doubleday.

———. 1984. "The Raven." In *The Complete Stories and Poems of Edgar Allan Poe*. New York: Doubleday.

* Roethke, Theodore. 1983. "The Bat." In *Collected Poems of Theodore Roethke*. New York: Anchor Books.

* Ruefle, Mary. 2001. "The Hand" In *Cold Pluto*. Pittsburgh, PA: Carnegie Mellon University Press.

Salerno, Joe. 2003. "October 3: 'Poetry Is the Art of Not Succeeding.'" In *Poetry Daily: 366 Poems from the World's Most Popular Poetry Website,* ed. Diane Boller, Don Selby, and Chryss Yost. Naperville, IL: Sourcebook.

Sandburg, Carl. 2003. "Chicago." In *The Complete Poems of Carl Sandburg*. Orlando, FL: Harcourt.

———. 2003. "Jazz Fantasia." In *The Complete Poems of Carl Sandburg*. Orlando, FL: Harcourt.

Sarton, May. 1993. "Now I Become Myself." In *Collected Poems 1930–1983*. New York: W. W. Norton.

Sears, Peter. 1978. "Accident." In *I Want to Be a Crowd: Poems and Commentary*. Portland, OR: Breitenbush.

Sexton, Anne. 1991. "Young." In *Preposterous: Poems of Youth*, ed. Paul B. Janeczko. New York: Orchard Books.

——. 2003. "Courage." In *Teaching with Fire: Poetry That Sustains the Courage to Teach*, ed. Sam M. Intrator and Megan Scribner. San Francisco: Jossey-Bass.

* Sheehan, Julie. 2004. "Hate Poem." *PLEIADES*, 24: 2.

Shelton, Richard. 1975. "Seven Preludes to Silence." In *Modern Poetry of Western America*, ed. Clinton F. Larson and William Stafford. Provo, UT: Brigham Young University Press.

Silverstein, Shel. 2004. Anniversary ed. *Where the Sidewalk Ends*. New York: HarperCollins.

Soto, Gary. 2003. "Saturday at the Canal." In *Teaching with Fire: Poetry That Sustains the Courage to Teach*, ed. Sam M. Intrator and Megan Scribner. San Francisco: Jossey-Bass.

Stafford, William. 1996. "Silver Star." In *Even in Quiet Places: Poems by William Stafford*. Lewiston, ID: Confluence Press.

——. 1999. "The Trouble with Reading." In *The Way It Is: New and Selected Poems*. St. Paul, MN: Graywolf Press.

——. 1999. "Traveling Through the Dark." In *The Way It Is: New and Selected Poems*. St. Paul, MN: Graywolf Press.

——. 1999. "You Reading This, Be Ready." In *The Way It Is: New and Selected Poems*. St. Paul, MN: Graywolf Press.

Taylor, Patrick. 2003. "February 1: 'Lighting Up Time.'" In *Poetry Daily: 366 Poems from the World's Most Popular Poetry Website*, ed. Diane Boller, Don Selby, and Chryss Yost. Naperville, IL: Sourcebook.

Veinberg, Jon. 2003. "March 25: 'Last Shot.'" In *Poetry Daily: 366 Poems from the World's Most Popular Poetry Website*, ed. Diane Boller, Don Selby, and Chryss Yost. Naperville, IL: Sourcebook.

* Wayman, Tom. 1993. "Did I Miss Anything?" In *Did I Miss Anything? Selected Poems 1973–1993*. Madeira Park, BC: Harbour.

Webb, Charles Harper. 1991. "The Time We Cherry-Bombed the Toilet at the River Oaks." In *Preposterous: Poems of Youth*, ed. Paul B. Janeczko. New York: Orchard Books.

Whitman, Walt. 1959. "I Hear America Singing." In *Complete Poetry and Prose by Walt Whitman*, ed. James Miller Jr. Boston: Houghton Mifflin.

——. 1959. "I Sit and Look Out." In *Complete Poetry and Prose by Walt Whitman*, ed. James Miller Jr. Boston: Houghton Mifflin.

——. 1959. "Song of Myself, Part I." In *Complete Poetry and Prose by Walt Whitman*, ed. James Miller Jr. Boston: Houghton Mifflin.

*Williams, Miller. 2003. "February 6: 'Love Poem with Toast.'" In *Poetry Daily: 366 Poems from the World's Most Popular Poetry Website*, ed. Diane Boller, Don Selby, and Chryss Yost. Naperville, IL: Sourcebook.

Williams, William Carlos. 1991. "Poem." In *The Collected Poems of William Carlos Williams, Vol. I: 1909–1939*, ed. A Walton Litz and Christopher MacGowan. New York: New Directions.

——. 1991. "This Is Just to Say." In *The Collected Poems of William Carlos Williams, Vol. I: 1909–1939*, ed. A Walton Litz and Christopher MacGowan. New York: New Directions.

* *Indicates poems that can be found on the Poetry 180 website: http://www.loc.gov/poetry/180*

RECOMMENDED RESOURCES IN SUPPORT OF TEACHING POETRY

Poetry Collections

Boller, Diane, Don Selby, and Chryss Yost, eds. 2003. *Poetry Daily: 366 Poems from the World's Most Popular Poetry Website.* Naperville, IL: Sourcebook.

Brewbaker, James, and Dawnelle J. Hyland, eds. 2002. *Poems by Adolescents and Adults: A Thematic Collection for Middle and High School.* Urbana, IL: National Council of Teachers of English.

Collier, Michael, and Stanley Plumly, eds. 1999. *The New Breadloaf Anthology of Contemporary American Poetry.* Hanover, NH: Middlebury College Press.

Drake, Barbara. *Love at the Egyptian Theatre: Poems by Barbara Drake.* East Lansing, MI: Red Cedar Press.

Janeczko, Paul B., ed. 1991. *Preposterous: Poems of Youth.* New York: Orchard Books.

Kenyon, Jane. 1996. *Otherwise: New and Selected Poems.* St. Paul, MN: Graywolf Press.

Larson, Clinton F. and William Stafford. 1975. *Modern Poetry of Western America.* Provo, UT: Brigham Young University Press.

Nye, Naomi Shihab. 1998. *Fuel: Poems by Naomi Shihab Nye.* Rochester, NY: Boa Editions.

Nye, Naomi Shibab, and Paul B. Janeczko. 1996. *I Feel a Little Jumpy Around You: Paired Poems by Men and Women.* New York: Aladdin.

Oliver, Mary. 1992. *New and Selected Poems.* Boston: Beacon Press.

Palmer, Parker J., and Tom Vander Ark, eds. 2003. *Teaching with Fire: Poetry That Sustains the Courage to Teach.* San Francisco: Jossey-Bass.

Piercy, Marge. 1992. *Mars and Her Children.* New York: Random House.

Wayman, Tom. 1993. *Did I Miss Anything? Selected Poems 1973–1993.* Madeira Park, BC: Harbour.

Books and Articles

Creech, Sharon. 2001. *Love That Dog: A Novel.* New York: HarperTrophy. A story of discovery and poetry in the classroom.

Eisenkraft, Stacey L. 1999. "Uncovering Voices: Middle School Poetry Anthologies." *Teaching and Learning: The Journal of Natural Inquiry* 14 (1): 24–33.

Flynn, Nick, and Shirley McPhillips. 2000. *A Note Slipped Under the Door: Teaching from Poems We Love.* York, ME: Stenhouse.

Heard, Georgia. 1989. *For the Good of the Earth and Sun: Teaching Poetry.* Portsmouth, NH: Heinemann.

Jago, Carol. 1999. *Nikki Giovanni in the Classroom.* Urbana, IL: National Council of Teachers of English.

Michaels, Judith Rowe. 1999. *Risking Intensity: Reading and Writing Poetry with High School Students.* Urbana, IL: National Council of Teachers of English.

Oliver, Mary. 1994. *A Poetry Handbook: A Prose Guide to Understanding Poetry.* San Francisco: Harvest Original.

Websites

Poetry 180 website: http://www.loc.gov/poetry/180

CHAPTER 7

Children's Literature and Picture Books

*Fine picture books exert a far more subtle influence in the
formation of reading habits than it is possible to estimate,
for their integrity is unshakeable.*

–ANNE CARROLL MOORE

"Please read us *Green Eggs and Ham*, Mrs. Campbell, please!" I was surprised by this request, which came from high school seniors during the
second week of class after I read aloud to them as an opening for reading
workshop. I acquiesced and read it to them the next week during my read-aloud
opener to reading workshop. As I read I found myself delighting in the rhyme
scheme, repetition, and illustrations. When I finished reading, thirty-six seniors
were eager to share their stories of Dr. Seuss and other favorites. I watched in
amazement as the room filled with laughter and glee as students connected
around favorite books. Our conversation served to open up communication
about the importance of reading and rereading books we adore. The discussion
also resulted in a number of students trying their hands at writing children's

175

books. Our community of readers was built on a foundation of shared children's literature.

Jamie Williams, a third-year teacher who works with high school students who are learning English or have been identified as struggling readers, finds children's literature is the invitation to reading her students need. She shares her own passion for children's literature by reading her favorite, *Where the Wild Things Are*. This reading inspires an ongoing sharing of favorite books.

Williams is not alone in her discovery of children's books' power to reach students. In a study of struggling adolescent readers, researchers found that focusing on children's literature resulted in increased motivation and in students' not only activating their early memories of reading but also seeing children's literature with new eyes.

> *Students' (re)interpretations of the children's books were revealing. . . . It was not surprising that students related the message of the book to their current circumstances, not to their childhood. For example, when reading and rereading* The Cat in the Hat, *students often identified with the cat as a trickster who does whatever he wants whenever he wants. (Taylor and Nesheim 2000/2001, 310)*

But children's literature is not just for struggling readers. This literature serves the needs of all adolescent readers. Reconnecting students with the literature from their childhood allows them to reconnect with why they like to read. It is important to create a classroom where reading children's literature is presented as a genre study of literature. As Jamie Williams notes, children's books have the same elements as short stories, poetry, or nonfiction, but their accessibility "levels the playing field for students and also reconnects them with the excitement of story-time" (2006).

A number of teachers I spoke with touted the value of reading children's books to open or close class. This reading can be connected to genre or theme study (which is how the next section of the chapter is arranged), or as Williams notes, "I read children's books for sheer pleasure. I want to expose students to as much written work as possible" (2006). All of the children's books listed here by genre or theme work well for sheer pleasure class read-alouds, but I have also put together a list of top ten children's books to read aloud gleaned from my experience and from recommendations from middle school and high school students (see sidebar).

TOP TEN CHILDREN'S BOOK READ-ALOUDS

AUTHOR/ILLUSTRATOR	TITLE
Maurice Sendak	Where the Wild Things Are
Dr. Seuss with help from Jack Prelutsky and Lane Smith	Hooray for Diffendoofer Day
Judith Viorst/Ray Cruz	Alexander and the Terrible, Horrible, No Good, Very Bad Day
Jon Scieszka/Lane Smith	The True Story of the Three Little Pigs!
Jon Scieszka/Lane Smith	The Stinky Cheese Man and Other Fairly Stupid Tales
Dr. Seuss	Oh, the Places You'll Go!
Mike Thaler/Jared Lee	The Teacher from the Black Lagoon
Diane Stanley	Rumpelstiltskin's Daughter
Jerry Seinfeld/James Bennett	Halloween
Byrd Baylor/Peter Parnall	The Other Way to Listen

Because children's books are accessible, students can read these texts to practice collaboration skills in support of literature circles, examine genre, explore themes, and analyze literary craft.

Children's Books in Support of Collaborative Literary Circles

Literature circles: in my mind I picture groups of students engaged in meaningful conversation about a book they have all read. The reality of literature circles in my classroom did not always reflect this ideal. Yes, students were in groups and were engaged in conversation, but it was not always about the book they had read.

I have learned from my interventions with literature circle groups that were off topic that accessible text and modeling strategies to support conversations about books are two keys to achieving successful literature circles. Children's books meet the requirement of accessibility and, as noted in this chapter's introduction, children's books invite students to respond to the story through storytelling of their own.

In support of children's books literature circles I typically select a theme to explore (see later sections of this chapter for more on children's books and

177

themes). I provide time in class for students to peruse children's books that reflect the theme. In an ideal world I would have several copies of each book, but it also works to have students in a literature circle share a copy of a children's book. After students have had class time to skim through the book selections I ask them to list their top three choices along with a reason for each choice. The rationale portion of this list is good data for me regarding what students know and understand from their initial skimming of the texts. It also helps me create groups made up of students who have some interest in the book. (I learned the hard way that if I don't provide this skimming and selecting time, students will pick groups based on who is in the group rather than what the group will be reading.)

After I have formed the literature circle groups based on students' input, we spend class time discussing the literature circle expectations. I want students to understand that they are coming together as a group to engage in conversation about the book, including sharing favorite passages, asking questions, identifying story elements and writing craft, and connecting the text with their own experiences, other texts, and the world.

With children's books, I usually provide time in class for the literature circle group to read the children's book aloud to each other. Depending on the group's reading abilities, I may assign a group reader or leave it up to the group to decide how they want to do the reading. I also require individual written work in preparation for the group discussion. Typically I require each student to select a quote to share, write two questions that the group should discuss, and identify a place in the text where they can make a text-to-text, text-to-self, or text-to-world connection. In support of making connections, Nancy Steineke (2002) prompts students as follows: "What does this book remind you of: another story, novel, personal experience, current event, television, program, play? Jot down one specific connection with detailed notes that explain it" (142). I find that requiring students to bring this preparatory writing to the literature circle discussion provides a starting point for conversations and allows me to assess individual students' understanding of the reading.

In addition to the written work that students generate, I usually provide groups with a note-taking format so I have a written record of the group conversation. I ask that students rotate note-taking duty so that one student doesn't spend the entire group meeting time writing. If needed, I will bring in a timer and set it for five-to-ten-minute intervals to remind students to switch note takers.

178

The note-taking format includes questions that build on the students' written preparation as well as reflective questions about their group process:

Questions About the Text:

- List a quote or passage from the book that illustrates the author's writing style. What did your group notice/appreciate about this quote?
- Think about point of view: Who is telling the story in your book? How do you think the story would change if it was told from a different point of view?
- What is the message or theme of this book?
- Think about audience: What is the age range you would recommend for this book? Why?

Group Process Questions:
- List something you did well as a group.
- Describe something you did less well and how you plan to address this challenge in future literature group discussions.
- If you had $100, how would you allocate this money as compensation for each group member's contribution? (I find this salary-based assessment gleans a more detailed assessment than asking students to grade their group or grade each group member.)

For children's book titles to use in literature circles, see the genre and theme sections of this chapter. For more information on creating, supporting, and assessing literature circles, see the resource list at the end of this chapter.

Children's Books by Genre
Children's books can be taught as a literature unit or they can be used in support of genre literature study.

POETRY
The use of sound devices such as rhyme, onomatopoeia, figurative language, and line breaks in children's books supports an exploration of poetry. For many of the students with whom I worked, their first introduction to poetry was through children's books, nursery rhymes, and Shel Silverstein's *Where the Sidewalk Ends* (2004).

Teaching Strategy: Recognizing Rhyme and Other Sound Devices

I build on students' appreciation of nursery rhymes and Shel Silverstein by using examples from these two favorites to examine rhyme. I've also found that a picture book version of Robert Frost's poem "Stopping by Woods on a Snowy Evening" is an effective way to explore rhyme and the powerful weave of poetry and illustrations (Frost 2001). Emily Dickinson's poetry is also brought to life in picture book form in *Emily Dickinson's Letters to the World* (2002).

In addition to rhyme, I use children's books to support students' recognition of other sound devices: alliteration, repetition, and onomatopoeia. Listed in the sidebar are children's books that can be used in the exploration of sound devices.

CHILDREN'S BOOKS IN SUPPORT OF SOUND DEVICES

AUTHOR/ILLUSTRATOR	TITLE	SOUND DEVICE
Audrey Wood	Silly Sally	*Rhyme*
Linda Williams/Megan Lloyd	The Little Old Lady Who Was Not Afraid of Anything	*Onomatopoeia*
Graeme Base	The Sign of the Seahorse: A Tale of Greed and High Adventure in Two Acts	*Rhyme Alliteration*
Lane Smith	The Happy Hocky Family	*Repetition*
Robert Munsch/Michael Martchenko	Mortimer	*Onomatopoeia Repetition*
Emily Dickinson/Jeanette Winter	Emily Dickinson's Letters to the World	*Rhyme*

NONFICTION

Children's books can also be used to explore nonfiction genres such as biography and memoir or stories on various issues and topics related to curriculum content areas. For purposes of this section, I chose to focus on biography and memoir because this has been my primary use of nonfiction children's books.

Often our exploration of biography and memoir was framed around a topic or theme: writers and heroes are two that frequently come up in middle school and high school curriculums.

Teaching Strategy: Children's Book Biographies and Memoirs About Writers

I am fascinated by the way writers live their lives. I have this fantasy of being a full-time writer, with a large desk near a window and an endless supply of really good coffee. I see myself writing every morning, wearing Nick and Nora pajamas, and then spending the afternoons preparing for appearances at bookstores and of course on *Oprah*. What is interesting about this fantasy is that there are no details of the words I am actually putting on paper, only the details that surround the actual writing process.

Those details of the writing life make for good children's books about writers.

In choosing children's books about writing, I try to find texts by or about authors we will be reading in our literature studies. For example, as part of our exploration of Emily Dickinson, I read the children's book *Emily*, by Michael Bedard, illustrated by Barbara Cooney. Students appreciate knowing that although Emily Dickinson was timid, she was known for lowering gifts of gingerbread to neighborhood children from her second-story window. I also appreciate how the author and illustrator based their book on the visits they made to Emily Dickinson's home in Amherst, Massachusetts. As I write this I am thinking about the possibility of children's books as a genre for research papers!

CHILDREN'S BOOKS ABOUT WRITERS

AUTHOR/ILLUSTRATOR	TITLE	WRITER FOCUS
George Ella Lyon/Chris K. Soentpiet	A Sign	*Story of author's own passion for writing*
Kathryn Lasky/Barry Moser	A Brilliant Stroke: The Making of Mark Twain	*Focuses on how Twain's life experiences were woven into his writing*
Henry David Thoreau; Steven Schner, editor/Peter Fiore	Henry David's House	*Thoreau's writing in picture book form*
Julie Dunlap and Mary Lorbiecki/ Mary Azarian	Louisa May and Mr. Thoreau's Flute	*A story of the young Louisa May and her encounter with Henry David Thoreau*
Cynthia Rylant/Diane Goode	When I Was Young in the Mountains	*Stories of author Cynthia Rylant's childhood*
Thomas Locker and Joseph Bruchac	Rachel Carson: Preserving a Sense of Wonder	*Illustrates Carson's passion for nature and writing*
Edgar Allan Poe and Gris Grimley	Edgar Allan Poe's Tales of Mystery and Madness	*Poe's work in a picture book format*
Emily Dickinson/Jeanette Winter	Emily Dickinson's Letters to the World	*Dickinson's poetry with illustrations*

Teaching Strategy: Children's Books Biographies and Memoirs About Heroes

The number of children's books that tell the story of past and present heroes is impressive. I appreciate how the use of story and artwork bring these people to life. Before we dive into this rich resource, I ask students to list the qualities they associate with heroes. We use their individual lists to compile a class list of heroic qualities. As we read children's books, we reference our list, often finding we need to expand it. This list is also used as we read fictional accounts of heroes.

One of my favorite children's book biographies is *Eleanor* by Barbara Cooney (I note Cooney's role as illustrator for the book *Emily*, described earlier). Cooney shows how Eleanor Roosevelt's loss of her mother at an early age required her to develop strength and courage but also imbued her with compassion and tenacity. These qualities served her well as she took on the role of first lady.

CHILDREN'S BOOKS ABOUT HEROES

AUTHOR/ILLUSTRATOR	TITLE	HERO FOCUS
David Adler/Robert Casilla	A Picture Book of Rosa Parks	*Rosa Parks*
Faith Ringgold	If a Bus Could Talk: The Story of Rosa Parks	*Rosa Parks*
David Adler/Samuel Byrd	A Picture Book of Frederick Douglass	*Frederick Douglass*
Doreen Rappaport/Bryan Collier	Martin's Big Words: The Life of Dr. Martin Luther King, Jr.	*Martin Luther King Jr.*
Patricia Polacoo	Thank You, Mr. Falker	*Committed teacher*
Faith Ringgold	Aunt Harriet's Underground Railroad in the Sky	*Harriet Tubman*

Children's Books by Theme

HOLIDAYS AND CELEBRATIONS

I recognize the challenge of reading and talking about holidays in ways that honor the cultural beliefs of the diverse students in our classrooms. I have found it helpful to include as many different holidays and cultural celebrations as possible in support of being inclusive rather than exclusive.

I begin the exploration of this theme and children's books by inviting students to write about their own holidays and celebrations. We share one to three lines from our writing with the class. I find most of my students are not familiar with lefse, which reflects my Norwegian culture. (For those of you who don't know about lefse, it is a potato flatbread with a tortilla-like texture. It is served in triangular pieces, spread with butter and sugar, and then rolled up and eaten as part of Thanksgiving and Christmas dinner.) Our community stories of holidays and celebrations set the foundation for an exploration of holidays and celebrations through children's books.

Several years ago I was pleased to be introduced to Laurie Halse Anderson's picture book *Thank You, Sarah: The Woman Who Saved Thanksgiving* (2002). I am a fan of Anderson's young-adolescent novels, particularly *Speak*, so I was delighted to find another genre she had authored. I was also delighted to learn the story behind our two-day Thanksgiving holiday, and I find students are interested in knowing the story as well. See the sidebar for children's books that discuss holidays and celebrations.

CHILDREN'S BOOKS ABOUT HOLIDAYS AND CELEBRATIONS

AUTHOR/ILLUSTRATOR	TITLE	HOLIDAY OR CELEBRATION
Jerry Seinfeld/James Bennett	Halloween	*Halloween*
Nancy Luenn/Robert Chapman	Un Regalo Para Abuelita/A Gift for Abuelita: En Celebración Del Día De Los Muertos/Celebrating the Day of the Dead	*Bilingual tale of love and loss centered around the Day of the Dead*
Byrd Baylor/Peter Parnall	I'm in Charge of Celebrations	*Exploration of why we celebrate*
Patricia Polacco	Rechenka's Eggs	*Ukranian Easter eggs*
Richard Ammon/Pamela Patrick	An Amish Wedding	*Amish wedding*
Eric Kimmel	Gershon's Monster: A Story of the Jewish New Year	*Jewish New Year*
Gary Soto	Too Many Tamales	*Southwestern Christmas*

FAMILY AND CULTURE

Children's books often explore families, highlighting unique and even humorous qualities but also illustrating how families from a variety of cultures have so much in common. I am always surprised and delighted by the stories we share in class about our own families after reading children's books describing a variety of families.

Teaching Strategy: Weird Families (Descriptive Detail in Support of Character and Setting)

I have yet to meet a student who doesn't think something about his or her family is weird. I have found that focusing students' attention on the details that make their families unique, even weird, allows us to revisit the power of descriptive detail to show character and setting. This lesson also allows us to discover that all of us have weird families and we can embrace what makes our families unique.

Reading children's books sets the tone for our exploration of families. I begin by reading aloud from Lane Smith's *The Happy Hocky Family* (1993). The stories' repetitive simplicity and use of stick-figure drawings and primary colors draw students in. We laugh aloud at stories of balloons, ants, chores, toys, and Cousin Stinky. Because the illustrations are stick figures, the Hocky family is everyone's family.

We discuss what we know about the Hocky family from the stories and pictures. I build on the details we identify by reading additional stories of family (see the sidebar).

Literature circles work well for exploring families. After reading and discussing *The Happy Hocky Family* and one or two other books, I ask literature circle groups to read several children's books about family. Their task is to capture with words and pictures what is unique to each family and what characteristics are universal across all families. Each literature circle group creates a visual representation of the "Unique" and "Shared" characteristics on butcher paper to share with the class.

As the groups present, I ask students to note the kinds of descriptive details authors use to show us the characters and setting. We note the following:

Characters:

　　Physical description, including hair and clothing

　　Activities

　　Dialogue

Setting:

　　House

　　Car

　　Town

　　Time of year

After generating our lists of shared characteristics, I ask students to list their own families' characteristics and use this list to write or draw a scene or two that would help us see their family or neighborhood. Sharing this writing is voluntary, but it's been my experience that students are eager to share. Because the children's books we have read model how to celebrate and enjoy our families' unique qualities but not to ridicule them, I have only once had to intervene with a student about what he was writing.

185

CHILDREN'S BOOKS THAT ILLUSTRATE FAMILY AND CULTURE

AUTHOR/ILLUSTRATOR	TITLE	FAMILY FOCUS
Audrey Wood	Weird Parents	*Quirky parents and an embarrassed son*
Cynthia Rylant	When I Was Young in the Mountains	*Growing up in Appalachia*
Judith Viorst/Ray Cruz	Alexander and the Terrible, Horrible, No Good, Very Bad Day	*Trials and tribulations of being the youngest on a very bad day*
Carolivia Herron/Joe Cepeda	Nappy Hair	*Uncle Mordecai's story of how Brenda's nappy hair came to be*
Sandra Cisneros	Hairs/Pelitos	*Bilingual story of hair*
Barbara Joosse/R. Gregory Christie	Stars in the Darkness	*Younger brother's story of family dealing with gangs*
Gary Soto	Too Many Tamales	*Daughter "borrows" mother's diamond ring during making of tamales*
Rukhsana Khan/Ronald Himler	The Roses in My Carpet	*Day in the life of a young Afghan in a refugee camp*
Marjorie Weinman Sharmat/Byron Barton	Gila Monsters Meet You at the Airport	*A boy moves from New York to the West*
Byrd Baylor/Peter Parnall	The Table Where Rich People Sit	*Story of a young girl who discovers that enjoyment of nature and the company of family are the real fortune*

READING, WRITING, AND SCHOOL

As I scoured our local library's children's book section in late August, I noted the selection of books about reading, writing, and school. A sign was posted that these books could be checked out only for one week from now until the end of September. I smiled at the thought that there was such an interest in these titles that the kind librarians wanted as many readers as possible to enjoy the books. I thought about the tension level at my own house, where my two teenaged children were preparing for high school: my daughter, a rising freshman, was already nervous about getting lost in the high school. And I noted that my own anxieties about the new school year had triggered nightly teacher dreams, dreams that included hearing my class but not being able to find them, teaching in a hideous prom dress (nine years of being the teacher in charge of prom has its price), and finding myself with a mouth full of gum.

What if I began the school year with children's books about school? What if I focused on books that highlight the joys of reading and writing, the focus of our time together in school? In talking with teachers who have used children's books to start the school year, I am now convinced that the local library is right in wanting to expose as many readers as possible to books that celebrate school and learning.

Teaching Strategy: Building Community with School Stories
I know how important it is to establish relationships with students as individuals and as a group of learners. I also know how much I balk at most community-building activities, including the pony dance, which was part of my daughter's freshman orientation experience. I want to know students and I want them to know me and their classmates through our class work; I want us to share stories.

So I propose opening the first day of class with a children's book and letting students know that the purpose in reading this book is to take them back to their earlier memories of elementary school. Our task will be to listen to the story and then list memories of school that come to mind through the use of the writing prompt "I remember." It's been my experience that at the beginning of the school year prompts that ask for lists encourage students to participate and share. These lists can be used to develop stories of school or in support of students' writing letters of introduction.

There are a number of children's books about school that can be used to tap into students' school memories. I am a fan of *Lilly's Purple Plastic Purse* by Kevin Henkes. I will confess that I look for books about school that emphasize the joys of reading and writing. In Henkes's book, Lilly's teacher provides in-class writing time known as "lightbulb lab." I draw on this reference in my later explanation of the writing we will do in writing workshop (see Chapter 2 for more on this). Listed in the sidebar are children's books about school—and reading and writing— that have received rave reviews from teachers and students.

187

CHILDREN'S BOOKS ABOUT SCHOOL

AUTHOR/ILLUSTRATOR	TITLE	SCHOOL FOCUS
Kevin Henkes	Chrysanthemum	*Learning to like your unique name*
Debra Frasier	Miss Alaineus: A Vocabulary Disaster	*Humbling story of vocabulary*
Sarah Stewart/David Small	The Library	*A love of books*
Sharon Creech/Harry Bliss	A Fine, Fine School	*A cautionary tale of what happens when school is extended to Saturday and focused on learning as hard work*
Sharon Creech	Love That Dog	*The heartfelt story, written in free verse, of how one boy discovers the power and pleasure of poetry*
Laura Numeroff/Felica Bond	If You Take a Mouse to School (English and Spanish versions)	*Humorous tale of a mouse and school*
Mike Thaler/Jared Lee	The Teacher from the Black Lagoon	*Surprising tale of how rumors can create a monster out of any teacher*
Mike Thaler/Jared Lee	The Librarian from the Black Lagoon	*Surprising tale of a librarian who is very different from what the students expected*
Natasha Wing/Mindy Pierce	The Night Before the 100th Day of School	*A humorous story that is a modern twist on Clement C. Moore's classic poem*

LIFE LESSONS

Last fall we lost our beloved cat, Rocky. He was seventeen years old and had lived a rich and full life, but we were still devastated when he died. Later that night I found myself searching my daughter's room for Judith Viorst's book *The 10th Good Thing About Barney*. I read this book every year to my students when I learned that one of them had lost a pet. Stories can bring us comfort and also serve to remind us of the knowledge that we have to deal with life situations.

188

Whether we are dealing with a student's situation, reading literature rich with life lessons (see the "Essays About Finding Our Way in Life" section in Chapter 4), or writing our own stories of advice, children's books are helpful resources. See the sidebar for lists of books that teach life lessons.

CHILDREN'S BOOKS THAT TEACH LIFE LESSONS

AUTHOR/ILLUSTRATOR	TITLE	LIFE LESSON FOCUS
Patricia Polacoo	Thank You, Mr. Falker	*Learning to learn with the help of a committed teacher*
Peggy Rathman	Officer Buckle and Gloria	*Safety tips* *Appreciating our buddies*
Dr. Seuss	Oh, the Places You'll Go!	*Discover your passion as you navigate the ups and downs of life*
Jon Scieszka/Lane Smith	The Stinky Cheese Man and Other Fairly Stupid Tales	*Learning from revised fairy tales*
Jon Scieszka/Lane Smith	Squids Will Be Squids: Fresh Morals, Beastly Fables	*Revised fables with morals*
Byrd Baylor/Peter Parnall	The Table Where Rich People Sit	*Story of a young girl who discovers that enjoyment of nature and the company of family are the real fortune*

SOCIAL JUSTICE

Equity. Justice. Fairness. I want students to grapple with these important concepts. In support of this I provide them with the humorous yet compelling book *Click, Clack, Moo: Cows That Type* by Doreen Cronin (2000). I admire the way this book highlights the power of writing in supporting requests for equitable conditions; in the case of the cows they type a note that reads:

> *Dear Farmer Brown,*
> *The barn is very cold*
> *at night.*
> *We'd like some electric blankets.*
> *Sincerely,*
> *The Cows.*

When Farmer Brown denies the cows' request, they go on strike, leaving a note on the barn door that reads:

> *Sorry.*
> *We're closed.*
> *No milk*
> *today.*

189

As the story continues, the cows become the "spokes-animals" for the chickens, who are also requesting electric blankets. As is the case with most strikes, settlement requires compromise by all parties: cows, chickens, and Farmer Brown.

Students appreciate the humor in this book, but they also are able to identify the issues of reasonable working conditions, forming a group (union) to achieve a goal, strikes, and the power of writing and compromise. Listed in the sidebar are other children's books that address social justice issues. See also the discussion of nonfiction children's books about heroes.

CHILDREN'S BOOKS ON SOCIAL JUSTICE

AUTHOR/ILLUSTRATOR	TITLE	TOPIC
Naomi Shibab Nye	Sitti's Secret	American child writes to president on behalf of her Palestinian grandmother
Florence Perry Heide/Judith Gilliland	Sami and the Time of the Troubles	Boy longs for peace in war-torn Beirut
Gloria Anzaldua/Consuelo Mendez	Friends from the Other Side/Amigos del Otro Lado	Various responses by Mexican immigrants in Texas to "illegals" from Mexico who are arriving in Texas
Barbara Joosse/R. Gregory Christie	Stars in the Darkness	Younger brother's story of older brother's transition into gang
Rukhsana Khan/Ronald Himler	The Roses in My Carpet	Day in the life of a young Afghan in a refugee camp
Ann McGovern/Marni Becker	La Señora de la Caja de Cartón	Story of a homeless woman and two youngsters who come to her aid
Jane Yolen/Barbara Cooney	Letting Swift River Go	Story of government purchase and flooding of town to create Quabbin Reservoir
Deborah Hopkinson/James E. Ransome	Under the Quilt of Night	Story of slave girl and her family escaping using the Underground Railroad
Candice Ransom/Ellen Beier	The Promise Quilt	Story of Southern family during the Civil War
Faith Ringgold	Aunt Harriet's Underground Railroad in the Sky	The fictional characters Cassie and her brother, BeBe, encounter Harriet Tubman and the Underground Railroad
Faith Ringgold	The Invisible Princess	A weave of fairy tale and American history that tells a story of conflict between slaves and their owner

NATURE

My father is a geologist, so I grew up looking at rocks—rocks in the house, the garden, by the side of the road, in the formations that lined the roads winding through the Rocky Mountains, in the volcano park in Hawaii. My father sent one of his favorite rocks, polished smooth by the waters off the coast of the Aleutian Islands, to my daughter for her birthday. She was in preschool and just beginning to discover what my father already knew: everybody needs a rock.

The notion of a special rock, and guidelines for finding such a rock, are explored in Byrd Baylor's book *Everybody Needs a Rock* (1974). I appreciate how this book invites the reader to take a close look at nature by focusing on ten rules for finding a rock. Not only does the book celebrate nature but it also celebrates the importance of a very personal relationship with nature.

I appreciate how children's books use words and pictures to celebrate our relationship with nature. Listed in the sidebar are children's books that focus on nature.

CHILDREN'S BOOKS ON NATURE

AUTHOR/ILLUSTRATOR	TITLE	NATURE FOCUS
Bryd Baylor/Peter Parnall	The Other Way to Listen	*Hearing nature*
Bryd Baylor/Peter Parnall	The Desert Is Theirs	*Relationship between people and the desert*
Cynthia Rylant	In November	*Sensory delights of November*
William Stafford/Debra Frazier	The Animal That Drank Up Sound	*Winter, sound, and the transformation that is spring*
Thomas Locker	Walking with Henry	*Illustrates Henry David Thoreau's writing about nature*
Thomas Locker and Joseph Bruchac	Rachel Carson: Preserving a Sense of Wonder	*Nature through the eyes of Rachel Carson*

191

Children's Books in Support of Literary Craft

SATISFYING ENDINGS

I enjoy picture books because the majority of them have happy endings, and I am always delighted when a children's book ending surprises me. I enjoy sharing with students *The Three Little Wolves and the Big Bad Pig* (Trivizas 1993). Students enjoy seeing the role reversal in this story, and they are surprised by the ending. Instead of the pig eating the wolves or the wolves eating the pig, the wolves discover that they are safest in a house of flowers. When the pig comes to destroy their house he is so taken by the house's fragrant scent that he changes his evil ways and chooses to become a big good pig.

I share several examples of children's book endings with my students. I invite them to categorize endings, as we did with intriguing leads (described in Chapter 3), in hopes they can draw on these categories when considering endings in their own writing. Ralph Fletcher's book *What a Writer Needs* (1993) is a wonderful resource for identifying types of endings and providing suggestions of children's books to share. Some of the "Satisfying Ending Categories" students in my classroom have identified include:

Surprise Ending

Heartfelt Ending

Full Circle or Coming Home Ending

Ironic or Humorous Ending

Lesson Learned Ending

BOOKS WITH SATISFYING ENDINGS

AUTHOR/ILLUSTRATOR	TITLE	TYPE OF ENDING
Doreen Cronin/Betsey Lewin	Click, Clack, Moo: Cows That Type	*Ironic/humorous*
Jerry Seinfeld/James Bennett	Halloween	*Lesson learned*
Kevin Henkes	Chrysanthemum	*Lesson learned*
Cynthia Rylant/Stephen Gammell	The Relatives Came	*Full circle/coming home*
Judith Viorst	Alexander and the Terrible, Horrible, No Good, Very Bad Day	*Full circle/coming home*
Candice Ransom/Ellen Beier	The Promise Quilt	*Heartfelt ending*
Jane Yolen/Diane Stanley	Sleeping Ugly	*Surprise ending*

POINT OF VIEW

Several years ago when I was in a political struggle as a high school principal, I was sharing my story with a veteran principal, hoping he would confirm that I was in the right and my opponents were the bad guys. So I was caught off guard when he asked me, "How would your opponents tell this story? What is their point of view?" I was stunned to realize I had never really considered their point of view. Taking time to consider it provided me with new insights. It didn't turn the situation around—or save my job—but it was a powerful lesson that has caused me to look at point of view with new eyes.

Teaching Strategy: Considering Point of View

I want my students to consider point of view from more than one perspective, in hopes they'll draw on this lesson when faced with their own challenges. So I look for literature that supports an examination of the questions: Who is telling this story? How would it be different if we heard the story from another character?

Jon Scieszka's *The True Story of the Three Little Pigs!* (1989) has served me well in examining point of view questions. In this delightful book with wonderful illustrations by Lane Smith we see the story of the three little pigs from the wolf's point of view. The wolf explains that he is not "bad." He is just a wolf with a bad cold who accidentally "blew down" his pig neighbors' houses and was shocked to find the poor pig's body in the rubble. The wolf explains, "It seemed like a shame to leave a perfectly good ham dinner lying there in the straw. So I ate it up. Think of it as a big cheeseburger just lying there."

I read Scieszka's book aloud to the students. After this first reading I ask them to jot down what they learned about this story from this new perspective of the wolf. I then read the story again, asking students to listen for places in the story they would want to ask follow-up questions of "Alexander T. Wolf." As students share their questions we explore the way the wolf's point of view colors this story. Students raise questions about his reliability as a narrator. We contrast the wolf's story with our recollections of the three little pigs' version of the story. To be sure we are all familiar with this original version, I invite students to share their recollections of the story. And if we have just read *The Three Little Wolves and the Big Bad Pig* (Trivizas 1993) described earlier, we contrast this version. I find students take pride in knowing the story (and those who don't know it can hear it from their peers). I always appreciate it when one of the students asks, "In the

193

original version, do the pigs tell the story or is it a narrator?" This leads us into a deeper discussion of point of view: first- versus third-person.

Scieszka's book provides a way for all the students in a diverse classroom to discuss the story. It's accessible, even fun. And there is much to explore in this "true story." In fact, this story works well for writing a literary essay (see pp. 266–267 of Heather Lattimer's *Thinking Through Genre* [2003]).

Closing Thoughts on Children's Books

As I began researching and writing this chapter, I was struck by the enthusiasm for children's books I felt from teachers and students. Children's books work well in middle school and high school classrooms because we can use their words and pictures to stimulate childhood memories, savor stories, and explore writing elements and craft. The fact that students and teachers have fun in the process is an added bonus. I think the most important reason to include children's books in our middle school and high school classrooms is that these books are a visual reminder of a time in our lives when we delighted in books. Teachers I spoke with described the energy they observed when middle school and high school students were given time to peruse children's books. Of course, they went on to note that this enthusiasm can be short-lived if they do not provide a rationale for why children's books are in the classroom. It's my hope this chapter has provided some rationale as well as some teaching strategies that will allow you to capture students' enthusiasm for children's books and build on it.

WORKS CITED

Adler, David. 1995. *A Picture Book of Frederick Douglass*. New York: Holiday House.

——.1995. *A Picture Book of Rosa Parks*. New York: Holiday House.

Ammon, Richard. 1998. *An Amish Wedding*. New York: Atheneum.

Anderson, Laurie Halse. 2002. *Thank You, Sarah: The Woman Who Saved Thanksgiving*. New York: Simon and Schuster Books for Young Readers.

Anzaldua, Gloria. 1993. *Friends from the Other Side*. San Francisco: Children's Book Press.

Base, Graeme. 1992. *The Sign of the Seahorse: A Tale of Greed and High Adventure in Two Acts*. New York: Henry N. Abrams.

Baylor, Byrd. 1974. *Everybody Needs a Rock*. New York: Aladdin Paperbacks.

——.1978. *The Other Way to Listen*. New York: Atheneum Books for Young Readers.

——.1986. *I'm in Charge of Celebrations*. New York: Charles Scribner's Sons.

——.1987. *The Desert Is Theirs*. New York: Aladdin.

——.1998. *The Table Where Rich People Sit*. Reprint ed. New York: Aladdin.

Bedard, Michael. 1992. *Emily*. New York: Scholastic.

Cisneros, Sandra. 1997. *Hairs/Pelitos*. New York: Dragonfly Books.

Creech, Sharon. 2001. *A Fine, Fine School*. New York: HarperTrophy.

——. 2003. *Love That Dog*. New ed. New York: Longman.

Cronin, Doreen. 2000. *Click, Clack, Moo: Cows That Type*. New York: Simon and Schuster Books for Young Readers.

Dickinson, Emily. 2002. *Emily Dickinson's Letters to the World*. New York: Farrar, Straus and Giroux.

Dunlap, Julie, and Mary Beth Lorbiecki. 2002. *Louisa May and Mr. Thoreau's Flute*. New York: Dial Books.

Fletcher, Ralph. 1993. *What a Writer Needs*. Portsmouth, NH: Heinemann.

Frasier, Debra. 2000. *Miss Alaineus: A Vocabulary Disaster*. New York: Harcourt.

Frost, Robert. 2001. *Stopping by Woods on a Snowy Evening*. New York: Dutton Juvenile.

Heide, Florence Perry, and Judith Heide Gilliland. 1995. *Sami and the Time of the Troubles*. New York: Clarion Books.

Henkes, Kevin. 1991. *Chrysanthemum*. New York: Mulberry Books.

——. 1996. *Lilly's Purple Plastic Purse*. New York: Greenwillow Books.

Herron, Carolivia. 1997. *Nappy Hair*. New York: Alfred A. Knopf.

Hopkinson, Deborah. 2005. *Under the Quilt of Night*. New York: Aladdin.

Joosse, Barbara M. 2002. *Stars in the Darkness*. San Francisco: Chronicle Books.

Khan, Rukhsana. 1998. *The Roses in My Carpet*. New York: Holiday House.

Kimmel, Eric. 2000. *Gershon's Monster: A Story for the Jewish New Year*. New York: Scholastic.

Lasky, Kathryn. 1998. *A Brilliant Streak: The Making of Mark Twain*. Orlando, FL: Harcourt Brace.

Lattimer, Heather. 2003. *Thinking Through Genre: Units of Study in Reading and Writing Workshops 4–12*. Portland, ME: Stenhouse.

Locker, Thomas. 2002. *Walking with Henry*. New York: Fulcrum.

Locker, Thomas, and Joseph Bruchac. 2004. *Rachel Carson: Preserving a Sense of Wonder*. New York: Fulcrum.

Lyon, George Ella. 1998. *A Sign*. New York: Orchard Books.

McGovern, Ann. 1997. *Le Señora de la Caja de Cartón*. New York: Turtle Books.

Munsch, Robert. 1985. *Mortimer*. New York: Annick Press.

Numeroff, Laura. 2003. *If You Take a Mouse to School*. New York: Scholastic.

———. 2003. *If You Take a Mouse to School*. New York: Rayo, Bilingual.

Nye, Naomi Shihab. 1997. *Sitti's Secret*. New York: Aladdin.

———. 1999. *The Invisible Princess*. New York: Crown.

Poe, Edgar Allan, and Gris Grimley. 2004. *Edgar Allan Poe's Tales of Mystery and Madness*. New York: Atheneum.

Polacco, Patricia. 1988. *Rechenka's Eggs*. New York: Philomel Books.

———. 1998. *Thank You, Mr. Falker*. New York: Philomel Books.

Ransom, Candice. 1990. *The Promise Quilt*. New York: Walker.

Rappaport, Doreen. 2001. *Martin's Big Words: The Life of Martin Luther King, Jr.* New York: Hyperion.

Rathman, Peggy. 1995. *Officer Buckle and Gloria*. New York: Scholastic.

Ringgold, Faith. 1995. *Aunt Harriet's Underground Railroad in the Sky*. New York: Dragonfly Books.

———. 1999. *If a Bus Could Talk: The Story of Rosa Parks*. New York: Simon and Schuster Children's Publications.

Rylant, Cynthia. 1985. *The Relatives Came*. New York: Aladdin Paperbacks.

———.1993. *When I Was Young in the Mountains*. New York: Puffin.

———. 2000. *In November*. New York: Harcourt Children's Books.

Scieszka, Jon. 1989. *The True Story of the Three Little Pigs!* New York: Puffin Books.

———.1992. *The Stinky Cheese Man and Other Fairly Stupid Tales*. New York: Scholastic.

———. 2003. *Squids Will Be Squids: Fresh Morals, Beastly Fables*. Reprint ed. New York: Puffin.

Seinfeld, Jerry. 2002. *Halloween*. Boston: A Byron Preiss Book.

Sendak, Maurice. 1963. *Where the Wild Things Are*. New York: HarperTrophy.

Seuss, Dr. 1990. *Oh, the Places You'll Go!* New York: Random House.

Seuss, Dr., Jack Prelutsky, and Lane Smith. 1998. *Hooray for Diffendoofer Day*. New York: Alfred A. Knopf.

Sharmat, Marjorie Weinman. 1980. *Gila Monsters Meet You at the Airport*. New York: Aladdin Paperbacks.

Silverstein, Shel. 2004. *Where the Sidewalk Ends*. Thirtieth anniversary ed. New York: HarperCollins.

Smith, Lane. 1993. *The Happy Hocky Family*. New York: Puffin Books.

Soto, Gary. 1993. *Too Many Tamales*. New York: G. P. Putnam's Sons.

Stafford, William. 1992. *The Animal That Drank Up Sound*. New York: Harcourt, Brace, Jovanovich.

Stanley, Diane. 2002. *Rumpelstiltskin's Daughter*. New York: HarperTrophy.

Steineke, Nancy. 2002. *Reading and Writing Together: Collaborative Literacy in Action.* Portsmouth, NH: Heinemann.

Stewart, Sarah. 1995. *The Library.* New York: A Sunburst Book.

Taylor, S. V., and D. W. Nesheim. 2000/2001. "Making Literacy Real for 'High-Risk' Adolescent Emerging Readers: An Innovative Application of Readers' Workshop." *Journal of Adolescent and Adult Literature* 44 (4): 308–318.

Thaler, Mike. 1989. *The Teacher from the Black Lagoon.* New York: Scholastic.

———. 1997. *The Librarian from the Black Lagoon.* New York: Scholastic.

Thoreau, Henry David, and Steven Schner, ed. 2002. *Henry David's House.* New York: Charlesbridge.

Trivizas, Eugene. 1993. *The Three Little Wolves and the Big Bad Pig.* New York: Margaret K. McElderry Books.

Viorst, Judith. 1972. *Alexander and the Terrible, Horrible, No Good, Very Bad Day.* New York: Aladdin Books.

Williams, Jamie. 2006. Interview with Kimberly Campbell. July 20.

Williams, Linda. 1986. *The Little Old Lady Who Was Not Afraid of Anything.* New York: HarperCollins.

Wing, Natasha. 2005. *The Night Before the 100th Day of School.* New York: Grosset and Dunlap.

Wood, Audrey. 1990. *Weird Parents.* New York: Puffin Books.

———. 1992. *Silly Sally.* New York: Harcourt Brace.

Yolen, Jane. 1992. *Letting Swift River Go.* Boston: Little, Brown.

———. 1997. *Sleeping Ugly.* New York: G. P. Putnam's Sons.

RECOMMENDED RESOURCES IN SUPPORT OF TEACHING CHILDREN'S BOOKS

Children's Books to Have in Your Classroom Library

Cronin, Doreen. 2000. *Click, Clack, Moo: Cows That Type.* New York: Simon and Schuster Books for Young Readers.

Scieszka, Jon. 1992. *The Stinky Cheese Man and Other Fairly Stupid Tales.* New York: Scholastic.

———. 2003. *Squids Will Be Squids: Fresh Morals, Beastly Fables.* Reprint ed. New York: Puffin.

Seinfeld, Jerry. 2002. *Halloween.* Boston: A Byron Preiss Book.

Sendak, Maurice. 1963. *Where the Wild Things Are.* New York: HarperTrophy.

Silverstein, Shel. 2004. *Where the Sidewalk Ends.* Thirtieth anniversary ed. New York: HarperCollins.

Smith, Lane. *The Happy Hocky Family.* New York: Puffin Books.

Viorst, Judith. 1972. *Alexander and the Terrible, Horrible, No Good, Very Bad Day.* New York: Aladdin Books.

———. 1973. *My Mama Says There Aren't Any Zombies, Ghosts, Vampires, Creatures, Demons, Monsters, Fiends, Goblins, or Things.* New York: Aladdin Paperbacks.

197

Books and Articles

Bishop, R. S., and J. Hickman. 1992. "Four or Fourteen or Forty: Picture Books Are for Everyone." In *Beyond Words: Picture Books for Older Readers and Writers*, ed. S. Benedict and L. Carlisle. Portsmouth, NH: Heinemann.

Daniels, Harvey. 2002. *Literature Circles: Voice and Choice in Book Clubs and Reading Groups.* Portland, ME: Stenhouse.

Fletcher, Ralph. 1993. *What a Writer Needs*. Portsmouth, NH: Heinemann.

Giorgis, Cyndi, and Kimberly J. Hartman. 2000. "Using Picture Books to Support Middle School Curricula." *Middle School Journal* 31 (4): 34–41.

Lattimer, Heather. 2003. "Fairy Tale." In *Thinking Through Genre: Units of Study in Reading and Writing Workshops 4–12.* Portland, ME: Stenhouse.

Steineke, Nancy. 2002. *Reading and Writing Together: Collaborative Literacy in Action.* Portsmouth, NH: Heinemann.

CHAPTER 8

Graphic Novels

*Certain books, paintings, films, plays, or pieces of music
can come into your life at just the right place and time, so
that they help you see the world in a different light, and
perhaps affect how you think and feel. I have found that
the same can also be true of the very best graphic novels.*

—PAUL GRAVETT

Graphic novels, which I have been told by the readers who love them are like comic books but longer and tell a more complete story, are new to me. To be honest, this is not a genre I read. It is not a genre I taught when I was a full-time high school teacher. Graphic novels entered my reading world through my son, John.

We read to John when he was little; he had his own library of picture books. But it was comic books that grabbed John's interest. His eyes lit up the first time he saw one, and his collection of comics soon overtook the picture books. My son loved superheroes, and comic books allowed him to read about his passion.

But comic books and superheroes were not part of John's school experience, so he learned early on how to tolerate the school reading he was assigned. In sixth grade I read John's book report on *Of Mice and Men*. As I read, it became clear that my son, the child of an English teacher and voracious reader, had fake-read this book. I asked John two questions that confirmed this for me: Where did this story take place? And what surprised you about the ending? I gave him the lecture about the power of literature to help us see ourselves and the world. He nodded politely. In his face I saw the faces of all the resistant readers I had failed to reach in my high school classroom.

As I read the research about boys and literacy (Newkirk 2002; Smith and Wilhelm 2002) and observed and interviewed John and his friends, I began to understand that my son, like many boys, was in fact a reader. He just didn't like to read the kinds of texts he was assigned in school. John and his friends read magazines, websites, film and music reviews (these reading choices are woven into the earlier chapters of this book), and graphic novels. His admiration for graphic novels was confirmed when John and I visited bookstores; he always went to the graphic novel section, which seemed to double in size between bookstore trips.

So I decided, with John's encouragement, to read a graphic novel. I was overwhelmed. Each page was a swirl of color. I tried to focus on the words but found myself caught up in trying to decide whether to look at the pictures first or the words. I knew the pictures were important and that there was a sequence to follow, but I felt lost. It was like trying to read a new language. I gave up!

But John didn't give up on helping me find my way into graphic novels. He shared with me Howard Zimmerman's *The Best of Ray Bradbury: The Graphic Novel* (2003), which is a collection of Ray Bradbury's short stories that has been recrafted into graphic novel format with Bradbury's enthusiastic support. In the introduction to this graphic novel, Bradbury tells of his own fascination with comics, in particular *Buck Rogers*, and goes on to write about his excitement in writing an introduction to a collection of his own stories told in graphic form: "For I still believe that there's nothing wrong with comics that a good idea and a good presentation can't cure, providing books whereby you yank kids, through excitement, into reading, by gosh, real live books. But you must start somewhere, mustn't you?" (5).

The Bradbury collection was my way into graphic novels, followed by *Persepolis*, a graphic novel by Marjane Satrapi that tells the story of a young woman growing up in Iran before and during the Fundamentalist Revolution. John selected this graphic novel for me because of its simple black-and-white format. After just a few pages I was engrossed in the story and captivated by the weave of words and pictures. I was thrilled that I could finally read this genre, and I recognized that graphic novels require different reading skills, skills that students—and I—needed to develop.

Graphic novels belong in this book on using short text to differentiate literature instruction, and graphic novels belong in our middle school and high school classrooms. The very issues I found challenging, pictures in relationship with text, are invitations for many high school readers. Stephen Krashen would agree. He writes that graphic novels can function as a gateway into reading for reluctant readers (2005).

A Foray into Graphic Novels in the Classroom

I repeatedly tell graduate education students that you cannot teach what you don't do. I had never taught graphic novels, so I knew that before I could write this chapter I would need to experience graphic novels in the classroom. Fortunately I had a colleague, a former graduate student of mine, who was willing, even enthusiastic. Sharon Klin had already included graphic novels in her classroom by offering *Persepolis* as a literature circle choice. She reported that students embraced this choice, and it was particularly helpful for ELL students.

In a questionnaire regarding their choice of *Persepolis* as their literature circle text, students in Sharon's class reported their appreciation for the way the words and pictures in the text worked together to tell the story. As one student wrote, "[Graphic novels] keep us interested in what we are reading instead of reading paragraph after paragraph, and it helps you to see and understand what you are reading."

The literature circle projects students who read *Persepolis* created also serve as compelling evidence that this genre provides students with an accessible read that also supports literary analysis. *Persepolis* readers shared what they learned about Iranian culture, discussed how the author's point of view contributed to but also limited the story, noted the author's writing craft by sharing quotes (and pictures) they admired, and developed new vocabulary based on their reading. Rather than limit literary discussion, *Persepolis* encouraged it across a varied group of readers.

I was excited to have the opportunity to build on the graphic novel work Sharon had done with her students, recognizing that not all of her students had

201

read *Persepolis* but they all had heard the presentation on this text. I arrived on a Thursday morning to talk with Sharon about what we might do with graphic novels. Sharon's sophomore students were in the midst of exploring poetry and were just about to begin reading *As I Lay Dying*. We had a very small window of time during which to try something with graphic novels. I had brought *The Best of Ray Bradbury: The Graphic Novel* with me. Sharon had an excerpt from *Maus* by Art Speigelman. This graphic novel explores the Holocaust through the use of animal characters.

We talked about wanting the students to experience reading an excerpt from a graphic novel and to share their reading process with us. Our challenge was to find a way to make multiple copies of a graphic novel. As freshman students arrived for their first-period study hall, we hit on the idea of using a story from the Ray Bradbury graphic novel. This would allow us to work with a complete text, and we could even have the students compare the graphic novel format with the original story. We flipped through the graphic novel and chose "Dark They Were, and Golden-Eyed." This story has wonderfully artistic illustrations that set the tone for the suspenseful story. We were off to the copy machine.

We discovered that making copies of a graphic novel is no easy task. The size of the pictures and text does not lend itself well to the size of copy paper, and black and white is not as compelling as color. But after several attempts we were able to cut and paste the copies in a way that we could make a class set of the story. As the copying continued, with the help of a wonderful instructional assistant, we were able to track down a copy of the original story in a collection of Bradbury's stories from the library. A freshman student volunteered to go get the book for us. As freshmen worked on their assignments in a required study hall, Sharon and I sat together and crafted a series of questions that would focus students' attention on their reading process. Sharon had taught her students about metacognition, so our plan was designed to build on this skill. We developed the following questions:

The Metacognition Questions

What did you notice about reading this story in graphic form?

How is it different from reading text-only pieces?

Do the pictures help? If so, how? If not, why not?

What do you notice about the pictures?

How did reading the story in graphic form affect your understanding and experience of it?

How did reading the story in text-only form affect your understanding and experience?

Our lesson plan was falling into place, but we also recognized we were living on the edge. Although we had both read the Bradbury story years ago, neither of us had read it recently. Neither of us had read the graphic novel version. We decided we would tell students this and let them know we were joining with them in the lesson today, exploring our own reactions as readers.

After a brief introduction during which I explained my interest in graphic novels and invited those in the class who had experience with graphic novels to share (turned out that those who shared were all boys), we handed out the graphic novel version of the story and began to read.

As I read I noted that I focused first on the words and then the pictures. In this graphic story there is typed text as well as handwritten text, and I found I preferred the typed text.

When I was finished reading I wrote in response to Question 5, "Reading the story in graphic form was more difficult. I had to infer much of what was happening, but it was also easier. I could focus on the basic elements of the plot, and I could feel the suspense as I read. I loved the scene where they went swimming in the canal." When I looked up from my own reading and responding to questions, I saw a classroom full of students with heads bent, pens and pencils writing. Students were picking up their copies of the graphic story, looking at them, flipping to key pages, and then returning to jot down a response to each question. The room was silent.

When the majority of students were finished reading, a buzz of conversation began to fill the room. As I listened I heard students talking about the story— talking about the text before we asked them to talk about the text! Sharon and I asked students to count off so they would be in groups of three. In their groups we asked them to share their responses to the metacognition questions about reading process. Sharon and I both circulated so we could eavesdrop on students' conversations. We heard students asking each other questions about the plot, particularly the ending. Several commented that they didn't like this graphic format; they felt like they were "cheating" as readers. One student commented, "It's like reading the Cliffs Notes version." After ten to twelve minutes of small-group talk, we pulled students back to a whole-group conversation about the questions. As Sharon facilitated the discussion, I attempted to take notes. Students' hands flew into the air; they seemed enthusiastic about sharing their reactions, which included the following:

> *"I liked the plot and ending, but I don't like the graphics."*
> *"I lose my own imagery because the pictures are there."*
> *To which another student responded, "I create better pictures in my head, so it ruined my thinking."*
> *Another noted, "I liked the pictures; they are not cartooney. They have lots of details."*
> *Followed by, "I liked the details of the people pictures, but I didn't like the landscape pictures; I wish they had left those up to the reader's mind."*
> *"I liked it. It reminded me of being a kid with a picture book."*
> *"It was in between a book and a movie; I had to balance the two."*

The energy in the room was palpable. As Sharon continued the discussion, she noted mostly boys were contributing. She asked the girls for their feedback. The girls' responses echoed the boys' earlier discussion—a mixed reaction:

> *"I really had to focus; it was hard to determine the order—what to read when." I readily agreed with her statement.*
> *"I found it easy to understand the story, but it was not fun to read."*
> *"The pictures were really helpful."*
> *"I found looking at the pictures made me think of more images."*
> *"I liked it, but I felt like I was reading sentence and then pictures. It was hard to follow the narrative."*

204

As the conversation continued I noted the energy level in the room. Students were leaning forward. Sharon could hardly keep up as she called on students. Stephan asked, "What is the difference between comic books and graphic novels?" The experts in the room were quick to respond, "Graphic novels are longer; they tell a complete story, whereas comic books focus on an event."

We stopped the discussion to show the students the actual illustrations from the graphic novel. As I circulated the room with the graphic novel open to the colorful artwork, students leaned forward to see.

We then handed out the text-only version of Bradbury's story. I read the opening section, and Sharon read the next one. With time in the class period running out, we stopped and asked for feedback. The first respondent, a girl, noted, "I like the text version. I get a 360-degree view from the story." Others nodded. But the majority of the class preferred the graphic novel version. A show of hands confirmed this. One young woman noted, "Is this the same story? Wow, this one [holding up Bradbury's story] has so many more words."

As the class came to a close, we were greeted with applause. Students stopped and said "thank you" to me as they handed me the story copy. Sharon and her instructional assistant both smiled and said, "That was amazing. Kids who almost never speak were active participants today."

As Sharon walked me to the high school's front door, she noted, "That was wonderful—a really great day of teaching. I am exhilarated and exhausted." What we realized is that although students' comments about the graphic text were mixed, their participation was evidence that this format had invited them into the conversation.

Students' written responses to the metacognition questions confirmed that they found the graphic version of the story accessible:

> "It gives you a clearer understanding, and it lets you comprehend the story faster."
>
> "I think it was better for me to have read with pictures because I actually understood and it made me think."
>
> "It was way easier to visualize and put into motion. Kinda like a movie in your head."
>
> "We can experience by our eyes. It's both reading and picturing the experience of the book."
>
> "I could understand the story better because I was using two ways to understand, visually and mentally."

205

For ELL students, the graphic novel seemed to work particularly well. Sharon commented on their active participation during our class discussion. Their written feedback shows that they appreciated being able to access and comprehend the story. The graphic version served to level the playing field: "It made it more interesting and perhaps funner because I could see something else not only the words. I understood it well, because it is well written and the pictures helped."

We also appreciated students' recognition that the graphic format had its limitations. Megan expressed this as follows: "The pictures made the story line easy to follow and understand. I think, however, reading too many graphic novels would take away from one's ability to be creative while reading. It feels like a watered-down version of literature, made easier to digest and comprehend." Bryan also expressed frustration: "It felt like a cheap substitute for text, as if it was for illiterate children instead of letting you make decisions and fill in the missing answers to the story, and it stops the story."

In looking at students' written responses we saw graphic novels' potential to support reading strategies. As students noted, the graphic novel format seems easier at first, but because there is not much text, readers are required to infer. We observed students at work with inferences. They raised a number of questions regarding the plot:

How long were they there?

How did he build a rocket by himself?

Why was there a war?

What was the ending trying to tell us?

The Bradbury graphic novel created a space and place for conversation about reading, drawing, science fiction, and Mars.

This brief foray into graphic novels opened my eyes to this genre's possibilities. Using graphic novels allows us to explore reading strategies as well as multiple literacies. It also creates a situation where the students are more likely to be the experts on the genre. It was eye-opening for me to be in the role of resistant reader when confronted with the challenge of reading a graphic novel.

My early failed efforts to read a graphic novel reminded me that it was not lack of motivation that caused me to stop reading; it was frustration. I needed help and support to learn how to read graphic novels. In the process I made discoveries about myself as a reader, about the graphic novel genre, and forged a connection with my son that has opened my eyes to what it means to create a community of readers.

Please note I am not advocating the use of graphic novels as a bridge to literature, although I think graphic novels may in fact be such a bridge. I am suggesting the use of graphic novels as a genre worthy of inclusion in our literature classrooms. Graphic novels serve several purposes:

They require complex reading skills and allow for the development of such.

They illustrate the importance of storytelling, a central theme in the study of literature.

They can be used to teach literary terms and writing craft.

They are a way to bring popular culture into the classroom, linking classroom literacies with students' out-of-school literacy.

They are a way into story for those who struggle with text-only literacy tasks.

They illustrate a link between language arts and art.

And I am not alone in my stance regarding the inclusion of graphic novels. The National Association of Comics Art Educators is gearing up for a new initiative to support K–12 educators and librarians in learning to use graphic novels. Go to their website, http://www.teachingcomics.org, for more information.

Ben Towle, who helped form the Association of Comics Art Educators, compares the use of graphic novels in the classroom today to the use of film in the classroom in the 1950s and 1960s. Stephanie Cromer, who has used graphic novels in both her high school and middle school classrooms, celebrates this genre for its ability to develop and reinforce reading strategies, its connection with visual literacy, its focus on key plot details, and its "level of metaphor," but she also recognizes that her appreciation for graphic novels buys her "street credibility" with her students. They trust her as a reader because she knows graphic novels.

Concerns About Graphic Novels

In talking about graphic novels with colleagues I have been struck by their concern that graphic novels don't provide the kind of rigor that novels require. As one colleague noted, "If they get in the habit of reading graphic novels, they may not want to go back to reading text-only books." I appreciate this concern, and I also see a role for using graphic versions of well-known literature (both novels and short stories) in support of understanding complex text. But neither of these uses are the rationale for introducing graphic novels; I believe graphic novels are a unique genre, worthy of study on their own.

"The graphic novel now offers English language arts teachers opportunities to engage all students in a medium that expands beyond the traditional borders of literacy" (Schwarz 2006, 58). To read a graphic novel, students need to understand traditional literacy, including character, plot, theme, and writing craft, particularly dialogue, but they also have the opportunity to explore "visual elements such as color, shading, panel layout, perspective, and even the lettering style" (Schwarz 2006, 59).

As for the concern that reading graphic novels will cause students to be less interested in text-only works, there is no current research regarding graphic novels to support this fear, but there is research that suggests just the opposite is true: comic book reading can be "a conduit to 'heavier reading'" (Krashen 2005, 1). A study conducted by Joanne Ujiie and Stephen Krashen found that "middle school boys who read comics read more in general than boys who did not read comics, read more books, and enjoyed reading more" (1996, 52). South Africa's Bishop Desmond Tutu credits comics for his interest in "heavier reading":

> One of the things my father did was to let me read comics. I devoured all kinds of comics. People used to say, "That's bad because it spoils your English" but in fact, letting me read comics fed my love for English and my love for reading. I suppose if he had been firm I might not have developed this deep love for reading and for English. (2004).

The research supporting comics provides a rationale for using graphic novels in the classroom, but I am also aware of the challenges using them will present. I offer the following suggestions in support of using graphic novels:

First and foremost, it is important that teachers read graphic novels and note their own reading experience in order to better understand literacy knowledge and skills that students use in reading comics and graphic novels.

Talk with your administration and your department about how the use of graphic novels supports students' reading skills development and analysis of literature elements while also developing their visual literacy skills. Reference the NCTE standards regarding visual literacy.

Select the graphic novel excerpts with care; many of them are not school appropriate.

Obtaining copies of graphic novels or excerpts is a challenge. As discussed previously, I think a black-and-white copy is better than not using any graphic novels.

The remainder of this chapter focuses on how to use graphic novels in support of reading skills and literature analysis. For information on teaching visual literacy skills, see the resources section at the end of this chapter. In selecting graphic novels, I focused on excerpts that would be school appropriate, although I recognize each school has its own community standards. I also focused on using graphic novels that could be readily obtained. All of the graphic novels listed were available through the public library system in Oregon.

Graphic Novels in Support of Reading Skills

As noted in students' responses earlier in this chapter, graphic novels appeal to students, and the research is clear that getting students to read is an essential first step in reading skills development (see Stephen Krashen's *The Power of Reading: Insights from the Research* for more on this). High school librarians confirm that graphic novels appeal to adolescents. A high school librarian from Florida found that while the graphic novel collection in the school library represented only 1 percent of its total collection, graphic novels accounted "for more than 25–30% of circulation" (Heckman 2004, 3).

Graphic novels also support visual language development by asking students to read pictures in addition to print. As mentioned earlier, to understand graphic novels, students have to pay attention to "color, shading, panel layout, perspective," and "lettering style" (Schwarz 2006, 59). Rachael Sawyer Perkins, an elementary teacher in California, reports on the use of graphic novels to support visual literacy: "For students who lack the ability to visualize as they read, it provides a graphic sense that approximates what good readers do as they read" (Council Chronicle 2005, 2). Graphic novels also support students who are learning to read or learning to read English as a second language by providing pictures along with text. This emphasis on visual literacy is consistent with standards for teaching English and language arts (NCTE and IRA Standard 3):

Students apply a wide range of strategies to comprehend, interpret, evaluate, and appreciate texts. They draw on their prior experience, their interactions with other readers and writers, their knowledge of word meaning and other texts, their word identification strategies, and their understanding of textual features (e.g. sound-letter correspondence, sentence structure, context, and graphics) [emphasis added].

In addition, graphic novels can be used to teach or reinforce inference. Inference is the creation of meaning based on predictions and interpretations of text. It requires readers to draw on background knowledge as well as what is in the text, making connections and adapting those connections as reading continues. Graphic novel readers use both pictures and text to infer what is happening. I certainly saw evidence of this in my work with the sophomores around the graphic version of the Ray Bradbury story "Dark They Were, and Golden-Eyed" (2003, 31). Sophomores pointed out details in the pictures that led them to speculate about what would happen next. They discussed how the text and the pictures together supported their interpretations. Because the graphic version of the story was rich in detail but also small in scope, students were able to look closely, to reread to test their understanding of the text with the pictures. Shelley Hong Xu speaks to the use of graphic novels to support inference: "Graphic novels can teach about making inferences, since readers must rely on pictures and just a small amount of text" (Council Chronicle 2005, 2). Graphic novels also provide opportunities for exploring storytelling elements, character, setting, plot, and theme as well as literary craft, including dialogue and metaphor.

Graphic Novels in Support of Story Elements

Because graphic novels are a new genre for me and for the majority of middle school and high school teachers with whom I work, I have focused my attention in this section on graphic novel excerpts and short stories in graphic form that can be used to teach story elements. My teaching strategies are based on interviews with teachers who have incorporated graphic novels into their classrooms as well as interviews with adolescents who want to encourage teachers to bring graphic novels into the classroom.

CHARACTER

In *Persepolis,* the narrator and main character, Marjane Satrapi, shows how her interactions with others, in particular her family, shape who she is. Her simple black-and-white drawings add to the power of her words. To support character exploration, students are invited to draw the main character and select two or three text excerpts that help the reader see the character.

SETTING

In the Ray Bradbury story "Dark They Were, and Golden-Eyed" (Bradbury 2003, 31) sophomore students commented on the artist's use of sketchy setting details at the beginning of the story. But as the story builds in suspense, the details of the setting increase and the picture comes to life. The graphic version of this story also uses color—shades of gold with accents of purple and shading going from light to dark—to develop setting. To support students in exploring visual literacy and color, students could color a black-and-white version of a graphic novel and be prepared to explain how their color choices contribute to setting creation.

PLOT

The concept of plot is well served by graphic novels. Michel Gagné, who drew the characters and special effects for the animated film *The Iron Giant,* has created several short graphic stories that contain only pictures. These stories are published in the anthologies *Flight,* volume 2, and *Flight,* volume 3 (Kibuishi 2005, 2006). Students read these picture-only texts and then work in small groups to identify the key plot points. Another option is to use a story students have read and ask them to draw panels to illustrate key plot points. There are a number of graphic novel collections based on short stories: *The Best of Ray Bradbury: The Graphic Novel; Graphic Classics: Mark Twain; Graphic Classics: Edgar Allan Poe;* and *Graphic Classics: H. G. Wells.*

Graphic Novels in Support of Plot

Pictures Only:

"Underworld" by Michel Gagné in *Flight,* volume 3

"The Rescue" by Phil Craven in *Flight,* volume 3

"Saturday" by Israel Sanchez in *Flight,* volume 3

"Message in a Bottle" by Rodolphe Guenoden in *Flight,* volume 3

"Snow Cap" by Matthew S. Armstrong in *Flight,* volume 3
(For publication information for *Flight*, volume 3, see Kibuishi 2006.)

Pictures and Text:
The Long Haul by Anthony Johnston and Eduardo Barreto
Courtney Crumrin and the Night Things by Ted Naifeh
The Young Indiana Jones Chronicles by Dan Barry

THEME

In the graphic novel *Maus* by Art Spiegelman, the story of the Holocaust is retold with animals: Jews are depicted as mice and the Nazis are cats. This graphic novel, which won the Pulitzer Prize, paints a story through pictures that encourages students to explore questions of relationships between groups. The series *Electric Girl* by Michael Brennan explores themes of peer pressure, with tales of a female protagonist who can harness and manipulate energy. *Bone: Out from Boneville: The Complete Bone Adventures 1* by Jeff Smith is a humorous tale that touches on themes of the hero's journey. This graphic novel is one of the few found in middle school libraries, so it also passes the "school-appropriate" test. *It's a Bird* by Steven T. Seagle and Teddy Kristiansen explores the relationship between man and Superman in this tale of a comic book writer who learns that life, even if short, is worth living.

Graphic Novels in Support of Literary Terms and Craft

DIALOGUE

I appreciate how the graphic novel format focuses students' eyes and ears on dialogue. The use of speech balloons over characters heads allows students to see who is talking. In *Electric Girl* by Michael Brennan the black-and-white format and multiple conversations between the main character, Electric Girl, and her father and peers are easy to see and follow, and the dialogue itself is realistic. I also enjoy the dialogue between Electric Girl and the gremlins who are responsible for Electric Girl and her special powers.

In *The Sandman* by Neil Gaiman and various artists varying styles and colors of ballons and lettering are used to represent different characters. After reading graphic novels that use the word-bubble format, students can then examine an excerpt from *Why I Hate Saturn* by Kyle Baker. This graphic novel utilizes a format in which the text is placed beneath the storyboard panels. The result is dialogue written with quotation marks under each character. Students can see how punctuation takes the place of word bubbles. (Note: Excerpts from *The Sandman* and *Why I Hate Saturn* can be found in Paul Gravett's book *Graphic Novels: Stories to Change Your Life* [2005]. See the resource list at the end of this chapter for more information about this book.)

METAPHOR

As is the case with dialogue, graphic novels allow students to "see" metaphor—words and pictures bring the comparison into focus. Art Spiegelman's graphic novels *Maus* and *Maus II* (1993) use animals as metaphors to capture the relationships of the Holocaust: Jews as mice and Nazis as cats. Like in Orwell's *Animal Farm*, the use of animals makes the context of the story less threatening but still allows for an examination of the important issues raised by the animals' interactions and dialogue.

SATIRE

The literary technique of satire, ridiculing foolish ideas or customs for the purpose of improving society, is alive and well in graphic novels. In *Batman: The Dark Knight Returns* by Frank Miller with Klaus Janson and Lynn Variey, the character of Batman, now aging—his costume and stomach sagging—considers leaving retirement and returning to crime fighting. Within this story, Miller satirizes the laws of society Batman is trying to defend as well as the role of television, ridiculing TV's banality with scenes of a gang leader's rant and an address from the president about imminent war (for an excerpt see Paul Gravett's *Graphic Novels: Stories to Change Your Life*).

Closing Thoughts on Graphic Novels

It's my hope this chapter will encourage you to read graphic novels and incorporate them into your classroom. I appreciate the challenges associated with this genre, but the enthusiasm I have seen students display as they explore graphic novels is compelling evidence that they belong in our middle school and high school classrooms.

213

WORKS CITED

Baker, Kyle. 1998. *Why I Hate Saturn*. New York: Vertigo.

Barry, Dan. 1992. *Young Indiana Jones Chronicles*. New York: Golden Press.

Brennan, Michael. 2003. *Electric Girl*. 2nd ed. San Francisco: AiT/PlanetLar.

Council Chronicle. 2005. "Using Comics and Graphic Novels in the Classroom." *The Council Chronicle* 15 (September).

Gaiman, Neil. 1990–1997. *Sandman* series. New York: Vertigo.

Heckman, W. 2004. "Reading Heroes for a New Generation." *Florida Media Quarterly* 29 (3).

———.2004. *The Power of Reading*. Portsmouth, NH: Heinemann.

Johnston, Anthony, and Eduardo Barreto. 2005. *The Long Haul*. Portland, OR: Oni Press.

Kibuishi, Kazu, ed. 2005. *Flight*. Vol. 2. Berkeley, CA: Image Comics.

———. 2006. *Flight*. Vol. 3. New York: Ballantine Books.

Krashen, Stephen. 2005. "The 'Decline' of Reading in America, Poverty and Access to Books, and the Use of Comics in Encouraging Reading." *Teachers College Record*, Feb. 14, 2005. Available: http://www.tcrecord.org, ID number 11740.

Miller, Frank. 1982. *Batman: The Dark Knight Returns*. New York: DC Comics.

Naifeh, Ted. 2003. *Courtney Crumrin and the Night Things*. Portland, OR: Oni Press.

Newkirk, Thomas. 2002. *Misreading Masculinity: Boys, Literacy, and Popular Culture*. Portsmouth, NH: Heinemann.

Pomplun, Tom. 2004. *Graphic Classics: Edgar Allan Poe*. 2nd ed. Mount Horeb, WI: Eureka Productions.

Satrapi, Marjane. 2003. *Persepolis*. New York: Pantheon.

Schwarz, Gretchen. 2006."Expanding Literacies Through Graphic Novels." *English Journal* 95 (6): 58–64.

Seagle, Steven T., and Teddy Kristiansen. 2004. *It's a Bird*. New York: DC Comics.

Smith, Jeff. 2003. *Bone: Out from Boneville: The Complete Bone Adventures 1*. Columbus, OH: Cartoon Books.

Smith, Michael W., and Jeffrey D. Wilhelm. 2002. *"Reading Don't Fix No Chevys": Literacy in the Lives of Young Men*. Portsmouth, NH: Heinemann.

Spiegelman, Art. 1986. *Maus: A Survivor's Tale: My Father Bleeds History*. New York: Pantheon.

———.1992. *Maus II: A Survivor's Tale: And Here My Troubles Began*. New York: Pantheon.

Tutu, Desmond. 2004, June 12. "Interview with Archbishop Desmond Tutu." Academy of Achievement. Available: http://www.achievement.org/autodoc/page/tut0int-1.

Twain, Mark, Rick Geary, Evert Geradts, and Skip Williams. 2004. *Graphic Classics: Mark Twain*. Mt. Horeb, WI: Eureka Productions.

Ujiie, Joanne, and Stephen Krashen. 1996. "Comic Book Reading, Reading Enjoyment, and Pleasure Reading Among Middle Class and Chapter 1 Middle School Students." *Reading Improvement* 33 (1): 51–54.

Wells, H. G., Antonella Caputo, Rod Lott, and Dan O'Neill. 2005. *Graphic Classics: H. G. Wells*. Mt. Horeb, WI: Eureka Productions.

Zimmerman, Howard. 2003. *The Best of Ray Bradbury: The Graphic Novel*. New York: Simon and Schuster.

214

RECOMMENDED RESOURCES IN SUPPORT OF TEACHING GRAPHIC NOVELS

Graphic Novels for Your Classroom Library

Brennan, Michael. 2003. *Electric Girl.* 2nd ed. San Francisco: AiT/PlanetLar.

Kibuishi, Kazu, ed. 2005. *Flight.* Vol. 2. Berkeley, CA: Image Comics.

———. 2006. *Flight.* Vol. 3. New York: Ballantine Books.

Naifeh, Ted. 2003. *Courtney Crumrin and the Night Things.* Portland, OR: Omni Press.

Pomplun, Tom. 2004. *Graphic Classics: Edgar Allan Poe.* 2nd ed. Mount Horeb, WI: Eureka Productions.

Satrapi, Marjane. 2003. *Persepolis.* New York: Pantheon.

Seagle, Steven T., and Teddy Kristiansen. 2004. *It's a Bird.* New York: DC Comics.

Smith, Jeff. *Bone: Out from Boneville: The Complete Bone Adventures 1.* Columbus, OH: Cartoon Books.

Zimmerman, Howard. 2003. *The Best of Ray Bradbury: The Graphic Novel.* New York: Simon and Schuster.

Books and Articles

Carter, James Bucky, ed. 2007. *Building Literacy Connections with Graphic Novels: Page by Page, Panel by Panel.* Urbana, IL: National Council of Teachers of English.

Eisner, Will. 1985. *Comic and Sequential Art.* Expanded ed. Tamarac, FL: Poorhouse.

———.1996. *Graphic Storytelling and Visual Narrative.* Tamarac, FL: Poorhouse.

Gorman, Michele. 2003. *Getting Graphic! Using Graphic Novels to Promote Literacy with Preteens and Teens.* Worthington, OH: Linworth.

Gravett, Paul. 2005. *Graphic Novels: Stories to Change Your Life.* New York: Collins Design.

Jacobs, Dale. 2007. "More Than Words: Comics as a Means of Teaching Multiple Literacies." *English Journal* 96 (3): 19–25.

McCloud, Scott. 1993. *Understanding Comics: The Invisible Art.* New York: Harper.

Schwarz, Gretchen. 2006. "Expanding Literacies through Graphic Novels." *English Journal* 95 (6): 58–64.

Weiner, Stephen. 2001. *The 101 Best Graphic Novels.* New York: NBM.

Websites

http://noflyingnotights.com. This site offers resources, reviews, and top ten lists of graphic novels for teens.

http://thelair.com. This site is created by the same folks who created "no flying/no tights." It focuses on graphic novels for adolescents and adults; note that all of the titles might not be appropriate for school.

http://my.voyager.net/~sraiteri/graphicnovels. htm. A list of more than one thousand comics for young adults compiled by Steve Raiteri, a librarian from Ohio.

www.nyccomicbookmuseum.org/education/ education.htm. Includes curriculum resources in support of using graphic novels in the classroom.

www.artbomb.net. This site contains a graphic guide to reading graphic novels as well as reviews and online graphic novels (not all of which are appropriate for school).

215

Index

adolescents
    research on reading and, 10
    short texts, relevance to
      and, 12
Allison, Dorothy, *Two or Three
    Things I Know for Sure*,
    119-120
American Childhood, An,
    (Dillard), 121-122, 135-136
Anderson, Laurie Halse, 13
Angelou, Maya, 103-104
    "Brutality is Definitely Not
      Acceptable," 104
    *I Know Why the Caged Bird
      Sings*, 132-133
    poetry and, 151
    *Wouldn't Take Nothing for
      My Journey Now*, 79-80,
      104
assessments, 16-19
    formal, 16
    informal, 17-19
Atwell, Nancie, *Side by Side*,
    145-146

Baker, Russell, *Growing Up*, 126
Bauer, Joan, "Letter from the
    Fringe, A," 63
Baylor, Byrd, *Everybody Needs a
    Rock*, 191
"Because I Could Not Stop for
    Death," (Dickinson), 164-
    165
Bedard, Michael, Emily, 181
Berriault, Gina, "Stone Boy, The,"
    49-51
"Best Against the Best, The,"
    (Deford), 99
Best American Essays: 2005, The,
    (Orlean), 78
*Best of Ray Bradbury: The Graphic
    Novel, The*,
    (Zimmerman), 200, 202-207

Bird by Bird, (Lamott), 91
Bradbury, Ray, "Dark They Were,
    and Golden-Eyed," 210
Brooks, Gwendolyn, "We Real
    Cool," 155
"Brutality is Definitely Not
    Acceptable," (Angelou), 104
Burke, Jim, "Plot the Action," 49

Call of Stories, The, (Coles), 52
Campbell, Bebe Moore, *Sweet
    Summer: Growing Up With
    and Without My Dad*,
    123-124
Candy and Me, (Liftin), 117-119
canon novels, short stories and,
    67-69
carousel graffiti, discussion and,
    30-31
Carver, Raymond, 35
character, graphic novels and, 211
character elements, teaching,
    44-46
*Childhood: The Biography of a
    Place in Modern American
    Memoirs, A*, (Crewe),
    138-139
children's literature and picture
    books
    collaborative literary circles
      and, 177-179
    genre and, 179-183
    nonfiction and, 180-183
    overview of, 36, 175–177
children's literature and picture
    books, by theme, 183-191
    family, culture, 184-186
    holidays, celebrations, 183-
      184
    life lessons, 188-189
    nature, 191
    reading, writing, school,
      186-188

    social justice, 189-190
children's literature and picture
    books, literary craft, 191-
    194
    point of view, 193-194
    satisfying ending, 191-192
children's literature and picture
    books, teaching strategies
    building community with
      school stories, 187-188
    children's book biographies
      and memoirs about
      heroes, 182
    children's book biographies
      and memoirs about
      writers, 181
children's literature and picture
    books, title lists
    family, culture, 186
    heroes, 183
    holidays, celebrations, 184
    nature, 191
    poetry, 179-180
    recognizing rhymes, sound
      devices, 180
    satisfying endings, 192
    school, 188
    social justice, 190
    sound devices, in support
      of, 180
    teaching life lessons, 189
    top ten read-alouds, 177
    writers, about, 182
Chopin, Kate, "Story of an Hour,
    The," 61-62
classroom structure, student
    supports, 15-32
    assessments and, 16-19
    discussion, 28-32
    framing objectives and, 16
    in-class reading, 19-23
    reading check-in, 24-25
    sticky notes, 23

writing in response to
  literature, 24
*Click, Clack, Moo: Cows That
  Type,* (Cronin), 189-190
Coles, Robert, 42
  Call of Stories, The, 52
collaborative literary circles
  children's literature and
    picture books and, 177-
    179
  group process questions and,
    179
  questions about texts and,
    179
Collins, Billy, 152
computers, reading and, 87
conflict, short story elements and,
  50-51
Cooney, Barbara, *Eleanor,* 182
Cooper, Bernard, 9
Crewe, Harry, *Childhood: The
  Biography of a Place,* 138-
  139
Cromer, Stephanie, 207
Cronin, Doreen, *Click, Clack,
  Moo: Cows That Type,*
  189-190
Crutcher, Chris, *King of the Mild
  Frontier,* 120

Dahl, Roald, "Lamb to the
  Slaughter," 1-2
Dance to the Piper, (DeMille), 129
"Dark They Were, and Golden-
  Eyed," (Bradbury), 210
Deford, Frank, 99
DeMille, Agnes, *Dance to the
  Piper,* 129
descriptive detail, memoirs and,
  133-134
details to support character,
  memoirs, 135-136
dialogue
  graphic novels and, 212-213
  journals, 27-28
  memoir and, 136-137
Dickinson, Emily
  "Because I Could Not Stop for
    Death," 164-165

"This Is My Letter to the
  World," 147-148
differentiated instruction, 12-14
Dillard, Annie, 77
  American Childhood, An, 121-
    122, 135-136
"Diner," *A Girl Named Zippy:
  Growing Up Small in
  Moreland, Indiana,*
  (Kimmel), 134
discussion, 28-32
  fishbowl, 31-32
  large-group structures and,
    30-32
  quote and question, 29
  small-group structures and,
    29-30
*Do I Really Have to Teach
  Reading? Content
  Comprehension, Grades
  6-12,* (Tovani), 127

Educative Assessment, (Wiggins),
  17
Eleanor, (Cooney), 182
Eliot, T. S., 155
Emerson, Ralph Waldo, "Self
  Reliance," 78-79
Emily, (Bedard), 181
essays, 28, 35, 77-78
  family, 101-103
  finding our way in life, 103-
    106
  issues, on, 98
  literary craft in, 106-109
  nature, 83-86
  overview of, 78-79
  political, 94-98
  response, books and
    literature, 86-90
  sports, 99-101
  writing, about, 90-93
essays, teaching strategies, 80-83
  advice, 104-105
  book review, 88
  close look, essays to
    persuade, 94-97
  creating book list, 87-88
  family, 101-102

locating information, 80-81
making connections,
  emphasis on text-to-text,
  81-83
observing nature, 84-86
parody, 106-107
reading to hear message, 94
review a review, 88-89
sports, 99-100
synthesizing ideas, 81
writing life, 91-93
essays, title lists
  advice, 106
  books and reading, 90
  family, 103
  how-to, 81
  issues, 98
  nature, 84
  parody, 108
  sports, 101
  writing, 93
Everybody Needs a Rock, (Baylor),
  191
exit/entrance notes, 27

fake reading, 4-5
family, culture, children's
  literature and picture
  books, 184-186
Faulkner, William, "Barn
  Burning," 64-65
figurative language, memoirs and,
  134-135
fishbowl discussion, 31-32
Fletcher, Ralph, *What Every
  Writer Needs,* 192
foreshadowing, short stories,
  craft of writing and, 59-60
*For the Good of the Earth and Sun:
  Teaching Poetry,* (Heard),
  154-155, 157-158, 163
Freire, Paulo, 10
Frost, Robert
  "Road Not Taken, The," 148
  "Stopping by Woods on a
    Snowy Evening," 145-146

genre, children's books
  nonfiction, 180-183

poetry, 179-180

genre, embracing with short texts and, 34-36

Goldberg, Natalie, *Long Quiet Highway: Waking Up in America,* 128

grabber leads, memoirs and, 132-133

graphic novels, 36, 199-201
classrooms, in the, 201-202
concerns about, 207-209
literary terms, craft and, 212-213
metacognition questions and, 202-207
reading skills, support and, 209-210
several purposes of, 207
story element support and, 210-212
visual language development and, 209

graphic novels, title list, in support of plot, 211-212

Gravett, Paul, 199

Hamilton, Carole, 35

Hansberry, Lorraine, 116

Happy Hocky Family, (Smith), 184-185

Hawthorne, Nathaniel
"Minister's Black Veil, The," 4-5, 67-68
Scarlet Letter, The, 67-68

Heard, Georgia, 138
For the Good of the Earth and Sun: Teaching Poetry, 154-155, 157-158, 163
Writing Toward Home: Tales and Lessons to Find Your Way, 127

holiday, celebrations, children's literature and picture books, 183-184

"How Reading Changed My Life," (Quindlen), 86-87

"How to Eat a Poem," (Merriam), 153

Hunger of Memory, (Rodriguez), 125

I Know Why the Caged Bird Sings, (Angelou), 132-133

imagery, short stories, craft of writing and, 57-59

imagery, poetry and, 157-159
poems rich in, 159

in-class reading, 19-23

International Reading Association (IRA), 6
standards, 15

"In the Blink of an Eye," (Mazer), 137

Inventing the Truth: The Art and Craft of Memoir, (Zinsser), 130

I Read It, but I Don't Get It, (Tovani), 3, 20

irony, short stories, craft of writing and, 61-62

"I Stand Here Ironing," (Olsen), 52

Kazin, Alfred, *Walker in the City, A,* 134-135

Kenyon, Jane, "Let Evening Come," 160

Kimmel, Haven, "Diner," *A Girl Named Zippy: Growing Up Small in Moreland, Indiana,* 134

"Kindness," (Nye), 155-156

King, Stephen, *On Writing: A Memoir of Craft,* 130-131

King of the Mild Frontier, (Crutcher), 120

Kratzke, Peter, 35

"Lamb to the Slaughter," (Dahl), 1-2

Lamott, Anne, *Bird by Bird,* 91

large-group structure, discussion and, 30-32
carousel graffiti and, 30-31
silent graffiti and, 30

leads, short stories, craft of writing and, 55-56

learning logs, 83

Le Guinn, Ursula, 88-89

"Let Evening Come," (Kenyon), 160

"Letter from the Fringe, A," (Bauer), 63

Let Your Life Speak: Listening for the Voice of Vocation, (Palmer), 129

life lessons, children's literature and picture books, 188

"Life You Save May Be Your Own, The," (O'Connor), 59-60

Liftin, Hilary, *Candy and Me,* 117-119

literary craft, children's books and, 191-192
point of view, 193-194
satisfying endings, 191-192

literary theory, 32

literature, teaching objectives and, 5-8

literature analogies, short texts and, 33-34

literature learning logs, 25-26

literature workshop, 15-23

Living the Word, (Walker), 131-132

Long Quiet Highway: Waking Up in America, (Goldberg), 128

Mayes, Frances, *Under the Tuscan Sun,* 138

Mazer, Norma Fox, "In the Blink of an Eye," 137

McTighe, Jay, *Understanding by Design,* 19

memoirs, 36
childhood, 121-122
family, 122-124
introducing, 117-121
overview of, 116-117
passion for one's work, 129-133
reading, life and the world, 124-126
writing, about, 126-129

memoirs, teaching strategies
defining memoirs, 120-121

memoir as inspiration for
memoir, 121-122
reading time line, 125-126
text-self connection, 123-124
what is memoir?, 119-120
writer's notebook, 127-128
writing, interviewing,
hobbies, passions, 129-
133
memoirs, title lists
character detail, 136
childhood, 122
dialogue in memoir, 137
family emphasis, 124
figurative language, 135
grabber leads, 133
passions, vocations, 130
place, 139
reading, about, 126
writing, about, 128
memoirs, writing craft, 130-139
descriptive details, 133-134
details to support character,
135-136
details to support place,
138-139
dialogue, 136-137
figurative language, 134-135
finding subject, small
moment and, 130-131
grabber leads, 132-133
memoirs, writing craft, teaching
strategies
analyzing characteristics of
grabber leads, 132-133
detailing detail, 134
graphing home, 138-139
highlighting similes and
metaphors, 134-135
small moment snapshots,
131-132
Merriam, Eve, "How to Eat a
Poem," 153
metacognition questions, graphic
novels and, 202-207
metaphor, graphic novels and, 213
"Minister's Black Veil, The,"
(Hawthorne), 4-5, 67-68

"Modest Proposal, A," (Swift),
106-107
Moffet, James, 28, 109
Moore, Anne Carroll, 175
Moore, Kathleen Dean, "Winter
Creek," 84-86
"Mr. Smith Goes to Heaven,"
(Quindlen), 101-102
Murray, Donald, 91

National Association of Comic
Art Educators, The, 207
standards, 15
National Council of Teachers of
English (NCTE), 6
nature, children's literature and
picture books, 191
NCTE/IRA standards, 15
Newman, Leslea, Writing from the
Heart, 136
Nonfiction Craft Lessons:
Teaching Information
Writing K-8, (Portalupi and
Fletcher), 132
Nye, Naomi Shihab, "Kindness,"
155-156

objectives
framing, 16
list, 6
teaching, 5-8
O'Connor, Flannery, "Life You
Save May Be Your Own,
The," 59-60
Oliver, Mary, 144
Poetry Handbook, A, 158-159
Olsen, Tillie, "I Stand Here
Ironing," 52
On Writing: A Memoir of Craft,
(King), 130-131
Orlean, Susan, Best American
Essays: 2005, The, 77-78

Paley, Grace, "Samuel," 55
Palmer, Parker, Let Your Life
Speak: Listening for the
Voice of Vocation, 129
Persepolis, (Satrapi), 200-201,
201-202

Piercy, Marge, "To Be of Use," 154
"Pit and the Pendulum, The,"
(Poe), 57-59
plot
graphic novels and, 211
short story elements and,
48-50
"Plot the Action," (Burke), 49
Poe, Edgar Allan, 155
"Pit and the Pendulum, The,"
57-59
poetry, 36
children's books and, 179-180
poems to read aloud, 150-151
reading aloud, 150-151
strategies for reading, 151-157
poetry, craft, 157-163
imagery, 157-159
sound and, 159-162
structure, format and, 163
poetry, craft, teaching strategies
chanting favorite words, 160
onomatopoeia through
concept attainment,
160-161
paying attention to the
"language of particulars,"
158-159
poetry corruption, imagery
and, 157-158
turning lines, 163
poetry, support for reading,
writing, 164-169
teaching strategies, live the
lines, 165-167
teaching strategies, music
video as poetry analysis,
164-165
teaching strategies, poem
as mentor, inspiration,
168-169
teaching strategies, poetry in
film, 164
poetry, teaching strategies
conversing through dialogue
journals and discussion,
155-157
finding poetry everywhere,
147-150

"found poem" of favorite
    lines, 154
poetry set to music, 155
reading poetry aloud, 152-153
snapping the beat, 154-155
poetry, title lists
    conversation support, 157
    imagery, 159
    read aloud, 150
    read-aloud, supporting of,
        153
    snapping, swaying, 155
    sound device, illustration, 162
    "turning of lines" illustration,
        163
Poetry Handbook, A, (Oliver),
    158-159
point of view
    children's literature and
        picture books, 193
    short stories, craft of writing
        and, 62-64
Portalupi, JoAnn, and Ralph
    Fletcher, *Nonfiction
    Craft Lessons: Teaching
    Information Writing K-8,*
    132
Probst, Robert, 32

Quindlen, Anna
    "How Reading Changed My
        Life," 86-87
    "Mr. Smith Goes to Heaven,"
        101-102
    "Three by Quindlen," 87
quote and question discussion, 29

reading, writing, school,
    children's literature and
    picture books and, 186-188
reading check-in, 24-25
reading choice, short texts and,
    10-12
research
    short texts, 10
    workshop approach writing,
        reading and, 15-16
resistant readers, 21

"Road Not Taken, The," (Frost),
    148
Rodriguez, Richard, *Hunger of
    Memory,* 125

"Samuel," (Paley), 55
satire, graphic novels and, 213
satisfying endings, children's
    literature and picture
    books, 191-192
Satrapi, Marjane, *Persepolis,* 200-
    201, 201-202
Scarlet Letter, The, (Hawthorne),
    67-68
Scieszka, Jon, *True Story of the
    Three Little Pigs!, The,*
    193-194
Sears, Peter, 157
Sedaris, David, "Us and Them,"
    102-103
selecting short texts
    children's books and, 36
    embracing genre and, 34-36
    essays and, 35
    graphic novels and, 36
    literature, 33-38
    literature analogies and,
        33-34
    memoirs and, 36
    poetry and, 36
    short stories and, 35
"Self Reliance," (Emerson), 78-79
setting
    graphic novels and, 211
    short story elements and,
        46-48
short stories, 35
    canon novels, in lieu of, 67-69
    conflict and, 51
    list, in lieu of novels, 69
    selection, 43-44
    students enjoy, 71
short stories, craft of writing and,
    55-67
    foreshadowing, 59-60
    imagery, 57-59
    irony, 61-62
    leads and, 55-56
    point of view, 62-64

    stream of consciousness,
        64-66
    title, 66-67
short stories, teaching strategies
    advice quotes in support of
        themes, 53-54
    column notes, 44-46
    focus on setting, 47-48
    marking plot, 49-50
    music as setting, 47
    reading leads aloud, quick
        write response, 55-56
    reading like detective, 59-60
    reading with eye for detail,
        57-59
    rereading to spot irony, 61-62
    selecting story based on title,
        66-67
short stories title lists
    conflict, 51
    focus on setting, 48
    foreshadowing, stories with,
        60
    intriguing leads, stories with,
        57
    novels, in place of, 69
    point of view and, 64
    stories students enjoy, 71
    stories with interesting
        punctuation, style, 66
    stories with irony, 62
short story elements
    character, 44-46
    conflict, 50-51
    plot, 48-50
    setting, 46-48
    theme, 52-54
short texts, 1-2
    fake reading and, 4-5
    selecting, 33-38
    value of, 3-4
short texts, case for, 10-15
    differentiated instruction
        and, 12-14
    NCTE/IRA standards and, 15
    reading choices and, 10-12
    relevance, adolescent's lives
        and, 12

221

writing models, effective and, 14-15

Side by Side, (Atwell), 145-146

silent graffiti, discussion and, 30

Silverstein, Shel

    Where the Sidewalk Ends, 148

small-group structures, discussion and, 29-30

Smith, Lane, *Happy Hocky Family*, 184-185

social justice, children's literature and picture books, 189

"Song of Myself," (Whitman), 165-167, 168-169

sound, poetry and, 159-162

Sports Illustrated, "The Best Against the Best," 99

Standards for the English Language Arts, 15

Steineke, Nancy, 178

sticky notes, 23

"Stone Boy, The," (Berriault), 49-51

"Stopping by Woods on a Snowy Evening," (Frost), 145-146

story elements, graphic novels and, 210-212

"Story of an Hour, The," (Chopin), 61-62

stream of consciousness, short stories, craft of writing and, 64-66

structure, format, poetry and, 163

subjects, finding, memoirs and, 130-131

Sweet Summer: Growing Up With and Without My Dad, (Campbell), 123-124

Swift, Jonathan, "Modest Proposal, A," 106-107

theme, children's books

    family, culture, 184-186

    holiday's and celebrations, 183-184

    life lessons, 188-189

    nature, 191

    reading, writing, school, 186-188

social justice, 189-190

theme, graphic novels and, 212

theme, short story elements and, 52-54

"This Is My Letter To The World," (Dickinson), 147-148

Thoreau, Henry David, *Walden*, 19-21, 86

"Three by Quindlen," (Quindlen), 87

Three Little Wolves and the Big Bad Pig, The, (Trivizas), 192, 193-194

titles, short stories, craft of writing and, 66-67

"To Be of Use," (Piercy), 154

Tovani, Cris, 13

    Do I Really Have to Teach Reading? Content Comprehension, Grades 6-12, 127

    I Read It, but I Don't Get It, 3, 20

Towle, Ben, 207

Trivizas, Eugene, *Three Little Wolves and the Big Bad Pig, The*, 192, 193-194

True Story of the Three Little Pigs!, The, (Scieszka), 193-194

Two or Three Things I know for Sure, (Allison), 119-120

Under the Tuscan Sun, (Mayes), 138

Understanding by Design, (Wiggins and McTighe), 19

"Us and Them," (Sedaris), 102-103

visual language development, graphic novels and, 209-210

Walden, (Thoreau), 19-21, 86

"Walden," (White), 81-83, 107

Walker, Alice, *Living in the World*, 131-132

Walker in the City, A, (Kazin), 134-135

"We Real Cool," (Brooks), 155

What Every Writer Needs, (Fletcher), 192

Where the Sidewalk Ends, (Silverstein), 148

White, E. B., 109

    "Walden," 81-83, 107

Whitman, Walt, 168-169

    "Song of Myself," 165-167

Wiggins, Grant,

    Educative Assessment, 17

    Understanding by Design, 19

"Winter Creek," (Moore), 84-86

"Winter Dreams," (Fitzgerald), 45

Wouldn't Take Nothing for My Journey Now, (Angelou), 79-80, 104

Writing from the Heart, (Newman), 136

writing in response to literature, 24-28

    dialogue journals, 27-28

    essays, 28

    exit/entrance notes, 27

    literature learning logs, 25-26

    reading check-in, 24-25

writing models, 14-15

Writing Toward Home: Tales and Lessons to Find Your Way, (Heard), 127

Xu, Shelley Hong, 210

Zimmerman, Howard, *Best of Ray Bradbury: The Graphic Novel, The*, 200, 202-207

Zinsser, William, 116, 120-121